Egypt

A Short History

Egypt

A Short History

JAMES JANKOWSKI

ONEWORLD

OXFORD

For Mary Ann

EGYPT: A SHORT HISTORY

Oneworld Publications
(Sales and Editorial)
185 Banbury Road
Oxford OX2 7AR
England
http://www.oneworld-publications.com

Oneworld Publications
(US Marketing Office)
160 N Washington St.
4th Floor, Boston
MA 02114
USA

© James Jankowski 2000

ISBN 1–85168–240–6

Cover design by Design Deluxe
Typeset by Saxon Graphics Ltd, Derby, UK
Printed and bound in Great Britain by Creative Print and Design

Cover photographs: Cairo skyline, © Travel Ink, 2000
22nd dynasty images and hieroglyphics, found inside
Ankhephenkhonsu Sarcophagus, © the art archive, 2000

Contents

Preface

Compressing five thousand years of Egyptian history into a survey of moderate size has been a daunting task. Obviously, much more could be said about any of the historical epochs discussed in the following pages. As with the other volumes in this series, the focus in this work is on the country's modern history (the nineteenth and twentieth centuries). Chapters 1–4, on the Pharaonic, Greco-Roman, Islamic, and Ottoman eras respectively, present the broad outlines of Egypt's development in each of these eras but do so in more broad-brush fashion than chapters 5–8, devoted to Egypt's evolution in the nineteenth and twentieth centuries.

By topic, the emphasis of the work is on Egypt's internal history. Egypt's external involvement in regional and world affairs receives some attention in each chapter, and is dealt with more systematically in chapters 7 and 8 on the post-1952 period when Egypt played a larger role in international politics. Yet most of what follows focuses on Egypt's domestic evolution. Particular attention is given to presenting a clear narrative of Egypt's political structure and dynamics under successive regimes, and to analyzing the dominant patterns and arrangements prevailing in the economic and social life of different periods. Conversely, intellectual and religious life receive less attention, with some exceptions (Egypt's unique religious beliefs and rituals under the Pharaohs; Egypt's place in the Hellenistic civilization of the Mediterranean; Egypt's cultural efflorescence under the parliamentary monarchy).

Transliteration of Arabic words into English differs from author to author, book to book. For most Arabic names and terms I have used a simplified version of the spelling system now conventional in Western scholarship (al-Azhar; Muhammad 'Ali; Anwar al-Sadat). For some frequently-cited place names (Alexandria; Cairo; Suez) and one individual (Jamal 'Abd al-Nasir = "Nasser") I have used the spellings which are best-known to a Western audience.

Save for portions of chapters 6 and 7, which overlap with my own previous research, this account of Egyptian history is based on the work of other scholars. Especially in the more detailed analyses found in chapters 4–8, I have attempted to draw primarily from the current generation of scholarship and to present at least some of the most recent new interpretations of Egyptian history. My debt to my colleagues is enormous, and is only partially indicated in the Notes which accompany the text. I hope I have accurately summarized their interpretations, and in doing so provided the reader with some understanding of current scholarly perspectives on the historical evolution of one of the oldest and most interesting countries in the world.

Pharaonic Egypt

The term "Egypt" conventionally denotes the stretch of fertile land along the lower course of the River Nile. To the east and west, historic Egypt was effectively bordered by deserts; its northern and southern limits were the Mediterranean Sea and the first cataract of the Nile. The fan-shaped delta created by the branches into which the Nile divides prior to emptying into the Mediterranean is "Lower Egypt" (the portion of the river valley closest to its mouth). "Upper Egypt" is the narrow tube of land stretching from Cairo south to Aswan.

Herodotus characterized Egypt as "the gift of the river." It has certainly been this in historical times. The break in the valley, on each side of the river, between the "Black Land" – well-watered, refreshed by the annual Nile flood, and eminently suitable for cultivation – and the "Red Land" – the barren deserts to the east and west – is an abrupt and unmistakable topographical distinction which has played a major role in shaping the rhythms of Egyptian life. The Nile has conditioned the course of Egyptian development in another way as well. With an almost imperceptible descent as it flows north towards the Mediterranean Sea, the river was navigable through all of Egypt. While the Nile's current carries vessels northwards, the prevailing winds blow in the opposite direction and thereby facilitate the movement of sailed ships in a southerly direction. Egypt's historical unity is in good part the result of the geographical unity created by the Nile.

The contrast between the Black Land and the Red Land has not always been as sharp as it has become in recent millennia. Both the climate and the forms of human land-use found in the lower Nile region have varied considerably over long periods of time. Rainfall and aridity show significant variation in prehistoric eras; there have been similar variations in the volume of the annual Nile flood. What today are deserts to either side of the river were rain-fed prairie in earlier eras, inhabited by hunters, pastoralists, possibly even agriculturalists. The volume of the annual Nile inundation has varied significantly from century to century; there is a partial link between periods of a high Nile and political centralization, as well as between those of a low Nile and political turbulence. Of special relevance for early Egyptian history is the fact that the period from roughly 5000 B.C.E. to 2350 B.C.E. was generally an epoch of greater rainfall than subsequently. As attested in early Egyptian art, flora and fauna were more diverse and abundant at the dawn of Egyptian history. Ancient Egyptian civilization emerged in an ecologically richer environment than the Egypt of today.

PREHISTORIC EGYPT AND THE TRANSITION TO CIVILIZATION

Egypt has long been a site of proto human and human habitation. The earliest tool finds in Egypt date to about 700,000 B.C.E.; there are numerous Paleolithic hunter-gatherer sites both along the banks of the Nile and in the surrounding steppe.

Precisely when and how the Neolithic Revolution – the development of agriculture and the domestication of animals – came to Egypt is a matter of scholarly debate. There is some evidence implying an independent genesis for agriculture in Egypt, possibly even earlier than its permanent development in southwest Asia; but farming seems to have been an abortive experiment in this radically new form of human adaptation to the environment. Pastoralism may have had its genesis in Egypt in the steppes west of the river, later spreading to the Nile Valley proper. In time the same plants and domesticated animals (emmer wheat and barley, sheep, goats, cattle, and pigs) that supported Neolithic communities in southwest Asia came to prevail in Egypt. Eventually, agriculture and pastoralism spread along the length of the Nile Valley as well as into favorable ecological niches in its borderlands. By 5000 B.C.E. Egypt was a land of many local Neolithic cultures, some primarily agricultural, others primarily pastoral, all co-existing in a formerly lush environment.

The pace of change quickened after roughly 4000 B.C.E. Archeological excavations from this time indicate larger settlements of agriculturalists, in some cases perhaps numbering several thousand people inhabiting one community. Finds from prehistoric tombs in Upper Egypt indicate a wider array of specialized products as well as luxury goods and imply the emergence of a degree of social stratification. Communication and trade both within the Nile Valley and with other regions seem to have been on the increase. Excavations at Maadi near modern Cairo reveal sustained trade with neighboring Palestine and the development of copper metallurgy by 3500 B.C.E.; finds in the Red Sea hills imply similar commercial contacts with early Mesopotamian civilization. In spite of these links, late Neolithic Egypt was still quite a diverse land of numerous small political units and local cultures, each following their own distinct traditions.

Egyptian civilization took shape when its politics became centralized and the Nile Valley unified into one state. How this happened is obscure. Ancient historians attributed the unification of Egypt to the legendary figure Menes, a ruler in Upper Egypt who is credited with conquering Lower Egypt and forging a unified kingdom in the Nile Valley. In reality, we know nothing definite about Menes. Historians today largely accept the probability that unification occurred through conquest and that it proceeded from south to north; they also suspect that unification may have been a gradual process which took decades if not generations to be accomplished, and that the unification attributed to Menes in conventional accounts was in reality the work of a succession of Upper Egyptian rulers.

The thrust of recent scholarship is that the formation of the Egyptian state and Egyptian civilization was primarily a social, rather than a technological, process. The "hydraulic" thesis sometimes posited for the emergence of ancient civilizations – that political centralization was generated by the need to construct and maintain large-scale irrigation works – finds little support in Egypt, where throughout the ancient period the prevailing system of basin irrigation was managed and maintained at local level and did not require national coordination. The emphasis given in early Egyptian art to the theme of containing disorder strongly implies that extended conflict brought about the formation of the state.

Economic factors undoubtedly played their part: an increase in trade and luxury goods generated by craft specialization appear to have stimulated an awareness of, and a desire for, products which could best be satisfied through the accumulation of political power. Common to most scenarios is an emphasis on the role of growing trade and craft specialization in breaking down egalitarian Neolithic social structures and producing a hierarchical society in which some men led and others followed. The political dynamic of competition for riches among the chieftains of such mini-states in turn produced a geographically larger, more stratified, and ultimately "civilized" form of society in Egypt around 3100 B.C.E.

OVERVIEW OF THE PHARAONIC EPOCH

Ancient Egyptians reckoned their history in terms of successive ruling families or dynasties. Modern historians prefer to group dynasties into clusters based on the criterion of the unity or disunity of the Nile Valley. The dates of dynasties and periods of unity/disunity are approximate for earlier periods; they become more definite as time progresses and data becomes more certain. The following is one approximate sequence of dates:

Name	Rough dates	Dynasties
Early Dynastic or Archaic	3100–2700	I–II
Old Kingdom	2700–2200	III–VI
First Intermediate Period	2200–2050	VII–XI
Middle Kingdom	2050–1800	XII
Second Intermediate Period	1800–1550	XIII–XVII
New Kingdom	1550–1080	XVIII–XX
Third Intermediate Period	1080–664	XXI–XXV
Late Period	664–332	XXVI–XXXI

The common features of the Archaic period and the Old, Middle, and New Kingdoms were that they were times of Egyptian unity, independence, and stability. In contrast, in the three Intermediate periods and for much of the Late period, Egypt was either effectively fragmented or dominated by foreigners.

Together, the Early Dynastic Period and the Old Kingdom comprise Pharaonic Egypt's formative era. For close to a millennium the country was politically stable. A semi-divine monarch, identified with the sun-god Re, presided over a unified government capable of maintaining both internal and external security. The essential outlines of the political institutions, social structure, and intellectual outlook which were to prevail for nearly three thousand years were laid down under these first six dynasties, as were the distinctive canons of ancient Egyptian art. Egypt's unique and involved pictograph-based system of writing, known as hieroglyphics ("sacred writing"), took definite form at this time, and remained in use for monumental and religious purposes until the close of the Pharaonic epoch. The Old Kingdom witnessed the construction of the most visible symbols of ancient Egyptian splendor, the colossal pyramids erected in the vicinity of the royal capital at Memphis. Externally, Egypt benefited throughout the third millennium B.C.E. from being the only sizable civilized state and society existing outside of Mesopotamia. Unlike in later periods, the country faced no serious external threats. Save for occasional trade expeditions and the establishment of border garrisons in the northeast and south, it could afford to pursue a policy of splendid isolation from its neighbors. Unified, prosperous, and unchallenged from abroad, the era of the Old Kingdom in particular was one of Egyptian optimism, confidence, and self-assurance – the Peaceable Kingdom of historical memory.

Environmental change, specifically increasing aridity late in the third millennium and consequent strains on agricultural productivity, may have contributed to the collapse of the Old Kingdom and the difficulties of the First Intermediate Period. The contrast between the Old Kingdom and the First Intermediate Period was not a total one. A monarchical institution, technically the ruling body of most of Egypt, continued to remain in place. The difference was that real power passed from the throne to provincial governors whose rivalries brought a greater level of instability than had existed previously.

Possibly benefiting from a period of stronger Nile floods and consequent stabilization of its agricultural base, Egyptian unity and prosperity were restored shortly before the close of the third millennium. For more than two hundred years under the Twelfth

Dynasty, ruling from a new capital at Ith-Tawy to the south of ancient Memphis, the country experienced internal peace, prosperity, and a revival of artistic and cultural productivity.

Unity did not prevail for long. The Second Intermediate Period was one of greater turmoil than the First. At first rival kings ruled in Upper and Lower Egypt; eventually the country was subdivided into several political units. The international context in which Egypt found itself was also changing by the Second Intermediate Period. Due to the migrations of originally "barbarian" peoples equipped with a more effective military technology (the horse-drawn chariot and the composite bow), waves of warlike new migrants swept across western Asia in the early centuries of the second millennium. Eventually this current affected Egypt. The later years of the Second Intermediate Period witnessed the northern parts of the country falling under the rule of the alien Hyksos ("rulers of foreign lands"), a Semitic warrior federation. Migrating into northern Egypt from Palestine, the Hyksos gradually conquered much of the country. They themselves left little by which we can evaluate the quality of their rule. Indigenous Egyptian sources certainly present them as despised aliens who, despite their eventual assumption of the traditional trappings of Egyptian royalty, were in reality uncouth barbarians who "ruled without Re."

The Hyksos' interlude marks the great fault-line in ancient Egyptian history. Egypt's place in the world changed significantly in the first half of the second millennium. The era of Egyptian isolation and security from external threats ended with the Hyksos. For the remainder of the Pharaonic epoch, Egypt and its rulers became, of necessity, deeply involved in the political affairs of the surrounding world.

Nowhere is this more evident than under the New Kingdom. Reunited and stabilized around 1550, Egypt became a Middle Eastern empire under the rulers of the Eighteenth, Nineteenth, and Twentieth Dynasties. A professional army, its cutting edge chariot-borne archers equipped with the composite bow, was now led personally by the Pharaoh (meaning literally "great house" referring to the king himself from the New Kingdom onwards). The Pharaoh waged frequent war with the rival empires of Mitanni and the Hittites across the breadth of the Fertile Crescent.

Under the New Kingdom Egypt conquered and ruled much of Palestine to the northeast and Nubia to the south. Booty from conquest, the tribute and taxation exacted by permanent Egyptian garrisons placed in the "Northlands" and "Southlands," and the products and profits obtained by royal trade expeditions abroad augmented the natural wealth of the Nile Valley and turned the New Kingdom into a second age of architectural and artistic magnificence. Along with the earlier pyramids further north, the monumental temples erected by New Kingdom rulers in and around their capital at Thebes in Upper Egypt stand as enduring symbols of the power and splendor of ancient Egypt.

The New Kingdom was the era of many of ancient Egypt's best-remembered rulers: Queen Hapshetsut, whose dramatic mortuary temple at Deir al-Bahri is arguably the most impressive Egyptian monument after the Pyramids; the religious revolutionary Akhenaten and his queen-consort the beautiful Nefertiti; young King Tutankhamon, made world-famous by the discovery of his unlooted tomb in 1922; Ramses II, whose imperial propaganda carved in stone upon the many temples in the vicinity of Thebes immortalized (and exaggerated the degree of) Egypt's military victories achieved in Western Asia during his sixty-seven year reign.

Particularly the Eighteenth, and to a lesser degree the Nineteenth, Dynasties were the height of New Kingdom power. Under the Twentieth Dynasty new invasions again shattered Egyptian stability. By 1200 B.C.E. Egypt was under repeated assault both by the invaders from the Aegean region known collectively to historians as the Peoples of the Sea and by migrating Libyans from the West. Egypt never fully recovered from the multiple assaults of the Libyans and the Peoples of the Sea. The early Pharaohs of the new Twentieth Dynasty, particularly Ramses III, were able to resist the invaders and reassert Egyptian control of the country. But thereafter Egyptian politics were an unending conflict between a weaker monarchy, a more assertive priesthood, and a more powerful military drawn in part from remnants of the invaders who had settled in Egypt. Before the end of the second millennium Egypt had fallen into the chaos of the Third Intermediate Period, for much of which the country was divided among rival and competing local rulers (eleven such rulers by the eighth century). Centralized government disintegrated; further Libyan as well as Nubian incursions added to the instability; sporadic civil war among regional strongmen, many of foreign origin, devastated Egypt.

By roughly 700 B.C.E. the main external menace facing Egypt was domination by and incorporation into the powerful new pan-Middle Eastern empires which emerged in the first millennium B.C.E. in Western Asia. The country was conquered by the Assyrian Empire in the seventh century, but only briefly; the rise of a new native dynasty, the Saites, based in the western Delta, soon saw the reemergence of Egypt as an independent political entity. After the precipitous collapse of Assyria, c.605 B.C.E., Saite rulers had to preoccupy themselves with fending off Chaldean domination for much of the sixth century. It was the new Persian Empire which eventually effected a longer-term subjugation of Egypt. The conquest of Egypt by Cambyses of Persia in 525 B.C.E. inaugurated over a century of Persian rule, a period in which a Persian Pharaoh now claimed the prerogatives of Egyptian kingship. Repeated Egyptian uprisings against Persia occurred through the fifth century B.C.E. The last of these in 404 B.C.E. reestabished a precarious Egyptian independence which lasted until 343 B.C.E., when Persian forces again reincorporated Egypt into the Empire. This proved to be the swan-song of Persian power; barely a decade later the new world-conqueror Alexander of Macedon entered Egypt, severing the Persian connection and beginning a new historical epoch in which Egypt found its destiny inextricably linked to the Greeks and later the Romans from across the Mediterranean.

For all the political vicissitudes of the long Pharaonic epoch, ancient Egypt demonstrates remarkable continuity in its fundamental features. Egyptian civilization was by no means static; both institutions and ideas evolved over time. Nonetheless, evolution largely occurred within the framework set down during the first several dynasties. To a greater or lesser degree subsequent dynasties were self-consciously archaic, attempting to recreate and to imitate the normative patterns originally established in the third millennium. This exceptional degree of historical continuity permits topical discussion of the characteristic features of ancient Egyptian civilization.

THE PHARAONIC STATE

The state and its ruler were central to ancient Egyptian life. From the Archaic Period onwards, Egyptian dogma presented Pharaoh as semi-divine. The king was identified with different deities in the Egyptian pantheon at different times. From an early date he was viewed as an incarnation of the falcon-god Horus, simultaneously a god of the sky and an image of a fighting predator appropriate for a time of strife. After unification he was the embodiment of "The Two Ladies," two goddesses representing Upper and Lower Egypt. As order became the norm he was seen as the son of the sun-god Re, supreme diety and giver of life. Identified with the gods, Pharaoh was nonetheless subordinate to them. In the Egyptian religion of propitiation revolving around veneration of super-natural beings, Pharaoh was the most effective officiant in ritual worship. His primary function was thus religious rather than secular: the preservation of the cosmic order.

In as far as any political ideology is discernible from Egyptian texts, it emphasized the themes of the unity of the Nile Valley as well as the preservation of stability and prosperity – all functions ultimately dependent on the ruler. A prevalent motif in Egyptian art is the tension between order and chaos and correspondingly the role of the monarch in maintaining the former while warding off the latter. A key term in ancient Egyptian thought was *ma'at*, a complex concept embodying ideas of "truth" and "righteousness", as well as denoting the role of Pharaoh in maintaining the proper condition of the universe as well as society. As an early text put it, Pharaoh was the "herdsman of this land," divinely designated to "keep it in order."

Ancient Egyptian social structure was defined in terms of the ruler. Inscriptions carefully distinguished between the bureaucracy – those connected with Pharoah – on the one hand, and ordinary Egyptians on the other. To serve the king was to be associated with the divine. Good and bad behavior were largely defined in terms of one's fidelity to the wishes of Pharaoh: "I acted so that His Majesty should praise me on account of it."

The most visible expression of the centrality of the state in ancient Egyptian civilization is the royal tombs of Egyptian monarchs. Even prior to the emergence of a unified Egyptian state, the erection of impressive tombs for regional chieftains was a prominent feature of Egyptian community life. In the late prehistoric period, tombs were underground burial chambers topped by earth mounds; during the Archaic Period, tombs became rectangular mud-brick structures called "mastabas;" under the Old Kingdom they took their classic form of a pyramid. Between the Third and the Thirteenth Dynasties, a period of nearly a thousand years, over forty massive stone or stone-faced pyramids were constructed as the final resting-place of Egyptian Pharaohs. The most impressive are those of the Third and Fourth Dynasties located to the west and south of modern Cairo. Built primarily of huge limestone blocks assembled with remarkable engineering precision, these "mansions of eternity" are among the most colossal structures ever created by human endeavor. The largest, that of Khufu (*c.* 2600 B.C.E.), originally had a base measurement of 755 feet and a height of 481 feet; today, with its facing removed, it still contains some 2,352,000 cubic meters of stone. The pyramids stand as the universally-recognized symbol of Egypt.

The social importance of the pyramids for third millennium Egypt cannot be overestimated. The pyramid itself was only part of a larger complex which usually included a valley temple nearer the river, a causeway providing access to the pyramid area, a large mortuary temple adjacent to the pyramid, and numerous smaller tombs of members of the royal family and state officials. The construction of gigantic pyramids, their associated structures, and the nearby tombs of relatives and bureaucrats was ancient Egypt's largest industry, the functional equivalent of the military-industrial complex in twentieth century societies.

Mobilizing raw materials and possibly labor from the length of the Nile Valley, building and furnishing the tombs of Egypt's kings and aristocracy created a national economic network centered around the state. Simultaneously it fostered greater and greater craft specialization, and more and more refined levels of luxury production. Since the products generated by the funerary industry were "consumed" in tombs each generation, fresh "demand" was created as monarch succeeded monarch. Royal mortuary cults thus provided "an economic stimulus broadly equivalent to 'built-in obsolescence' in modern technological societies."[1] Much of the glorious cultural heritage left by Egypt's early dynasties was fuelled by the continuing effort to outfit Egypt's ruler, relations, and elite for their passage into the hereafter.

A distinction must be made between the theoretical and the actual position of the Pharaohs of ancient Egypt. While much the same semi-divine status and role as maintainer of the cosmic order were ascribed to all Pharaohs from the third through the first millennium, the actual position and power of the royal institution fluctuated of course over nearly three thousand years. Effective royal authority was strongest under the Old, Middle, and New Kingdoms, and was challenged or in eclipse during the three Intermediate Periods and in the Late Period. A clear trend of diminishing royal power is apparent from the middle of the New Kingdom onwards. Personal Pharaonic rule substantially ended with the defeat of the royal revolutionary Akhenaten by the priesthood late in the Eighteenth Dynasty. In practice, later Pharaohs had to contend with a more entrenched and powerful priesthood and a larger and more autonomous military class internally, as well as with repeated bouts of invasion from abroad externally.

ANCIENT EGYPTIAN RELIGION

"Religion" is a somewhat inadequate term for ancient Egyptian beliefs and practices relating to the supernatural. The central features of later religions – a commonly shared body of doctrine about the nature of the cosmos and man's place in it, an explicit ethical code, and a tradition of pastoral care and ministry – had no counterpart in ancient Egypt. What did exist was a wide spectrum of differing beliefs about a bewildering array of supernatural beings, as well as numerous regional or family cults defining how mortals needed to behave towards the gods.

In the prehistoric period religious multiplicity prevailed, with different areas and emerging city-states each having its own deity or deities believed to be in control of the natural order and therefore in need of propitiation. Political unification brought a measure of harmonization among previously distinct supernatural figures. Gods and goddesses from different places became associated with others by means of a presumed family connection, by combining their physical images into a composite figure, or by merging specific characteristics of different deities into a being with multiple attributes.

Egyptian deities took many forms. Some were nature-gods (the sun-god Re). Others were portrayed in human form (Ptah, a beautiful youth), or as an animal (the crocodile-god Sobek) or in part-human, part-animal form (Thoth, a male body with the head of an ibis; Sekhmet, a female figure with the head of a lioness). Many were associated with particular crafts or skills (Ptah the god of artists and smiths, Thoth the god of learning, Hathor the goddess of love and joy). Throughout ancient Egyptian history the Egyptian pantheon was a fluid rather than a static one. The attributes of individual gods and goddesses and their perceived relationship to each other shifted over time in accord with the changing fortunes of different regions and temples.

Ancient Egyptian "religion" had a decidedly pragmatic bent. Its central feature was various rituals of propitiation in which the gods, in control of nature, were worshipped with sacrificial rites in order to maintain the order and prosperity of the world. The most effective worshipper was the king. But Pharaoh could not be everywhere at once, so in his absence priests carried out the rituals of worship. Twice a day the statues of the numerous deities resident in the hundreds of temples dotting the Nile Valley would be washed, anointed with oils, dressed in fine clothing, amused with song and dance, and presented with a sumptuous repast from which they would take spiritual nourishment, leaving the physical remains to be divided among the worshippers. Gods and goddesses were periodically brought out of their temples to bless the community and to arbitrate disputes. Sometimes they visited each other, travelling in procession from one temple to another. Eventually all-Egypt seasonal festivals became the occasion of ritual worship, public celebration, and feasting. Thus religious observance shaped much of the texture of ancient Egyptian life.

New Kingdom Egypt witnessed a major attempt at religious innovation. In the sixth year of his reign, the young Pharaoh Amonhotep IV ("Amon is Satisfied") changed his name to Akhenaten ("Servant of the Aten"). The change of name heralded an attempt at religious revolution. Akhenaten's aim was to replace the worship of the numerous deities previously venerated in Egypt with the exclusive worship of the sun-disk Aten and of himself as its living embodiment. Existing temples were neglected or in some cases desecrated, and the power of the state employed to root out the worship of deities other than the sun-disk. In place of the names of other gods was substituted the image of the sun-disk, with its rays stretching in all directions. The capital was moved from Thebes to the new city of Tell-el-Amarna, where the temples – now vast courtyards open to the sun rather than the earlier structures centered on enclosed shrine-rooms – were dedicated solely to the worship of the Aten. A drastically different artistic style rapidly developed to express this new outlook. Rather than the somber formalism of the past, Pharaoh and his family were portrayed in informal and starkly naturalistic terms; the bust of Akhenaten's queen-consort Nefertiti is the most famous example of the Tell-el-Amarna style.

Conceptually Akhenaten's new religion came close to monotheism. The power of the Aten was clearly perceived as extending to all peoples; the sun-disk was the universal source of all life. A renewed emphasis was also placed on the older concept of *ma'at*, here best translated as "truth" rather than as "justice." Being faithful to *ma'at* in the sense of leading a natural and open life was the proper form of worship of the life-giving sun-disk. The Aten was termed "he who is satisfied with *ma'at*," his embodiment Akhenaten envisaged as a living god "who lives on *ma'at*." Yet it is arguable whether or not the worship of the Aten can properly be termed monotheistic. It involved the worship of two figures – the Aten, and his human embodiment the Pharaoh Akhenaten. The personalization of the supernatural which permeated ancient Egyptian thought was not completely transcended in Akhenaten's new vision.

Interpreting Akhenaten and his new religion has been an historian's delight. Where did these ideas come from? One tantalizing hypothesis is the suggestion that Akhenaten's radical rejection of the Egyptian religious heritage was the intellectual accompaniment to Egypt's physical integration into the wider world of the Middle East under the New Kingdom. From this perspective Akhenaten's new religion signified a growing Egyptian awareness of the interconnected nature of the world and beyond that of the universe. With recent experience demonstrating that Egypt's destiny was inextricably linked to the lands and peoples beyond the Nile Valley, it was perhaps not too great a conceptual leap to postulate the existence of one supreme force whose power extended everywhere.

Equally intriguing is the issue of the historical impact of Akhenaten's ideas. The idea that one, and only one, supreme being was the source of everything in existence certainly bears a resemblance to the core belief of later Middle Eastern monotheistic religions. This resemblance, combined with the Biblical account of the Hebrew sojourn in Egypt, itself sometimes assumed to have occurred during the period of the New Kingdom, has fuelled speculation of an intellectual link between Akhenaten's religious ideas and the historical evolution of Judaism. This issue is deeply contested in contemporary scholarship. Sceptics note both historical and philosophical problems in identifying an Egyptian influence in the genesis of Judaism. In terms of history, the Biblical narrative of the Israelite sojourn in, and exodus from, Egypt demonstrates little knowledge of Old Kingdom Egypt; the narrative also finds little echo in the available Egyptian archeological and literary evidence. In terms of philosophy, there are appreciable conceptual differences between Akhenaten's image of the sun-god Aten, an abstract and timeless solar deity who simultaneously manifested himself in the person of Akhenaten, and the later Judaic understanding of the character of Yahweh, a passionate God constantly intervening personally and directly in history rather than through human avatars.[2]

However we interpret the roots and results of Akhenaten's attempt at religious revolution, within Egypt it failed. Institutionalized in a network of temples existing up and down the length of the Nile and supported by a large priesthood, the existing religious order could not be eradicated in the reign of one Pharaoh. Even in his last years, Akhenaten had to temper his religious iconoclasm; his successor the boy-king Tutankhamon proved too weak to carry his vision forward. After Tut, the priesthood, especially the priests of Amon at Thebes, regained much of their power over both religion and society. By the Third Intermediate Period parts of the country were effectively ruled by temple establishments. Intellectually the dominant note in Egyptian religious life after the failed revolution of Ahkenaten was cultural conservatism – the scrupulous imitation and repetition of earlier patterns of religious and intellectual expression. Pharoahs continued to rule and to be accorded semi-divine status; but an equally if not more powerful force in later Pharaonic times was the priestly class.

PHARAONIC ECONOMY AND SOCIETY

We have only rough estimates for the population of ancient Egypt. It has been tentatively calculated at between one and two million under the Old and Middle Kingdoms, fluctuating considerably from century to century according to long-term variations in the volume of the annual Nile flood. Somewhat harder estimates for the size of the population under the New Kingdom range from three to four and a half million, probably declining to the lower figure by the Late Period. The long-term growth of population over the Pharaonic epoch as a whole was primarily the result of internal colonization and the opening of new agricultural lands in the marshes and along the coastline of the Delta, as well as in previously unexploited portions of the Nile floodplain in Upper Egypt.

Even before the creation of the state and the emergence of civilization, Egypt had become a land of sedentary agricultural settlements. Decorative reliefs on tombs offer a rich portrait of rural daily life. Wheat and barley were the main food crops providing raw material for the baking of bread and the brewing of beer, the two staples of the ancient Egyptian diet. A grain-based diet was supplemented by a rich assortment of fruits and vegetables (onions, lettuce, beans, melons, dates, figs, and grapes), animal products provided by a variety of domesticated animals (cattle, sheep, goats, pigs, ducks, geese), and fish obtained from the river.

The Nile defined the agricultural year. The ancient Egyptian calendar knew three seasons – those of Inundation, Seed, and Harvest. The annual Nile flood of late summer was the time of inundation, after which the laborious process of preparing the soil for planting followed. A wooden plough drawn by oxen broke the soil. Planting was done by seedsmen dropping seeds into the open furrows, sometimes followed by teams of rams who trampled the seeds into the ground. Irrigation techniques were primitive in earlier periods, relying on the flooding of natural basins to supplement hand-drawn water carried to the fields. Only under the New Kingdom is there evidence of the use of the labor-saving *shaduf*, a pole balanced on a pivot allowing a bucket to be dipped into water and swiveled to drop its load on the soil. The harvesting of crops in late winter and spring was a busy time in which men, women, and children all worked at the tasks of cutting, gathering,

and winnowing the grain. The harvest was also a time of celebration and offerings to the gods, as well as the occasion when
scribes assessed the crop for taxation purposes.

Although private landownership existed, most rural cultivators
appear not to have owned the land which they worked but to have
been tenants on royal, temple, or private estates. What they
produced was often the property of the state, the temple, or the
landlord, their own subsistence needs being met through a
centralized system of allocation in which they received
commodities in exchange for labor. It was the annual tax on the
harvest or the rent due to temple or landlord, as well as the obligatory labor of the peasantry on various estates, which provided the
necessary support for the non-agricultural sectors of society.

A third kind of community stood midway between the
centralized state and local villages. These were the temples of
ancient Egypt. Some temples presumably have their origins in local
cults that existed along the Nile since the prehistoric period.
Others were spawned by the efforts of both rulers and private individuals to commemorate themselves and to ensure perpetual maintenance of their funerary cults. A gradual broadening of the
concept of immortality occurred over the Pharaonic epoch.
Whereas under the Old Kingdom only Pharaoh was generally
assumed to pass on to eternal life in another sphere after death,
from the Middle Kingdom onwards the idea of passage to a better
hereafter gradually expanded to become accessible to at least the
upper and middle classes of Egypt. With this democratization of
the afterlife temple communities proliferated, becoming more
prominent in Egyptian society as time passed.

The economic basis of an Egyptian temple community was a
perpetual endowment of real property, usually agricultural land. A
priestly class, its pre-eminence based on literacy and hence its
mastery of cultic knowledge, directed the religious ceremonies and
festivals which were the raison d'être of the temple. Yet the
performance of many of the tasks associated with temple maintenance were not monopolized by a small elite. Temple records
indicate a system of part-time, rotating service in which private
individuals would serve the temple one month during the year,
receiving an allowance for their service. Thus the temple system
was by no means one of unmitigated priestly exploitation of the

illiterate masses; both the spiritual and the material benefits attached to temple service were widely, although not equally, shared through this labor rotation.

Parallel to the diminution of central political authority over time was the secular trend, over the long Pharaonic epoch, of the expansion of temple, as well as private, control of agricultural land. By late in the New Kingdom, temples are estimated to have owned one-third of the arable land and to have had one-fifth of the country's population dependent on temple economies. Significant amounts of land from the New Kingdom onwards were also handed over to the burgeoning professional military in exchange for military service. Such estates in time became the basis of the political power of the increasingly autonomous local magnates of later Pharaonic times.

Temples often formed the original nucleus of Pharaonic Egypt's larger-than-village-size settlements or towns. The exchange of goods and services in ancient Egypt was usually more on a command basis (through taxes, rent, or obligatory labor service) rather than via the mechanism of the marketplace. The absence of coinage until late in the Pharaonic era restricted the possibility of commerce, although a lively exchange of goods via barter is indicated. Foreign trade also existed, but on a lesser scale in earlier periods than in later ones, and primarily to meet the luxury needs of the state and the ruler. In these conditions, communities bigger than an agricultural village originally came into being less because of trade or commerce than through the congregation of people in one place in the service of Pharoah or deity. Such were the "pyramid towns" of ancient Egypt, communities of priests, retainers, and laborers assembled around royal burial complexes. Lesser temples also gave birth to permanent settlements with a disproportion of religious and craft specialists among their population. Late in the Pharaonic epoch, internal turmoil and repeated external invasions served as a stimulus to urbanization. Walled and fortified towns became more prominent, with more of the country's population clustering within their walls for security in a time of troubles.

The class structure of ancient Egypt reflected the prevailing politico-religious order. Literary sources often rank individuals in terms of their function and relationship to the state: bureaucrats, priests, warriors, and "commoners" (everyone else). Social reality was undoubtedly more complex. Pharaoh and the royal family always stood at the apex of the social pyramid, a long way above the rest of the population. At a significantly lower but still privileged level were high officials of the central government, provincial notables, and temple dignitaries, the latter two groups becoming larger and larger over time. Lesser bureaucrats and priests, military officers, and landowners formed an Egyptian middle class of uncertain size. The bulk of the population – minor officials and priests, soldiers, tenant farmers, the huge mass of peasants bound to the land on royal or temple estates, slaves – formed the lower classes.

A notable feature of the ancient Egyptian social order was the relatively favorable position of women. In contrast to most of the patriarchical civilizations of the ancient Middle East in which women possessed few if any legal rights and stood firmly under male control, women and men in ancient Egypt were legal equals under the law. Women had the right to inherit, to hold, purchase, and sell real property, and to enter into legal contracts. Scattered legal records indicate that women were active participants in court cases. Although instances of polygamy have been identified, multiple marriage was apparently rare, as in many other societies the prerogative of the upper classes. The gendered division of labor customary within the institution of marriage – husband as the breadwinner involved with the outside world, and wife in charge of domestic duties – was certainly the norm in ancient Egypt. Yet within marriage a woman remained an independent being, not confined within the home, and legally controlling her own property; property that accumulated during marriage became the joint possession of husband and wife. Divorce was a relatively easy process which at least from the New Kingdom onwards could be initiated by either husband or wife.

The benefits available to women in ancient Egypt should not be overstated. The social expectations placed upon men and women clearly differed, with the male having more authority within the family and more freedom in society. The difference is reflected visually in the artistic convention whereby male figures are often colored brown to indicate exposure to the sun whereas female figures are white, denoting their life within the home. There is no evidence of girls receiving formal education once schools had developed by the Middle Kingdom, although there are examples of privately educated literate women. Only a limited range of occupations outside the home – domestic servants as well as supervisors of women's work within palace and temple establishments, weavers, musicians, prostitutes – have been documented as available to women. In the heavenly pantheon no goddess was as powerful as the most prominent male deities; in the Peaceable Kingdom on earth only three women (a possibly-legendary Nitocris during the Sixth Dynasty; Hapshetsut during the Eighteenth Dynasty; Twosret during the Nineteenth Dynasty) have been identified as having assumed the title and prerogatives of Pharaoh over the nearly three millennia of the ancient epoch.

Greco-Roman Egypt

The long Pharaonic epoch came to an end in 332 B.C.E. Alexander the Great's conquest of Egypt had far deeper repercussions than the earlier Assyrian and Persian interludes. It marked the beginning of a period of almost a millennium (332 B.C.E.–642 C.E.) in which Egypt fell under either Macedonian/Greek or Roman/Byzantine political domination, and in which the population, institutions, and culture of the country came under strong Greco-Roman influence. For a thousand years, Egypt was an integral part of the Mediterranean *oikoumene* (civilized world) created by the Greeks and maintained by the Romans.

THE PTOLEMIES

Alexander himself did not remain in Egypt for long. After personally supervising the establishment of the new city on the Mediterranean shore which was to bear his name, he left Egypt in 331 B.C.E. to complete the subjugation of the Persian Empire. In the initial subdivision of Alexander's conquests upon his premature death in 323 B.C.E., Egypt went to his Macedonian general Ptolemy. A generation-long struggle for permanent possession of the spoils ensued. By the time the dust had settled at the close of the fourth century B.C.E., Ptolemy had succeeded in repelling the challenges of his erstwhile Macedonian companions and in retaining control of Egypt, of Cyrenaica, of Cyprus, and of part of the Palestinian coast. Formally declaring himself king in 305 B.C.E., Ptolemy I Soter ("Saviour") was the founder of the

Ptolemaic dynasty which was to rule Egypt for almost three hundred years.

The height of Ptolemaic power and splendor was the third century B.C.E., under the first three Ptolemies (323–222). Internally the country was both prosperous and stable, as well as free of the debilitating royal family rivalries which were to vex the dynasty in later years. Externally the early Ptolemies were strong enough to maintain control of their foreign possessions and to repel Seleucid invasions of the Nile Valley. The prosperity of Egypt and the dynasty's lavish patronage of their new capital Alexandria served as a magnet attracting large-scale immigration from Greek communities around the Mediterranean, as well as considerable Jewish immigration from neighboring Palestine. It was in the early Ptolemaic period that Egypt's institutions and culture assumed the Greek patina which was to persist until well into the Roman period.

Foreign conquerors ruling Egypt from a capital located at one edge of the country ("Alexandria-by-Egypt" in contemporary parlance), the Ptolemies were unquestionably alien overlords. Although they, like the Persians before them, were careful to present themselves as Egyptian Pharaohs, their regime was dominated by Macedonians or Greeks and was oriented towards exploiting Egypt for the benefit of the country's new ruling class. Their army originally comprised Macedonian or Greek mercenaries who were given grants of land and in time became a rural elite. Their administration was staffed at the higher levels by Macedonians or Greeks and conducted its business in Greek. Higher officialdom related to Egyptian-speaking scribes at the local level through interpreters. The first Ptolemaic ruler who is known to have spoken Egyptian was the last of the line, Cleopatra VII.

The dynasty's control over both Egypt and its external outliers weakened after the first three Ptolemies. Several internal revolts against the dynasty occurring from the late third century onwards contributed to periodic loss of control over parts of the country, to economic turmoil, and to a consequent diminution of the regime's financial base. They also weakened the regime externally. Palestine was lost permanently at the end of the third century. Thirty years later a Seleucid army briefly occupied Egypt itself, only to be ousted by an ultimatum delivered from the new Mediterranean hegemon Rome. From the middle of the second century B.C.E.,

Ptolemaic Egypt increasingly became a Roman protectorate surviving on the sufferance of Rome.

The second half of the Ptolemaic era was a descending spiral into internal instability and external dependency. The practices of brother-sister marriage within the royal family and of joint rule by brother-sister/husband-wife teams (successive Ptolemies on the male side; several Cleopatras on the female) served as a fertile source of family rivalry, intrigue, and occasional civil war. From abroad Rome played a greater and greater role in Egyptian affairs as time progressed, supporting one or another claimant in the internecine warfare within the royal family and eventually itself taking control of the Ptolemaic dependencies in Cyrenaica (74 B.C.E.) and Cyprus (58 B.C.E.). The climax came in the mid-first century B.C.E., when Rome intervened with military force in the increasingly chaotic dynastic politics of the Ptolemies. First Pompey, then Caesar, then Mark Antony went to Egypt partially in a Roman effort to stabilize the situation in the country, partially in pursuit of their own ambitions; the latter two took that involvement in Egyptian affairs to the point of marriage with the last and most capable of Ptolemaic queens, Cleopatra VII (she of the asp). It was the joint effort of Mark Antony and Cleopatra to use Egypt as the base for a challenge to Rome itself which prompted the Roman counter of sending the consul Octavian to defeat Antony's and Cleopatra's forces at Actium, leading to the suicide of Mark Antony and Cleopatra. In 30 B.C.E., Egypt was at last formally incorporated into the Roman Empire.

EGYPT UNDER ROMAN AND BYZANTINE RULE

Rome's annexation of Egypt substantially depoliticized the country. For the next several centuries Egypt was not an independent state but a Roman, later a Byzantine, possession. High politics took place in Rome or in Byzantium/Constantinople, not in Alexandria. The main benefit of this depoliticization was a greater measure of internal stability than had existed when Ptolemy had plotted against Ptolemy, Cleopatra against Cleopatra. The drawback was the determination of national policy outside the country and possibly an even greater measure of exploitation of the resources of Egypt for the benefit of foreigners.

In its broad outlines, the system of rule and administration introduced by the Emperor Augustus (formerly Octavian) after his conquest of Egypt remained in effect until the late third century c.e. Roman Emperors continued the polite fiction of having themselves presented as Pharaoh and of patronizing Egyptian temples. The realities of rule, however, were quite different. Responsible for supplying one-third of the annual supply of grain for the city of Rome, Egypt was simply too important to be administered like other Roman possessions. Unlike other Roman provinces, Egypt's chief administrator or prefect was a direct appointee of the Roman Emperor drawn from the equestrian class rather than from the Senate and personally accountable to the Emperor. Only the upper levels of the bureaucracy, centered at Alexandria, were Roman. Local administration was staffed primarily by the Greco-Egyptian elite which had emerged under the Ptolemies. Except within the central administration where Latin was used, Greek was the language of government in "Roman" Egypt. At the local level, taxes were assessed and collected by village notables, some Greco-Egyptian, some native Egyptian. The internal and external security of Rome's Egyptian possession was maintained by the stationing of first three, and later two, Roman legions in Egypt.

The ups and downs of Egyptian politics under Roman domination in large part paralleled with the political vicissitudes experienced by Rome itself. Egypt was largely placid during the early centuries of Roman rule, when the Empire was most stable. Despite the various tax obligations imposed on its rural population – taxes made more burdensome by the centralization and efficiency of Roman tax collection – we hear of no major outbreaks of unrest through the first century c.e. What has entered the historical record are numerous reports of peasant flight in response to onerous taxation demands and the resultant growth of rural brigandage; the latter remained endemic in the Egyptian countryside throughout the Roman era.

Only in the second century c.e. were there major uprisings against Rome which shook Roman control over parts of the country: a Jewish revolt in 115–117 generated by Jewish-Greek animosity in Alexandria resulting in the extermination of much of Egypt's sizable Jewish community, and native Egyptian uprisings of considerable scope in 152 and again in 172–173. Unrest accelerated in the third century, as the Empire experienced its own time of troubles. Major internal revolts erupted late in the century, one producing a self-declared "emperor" who controlled most of Egypt until a military expedition led by the Emperor Diocletian retook Alexandria and restored Roman dominion.

Diocletian's reign also marks the beginning of the transition from the Roman to the Byzantine era in Egypt. Diocletian and his successor Constantine both undertook major administrative reforms which affected Egypt. Diocletian ended Egypt's unique administrative status within the empire; simultaneously he divided what had been one unit into three separate provinces. Constantine continued the devolution of administrative responsibilities, giving local municipalities greater authority over both themselves and their rural hinterlands. The net result of Diocletian's and Constantine's reforms was a more fragmented Egypt in which local urban communities and elites had greater political leeway than had been the case in the more centralized early centuries of Roman rule. Reinforced by the emergence of new institutions spawned by the rise of Christianity, power in Byzantine Egypt was more diffused than had been the case when the Empire was centered in Rome.

ECONOMIC EXPANSION AND EXPLOITATION

Egypt's economy and population both expanded over much of the Greco-Roman period. Thanks in part to the introduction of more effective irrigation devices (the ox-powered water-wheel and the Archimedean screw) and to the construction of a dense network of irrigation canals in the Fayyum depression to the west of the Nile under the Ptolemies, the agricultural productivity of the country may have reached its greatest level, prior to the nineteenth century, by the Roman period. A richer resource-base apparently generated a considerable growth in population. The classical author Diodorus of Sicily estimated Egypt's population at the end of the Ptolemaic period at about seven million; a century later the Jewish historian Josephus offered an estimate of seven and a half million excluding the city of Alexandria. These frequently cited estimates must be regarded as possible but unproven. Egypt's metropole throughout the entire Greco-Roman period, Alexandria, may have reached a population of half a million in the later Ptolemaic and early Roman periods. Political and economic difficulties from the second century C.E. onwards are believed to have produced a decline in population. A cautious estimate for the fourth century is a population of something over four million for the country as a whole.

Under Greek and Roman rule Egypt became a monetarized and market-oriented economy. While the bartering of goods and services continued at village level, and while some taxes (particularly the all-important levy on grain) were assessed and collected in kind, a money economy prevailed in Egypt's urban communities and in regard to some forms of exchange between town and country (e.g. taxes other than those upon grains; the sale of manufactured goods). The urban economy of Greco-Roman Egypt was a complex, differentiated one with various highly-specialized occupations regulated by guilds and a market-based system of exchange. On the one hand, towns were linked with their rural hinterlands through urban ownership of agricultural lands and the concomitant flow of rural resources to urban areas; on the other hand, towns were thoroughly integrated into an international trade network extending across the Mediterranean, east into western Asia and south into Africa, and by the Roman period to India.

A central concern of both the Ptolemies and the Romans was the exploitation of the resources of Egypt for their own benefit. They did so in different ways. Most agricultural land in Ptolemaic Egypt was theoretically the property of the ruler. Worked primarily by smallholding tenant families, the bulk of the surplus from Egyptian agriculture accrued to the state. Privately-owned rural land was at first limited, although the dynasty's grants of agricultural plots to soldiers in exchange for military service eventually created a privileged Greek landlord class in the countryside. Parts of the urban economy were also dominated by the state through royal monopolies of important goods and services such as olive oil and banking. Taxation of the private sector was geared to extracting the maximum revenue possible, revenue which in turn was spent not for the benefit of native Egyptians or on economic reinvestment but on the dynasty, on the costs of security, and on patronage of institutions serving primarily the Greek population of Alexandria and other Greek enclaves within Egypt.

Roman exploitation of Egypt, at least from the Roman annexation in 30 B.C.E. to the third century C.E., is generally considered to have been even more efficient than that of the Ptolemies. The long-term trend in landownership under Roman rule was the extension of private property rights. With an eye towards encouraging private investment and economic development, the state-owned estates of the Ptolemies were gradually sold off to private citizens. By the later Roman or Byzantine period most land in Egypt had passed into private ownership.

Rome got the bulk of what it wanted from Egypt not through state ownership of economic resources but through taxation. The Roman system of tax collection was centrally-organized and tightly-controlled. Grain fell in a special category. With Egypt responsible for providing one-third of Rome's grain supply, the tax on grain was collected in kind. Each stage of its movement – from village to state granaries; from state granaries to Alexandria; from Alexandria to Rome – was effected by compulsory labor services and carefully monitored by the state. Taxes on agricultural products other than grain were generally collected in money, necessitating village involvement in the urban-oriented market economy in order to obtain cash for the payment of taxes. Until the grant of Roman citizenship to all residents of the Empire in 212 c.e., a head-tax was imposed on all male Egyptians between the ages of fourteen and sixty (but not levied on Romans, citizens of Greek cities, or Jews), adding to the tax burden. Official requisitioning of food, equipment, and transport and a wide variety of compulsory labor services – for canal maintenance or grain transport for villagers, for staffing local government offices, or urban upkeep on townsmen – formed non-monetary forms of "taxation" imposed by Rome upon both Greek and Egyptian residents of the country.

The overall burden which Ptolemaic landownership/monopolies and Roman taxation placed upon Egypt's population is difficult to assess. On the one hand, the sources contain frequent references to a resort to coercion by the government and tax-farmers to extract revenues and services from the countryside, and even more numerous accounts of both rural and urban flight occasioned by the rent or tax obligations imposed upon producers. On the other, there is also evidence of tax relief being provided to cultivators in years of a low Nile, of the persistence of a vibrant and highly specialized urban economy, and of the production of a wide range of luxury products for export. Against tales of woe must be set the increase in the agricultural carrying-capacity of the country due to technological improvements under the Ptolemies and of the effects of the closer economic integration of Egypt into the wider world of the Greco-Roman *oikoumene* under both Ptolemies and Romans. Whatever the predatory intentions of some of Egypt's masters in the era of Greco-Roman domination, recent estimates of the overall level of the economic exploitation of Egypt are more tempered than previous ones: "The longevity of Egypt's general prosperity suggests the obvious conclusion that, despite the endemic complaints from taxpayers, government control assured a revenue yield which was, in general, not so extortionate as to drive the producers to the wall."[1]

GREEKS, ROMANS, AND EGYPTIANS

Alexander's conquest of Egypt marked the beginning of a social revolution in Egypt. Tens if not hundreds of thousands of foreigners – mainly Greeks from the Greek diaspora around the Mediterranean, but also Jews from Palestine and immigrants from other parts of western Asia – flocked to this new "Eldorado on the Nile" under the Ptolemies. Immigration created a new society in Egypt, one in which Greeks ruled and native Egyptians served. After their annexation of Egypt, Romans formed a similar separate and distinct ruling elite. Sharp distinctions of status and privilege first between Greeks and Egyptians, later between Romans and both Greeks and Egyptians, persisted until the Byzantine period when a greater measure of social integration based in part on the spread of a new religion was achieved. The social history of Egypt through the Greco-Roman period is largely one of defining the differences among ethnic communities.

Unquestionably, Greeks formed a privileged group in Ptolemaic Egypt. The bulk of Greek immigrants lived in their own cities with citizenship largely restricted to Greeks and with distinctive institutions modelled on those of Greece. Greek cities were laid out on the grid pattern typical of Greece; colonnaded Greek temples open to the outside world contrasted sharply with the enclosed fortress-like temples of Pharaonic Egypt; Greek gymnasia for physical training were open only to Greeks until late in the Ptolemaic period and had no Egyptian counterpart. Greek became the language of both administration and higher culture. The impressive civilization of Hellenistic Egypt had little or no meaning for the vast majority of the population of the country.

In the three centuries of Ptolemaic rule some measure of Greco-Egyptian assimilation was inevitable. The two main avenues of Egyptian passage into the Greek world of power were through the bureaucracy and the military. Since Greek was the language of administration and since many Greeks at least at first knew no Egyptian, bilingual native Egyptians formed a necessary stratum in the bureaucracy. In time the regime also found it necessary to enroll native Egyptians in the military. Yet in both the bureaucracy and the army, Egyptians did not acquire a position equivalent to Greeks. Only a few native Egyptian provincial governors have been identified, and no native Egyptian served the Ptolemies as an ambassador abroad. Egyptian soldiers received smaller land grants than Macedonians or Greeks, and the number who held officer rank was closely monitored and restricted in order not to offend Greek sensibilities.

A degree of Egyptianization of the originally separate Greek elite occurred over time. Possibly to counter native resentment, the dynasty itself eventually placed greater emphasis on the "Egyptian" nature of its authority. From Ptolemy V onwards rulers were ceremonially crowned as Pharaoh at the ancient Egyptian capital of Memphis. Non-Greek social practices such as brother-sister marriage were adopted by some Greeks (particularly within the ruling family itself). Syncretic cults which combined indigenous Egyptian cult figures with Greek concepts were fostered by the state. Intermarriage mainly between Greek soldiers, assigned rural land grants, and Egyptian women in time created an intermediate Greco-Egyptian class within Ptolemaic society. The offspring of such unions were Greek in legal terms, but often more Egyptian in social practices (speaking Egyptian at home, using Egyptian names within their local milieu, employing the indigenous demotic script for contracts).

But Greek-Egyptian assimilation had definite limits. Only a minority of Greeks or Egyptians learned each others' language or intermarried. Most Greeks lived in cities, most Egyptians in the countryside. The extant papyri of the period indicate a prevailing Greek disdain for native Egyptians who knew not the ways of

Greece: "They have treated me with contempt because I am a barbarian ... I do not know how to behave like a Greek."[2] For their part native Egyptians frequently resented the pretensions and privileges of their Greek masters, and acted out their resentment in occasional attacks upon Greeks. "Ptolemaic Egypt, in other words, remained throughout its history a land of two cultures which did coexist but, for the most part, did not coalesce or blend."[3]

Rome's annexation of Egypt in 30 B.C.E. originally did little to alter the social structure of Egypt. Through the first and second centuries C.E. the Romans largely maintained existing divisions, merely inserting themselves at the top of the social pyramid. Greek cities with restricted rights of citizenship retained their separate status under Rome. Different legal regimes continued to exist for Egyptians, the citizens of Greek cities, and (until their revolt in 115–117 C.E.) Jews; the mixed Greco-Egyptian population which had emerged under the Ptolemies was now reduced to the status of "Egyptian." Roman legislation in effect from the reign of the Emperor Augustus attempted to limit social mobility and inter-marriage among different legal categories. The pecking order was clear: a small number of Roman citizens at the top, urban Greeks and Jews in the middle, everyone else below. The evidence of the papyri indicates that Romans living in Egypt were often as disdainful of Egyptians as Greeks had previously been: "... as I am a Roman man suffering such indignities at the hands of an Egyptian, I ask ... ."[4]

The sharp edges of this ethnically-divided social order eventually blurred. The grant of Roman citizenship to most residents of Egypt in 212 C.E. brought a greater equalization of status among previously segregated communities. At the same time social changes were operating to transform the social structure from below. With the financial and other difficulties of the Empire in the third century, the ancient temple communities, which through the Ptolemaic and early Roman periods had survived through the receipt of state financial support, began to decline. Old temples fell into disuse; new temples ceased to be built. This decay of a millennial Egyptian institution with deep roots in the countryside was accelerated by the spread of the new religion of Christianity in the third and fourth centuries. Simultaneously in the cities of Egypt a largely Greek urban elite with wealth in land was gaining greater political responsibility and authority from the reforms of Diocletian and Constantine.

By the fourth century, a new social structure was coalescing in Egypt. The institutional vacuum produced by the decline of temples was progressively filled by the new institutions of the Christian church (village churches, bishoprics, monasteries); by the closer relations forged between villagers and the new landed elite in the cities as a result of tenant farming and land-leasing; and by the devolution of administrative responsibilities to urban notables. A new social configuration "consciously both Egyptian and Greek" was emerging.[5] Byzantine Egypt of the fourth, fifth, and sixth centuries C.E. was a more integrated society than either that of Greek-dominated Ptolemaic Egypt or the stratified Egypt ruled by Rome.

FROM HELLENISM TO CHRISTIANITY

Alexandria was the center of intellectual life in Egypt under both the Ptolemies and the Romans. Thanks to lavish state patronage of its cultural institutions, Alexandria under the Ptolemies attracted intellectuals from all over the Hellenized Mediterranean. Two facilities established early in the Ptolemaic period were particularly important in fostering higher culture at Alexandria. One was the Museum, a cult center dedicated to the worship of the Greek Muses, which in effect functioned like a modern research institute with resident scholars and seminars. The other was the famous Library, a state-supported entity dedicated to preserving and disseminating the Greek cultural heritage. At its peak, the Library may have housed close to half a million papyrus rolls. Important scholarship in numerous fields – history, biography, philology, philosophy, various areas of the natural sciences – was undertaken by Hellenistic scholars working at Alexandria. Euclid, Archimedes, and Eratosthenes all spent part of their intellectual careers in the congenial atmosphere of the Ptolemaic capital. Nor was Alexandrian scholarship exclusively based on Greek texts. Members of the large Jewish community of Egypt were responsible for the translation of the Hebrew Bible into Greek, and at the beginning of the Roman era the Jewish philosopher Philo of Alexandria undertook his monumental attempt to reinterpret the Jewish religious tradition within a Hellenistic philosophical frame.

Ptolemaic Egypt also gave birth to new syncretic trends, such as the worship of the god Sarapis and the goddess Isis, associated cults of death and regeneration that transposed myths and rituals from the Egyptian religious reservoir into a Hellenistic vocabulary. Such syncretic cults spawned by Greco-Egyptian interaction appears to have appealed mainly to the Hellenized peoples of the Mediterranean rather than to native Egyptians, whose religious needs through the Ptolemaic and into the Roman era continued to be met primarily by the divinities, temples, and rituals which had developed in Pharaonic Egypt.

Although diminishing over time, under Roman rule Egypt and especially its metropole Alexandria continued to occupy an important place in the intellectual life of the Roman world. The country remained a center of classical learning in the early Roman centuries; the astronomer Claudius Ptolemaus, the physician Galen, and the Neoplatonic philosopher Plotinus trained or worked in Alexandria. Due partly to the Empire's own difficulties and the consequent decline of state patronage, partly to internal turmoil, Egypt's prominence in the cultural life of the Mediterranean *oikoumene* faded from the third century onwards. The Museum was out of operation by the fourth century c.e. Part of the collection of the great Library was lost in the course of civil strife in the 270s, the remainder apparently destroyed along with the temple of the uniquely Hellenistic deity Sarapis in the 390s. An active school of Greek philosophy continued to exist in Alexandria until the early Islamic period; but the great days of Hellenistic Egypt were over well before the Arab conquest.

Yet, even as Egypt was coming to play a smaller role on a shrinking pagan stage, it was assuming a prominent place in the new religious and intellectual world of Christianity. Church tradition attributed the foundation of Christianity in Egypt to the Evangelist Mark. Christian texts have been dated to the early second century. Only in the mid-third century is there clear evidence, in the form of Roman persecutions, of an appreciable community of Christians in Egypt. Contemporary scholarship estimates that close to half of the population of the country may have adopted Christianity by the time of the official conversion of the Roman Empire to the new faith in the early fourth century, and that the mass of Egyptians were at least nominally Christian by the close of the fourth century.

Within church history Egypt is usually credited as a pioneer in the evolution of Christian monasticism, the site of the first recorded experiments in both solitary (St. Antony) and communal (St. Pachomius) monastic life. In high church politics Egyptian clerics were deeply involved in the definition of Christian doctrine. During the fiery controversies over the nature of Christ in the fifth century the Egyptian hierarchy took a different position from the gradually-evolving orthodoxy of the Byzantine establishment, adopting the doctrine not of the inseparably united dual nature of Christ, but rather of the singularity and unity of His divine figure. The resulting position, generally termed "Monophysitism" ("one nature"), has been the distinguishing doctrinal mark of Egyptian Christianity.

In time the Christian church became the dominant institution in Byzantine Egypt. Headed by a Patriarch at Alexandria and organized into numerous bishoprics, by the fourth century it had penetrated to the village level. Christian facilities – churches, hospitals, monasteries – acted as social service centers as well as venues of spiritual enlightenment and guidance. Locally its clergy played an important social role of mediation, arbitration, and care of the needy. On a larger stage its bishops acted as intermediaries with state authorities on behalf of the people of their dioceses; nationally the Patriarch of Alexandria was the most powerful figure in Egypt.

Just as a more integrated society was taking shape in Byzantine Egypt, so at last a more unified culture was developing. Its intellectual basis was the shared, although sometimes differently interpreted, premises of Christianity; its medium of expression was the new liturgical script of Coptic (Egyptian infused with Greek terms and written in the Greek alphabet) which superseded Greek with the rise of Christianity. After almost a millennium, the social and intellectual chasms characteristic of Greco-Roman Egypt were being overcome. In the long sweep of Egyptian history, however, this period of social and cultural coalescence was to prove a short-lived phase, a brief interlude which soon gave way to a new era in which different and quite unanticipated patterns of social and cultural as well as of political cleavage came to prevail in Egypt.

THREE

Islamic Egypt

Egypt began a new era of its long history in 639 C.E., when an Arab military detachment invaded the country. It took fully three years of maneuver in the field, of intermittent fighting including one major battle at Heliopolis, and of extended sieges of the strategic fortress of Babylon and of the provincial capital at Alexandria, before the Arab invaders succeeded in wresting control of the country from the Byzantines. Their success in doing so was in part a function of their own military ability and mobility, in part the result of demoralization and divided counsels among the Byzantine leadership in the wake of repeated defeats by the Arabs and the death of the Emperor Heraclius in 641. The eventual Byzantine surrender of Alexandria was negotiated by a treaty guaranteeing the safe evacuation of part of the city's Greek population and the religious rights of those who remained.

EGYPT UNDER THE RASHIDUN, UMMAYAD, AND ABBASID CALIPHATES

From its conquest in the 640s until the late ninth century, Egypt was a province of the Rashidun (632–661), the Ummayad (661–750), and the Abbasid (750–1258) Caliphates. Arab-Muslim conquest and rule initially brought little change to the lives of most Egyptians. While some of the Greek elite left the country upon its conquest by the Arabs, the bulk of the population remained in place and in possession of their property. The new regime governed the country from the new settlement of Fustat (today part of

Cairo), a garrison-town established in the 640s to house the Arab army of occupation and serve as a base for further expansion in North Africa. Through the seventh century the Arab government retained the existing Byzantine administrative structure; Greek remained the language of government and record-keeping. The main tie between the new regime and the indigenous population was taxation which in most cases was left in the hands of native officials. In exchange for a head-tax levied on the native population, the new rulers also tolerated Egyptian Christianity and recognized the religious authority of the existing Monophysite church hierarchy. Arab-Muslim migration into Egypt was limited through the seventh century.

In time, of course, Egypt became a predominantly Arabic-speaking and Muslim country. The adoption of Arabic and the conversion of the majority of Egyptians from Christianity to Islam were processes which took centuries. Arabic became the official language of administration in Egypt only in 706, when the use of Greek for official purposes was prohibited. Coptic, the everyday language of most Egyptians, demonstrated greater resiliency but also eventually succumbed to Arabic. Some tax records continued to be written in both Coptic and Arabic until the eleventh century. Yet by the tenth century Coptic was falling into disuse even among Egypt's still-sizable Christian population; by the eleventh, Coptic bishops were using Arabic to reach their flocks; by the thirteenth, Coptic had become a mainly liturgical language employed in religious purposes but no longer extensively used in daily life.

The conversion of the bulk of Egyptians from Christianity to Islam appears to have taken even longer. In a world where religion defined personal identity and where the religious community structured social life, conversion from one faith to another meant much more than merely professing new beliefs. Nor did the Caliphal regime, interested mainly in the collection of the head-tax imposed upon non-Muslims in exchange for recognition of their religious autonomy, at first encourage conversion to Islam. Conversion through the Ummayad century seems to have been quite limited. It apparently accelerated in the early Abbasid period after the failure of repeated Coptic revolts in the late eighth and early ninth centuries established that the durability of the new Islamic order was no longer in question. The economic as well as social advantages of becoming Muslim operated upon more and more individuals over time.

The form of Islam which took hold in Egypt was Sunnism, the branch enforced and patronized by the Ummayad and Abbasid dynasties. Despite growing numbers of conversions, Egypt retained a sizable Coptic Christian population through the Fatamid and Ayyubid periods (mid-tenth to mid-thirteenth centuries). The most extensive wave of Coptic conversions to Islam may have occurred only in the early Mamluk period (mid-thirteenth to mid-fourteenth centuries). Popular Muslim resentment against Christians, due both to recent Crusader assaults upon Egypt and to Christian prominence in the financial bureaucracy, produced several state-directed campaigns of forced conversion. By the fifteenth century Egypt had become what it has been ever since – a mainly Muslim country with a Christian minority of uncertain size.

The Caliphate's demands upon Egyptians increased over time. The eighth century saw financial reforms which increased the tax obligations levied upon the population and consequently which produced more local discontent than had been evident before 700. Agricultural censi from the early eighth century onwards were designed to better estimate, and thereby more efficiently exploit, the country's rich agricultural resources. In an effort to obtain more revenue for the state, tax rates were also periodically increased in the later Ummayad and early Abbasid periods. The result was a series of local uprisings, first by Coptic peasants protesting against increased taxation, and later by both Coptic and Arab agriculturalists resentful of the rising exactions of the central government. The cycle of revolt and repression through the eighth and early ninth centuries worked in two directions. On the one hand, higher taxes and persistent civil unrest upset the economic stability of the country, producing commercial disruption, peasant flight, and the consequent decline of both agricultural output and tax revenue. On the other hand, the harsh suppression of revolt by the forces of the central government had the effect of demonstrating the permanence of the new order. It thereby may have contributed to the gradual adoption of both Arabic and Islam by Egyptians.

A measure of relief from increasingly exploitative Caliphal rule came in the late ninth century. The century as a whole witnessed the crumbling of the centralized Abbasid state, as provincial generals and strongmen assumed real power in many of the provinces of the far-flung empire. The process of decentralization reached Egypt in 868, when the central government appointed the Turkish general Ahmad ibn Tulun (*d*.884) as governor. Through building up his own slave military loyal to himself, and by combining the power of the treasury as well as control of the army in his own hands, ibn Tulun soon acquired a measure of personal authority no previous Muslim governor of Egypt had possessed. Although he continued to acknowledge the suzerainty of the Abbasid Caliph at Baghdad and to dispatch an annual tribute to the capital, ibn Tulun became in effect an autonomous Egyptian ruler.

Ibn Tulun was also successful in arranging the transfer of the governorship of Egypt to his descendants upon his death. Members of the Tulunid family governed Egypt until 905, when the Abassids dispatched a military expedition and reasserted direct Caliphal control. This rule lasted only thirty years. By 935 another military appointee as governor, Muhammad ibn Tughj "the Ikhshid" (a title derived from his family's Central Asian roots), was appointed governor and soon centralized effective authority in his own hands. Like ibn Tulun he too was able to pass his position to his sons who nominally governed Egypt until the 960s. Real power under the later Ikhshidids was exercised by a family retainer of slave origin, Kafur.

The Tulunid-Ikhshidid interlude from the late ninth to the late tenth centuries set several precedents for the way Egypt was to evolve through much of the remainder of the medieval era. Most importantly, henceforth the country was substantially an independent political unit. This should not be taken to mean that Egyptians controlled their own destiny; under Tulunids and Ikhshidids, as well as under many of their successors, both ruler and ruling elite were largely non-Egyptian, with a considerable political and social gulf separating them from the indigenous population whom they ruled. But now, governed by individuals who identified their interests with those of Egypt, the quasi- or fully-independent regimes that began with the Tulunids often governed the country with a greater ability to foster its internal stability and economic prosperity than had been the case when Egypt had been an Ummayad or Abbasid province. Thus ibn Tulun is credited with paying close attention to the economic productivity of his new domain, supervising the restoration of the irrigation system, which had deteriorated in the course of peasant uprisings against the Abbasids, and eliminating some of the excesses in tax collection which had developed under Caliphal rule. A similar concern for the economic productivity of the country characterized many later autonomous regimes.

THE FATAMID DYNASTY

A very different sort of regime assumed control of Egypt in the late tenth century. The Fatamids, a revolutionary movement professing the Isma'ili variant of Shi'ism, had established itself in power in Tunisia in 909. Asserting that legitimate leadership of the Islamic community rested in the family of the Prophet Muhammad through his daughter Fatima and her husband 'Ali, the movement set out to conquer the Islamic world. The first three Fatamid attempts to conquer Egypt failed. The fourth succeeded. In 969, with the country adrift and the existing elite willing to reach an accommodation in exchange for the preservation of their own positions, a Fatamid army led by the general Jawhar entered Egypt and almost peacefully took control of the country in the name of the Fatamids. For the next two centuries (969–1171), Egypt was the hub of an Isma'ili Shi'ite empire.

The Fatamid conquest was immediately followed by two initiatives which have left a permanent mark upon Egypt. One was Jawhar's establishment of a new city north of the existing urban settlements at and near Fustat. Al-Qahira ("the Victorious") in Arabic, we know it as Cairo. Originally a walled royal residence and garrison-town for the Berber army of the Fatamids, Cairo did not immediately displace Fustat as the national center of commerce and population. In time it did so, engulfing Fustat and becoming the metropolis of Egypt through the later medieval, and into the modern, eras. The other initiative was the establishment in Cairo of al-Azhar, a new mosque intended to serve as the center of Fatamid religious life. Al-Azhar eventually became the preeminent Muslim religious and educational institution in Egypt.

The two hundred years of Fatamid rule over Egypt divide neatly into a century of power and prosperity followed by a century of turmoil and decline. The dynasty itself soon moved its base from Tunisia to Egypt. Egypt was now indisputably an independent state. Fatamid dominion over Egypt was enforced by a large and largely alien military comprising various Berber, Sudanese, and Turkish units. It was implemented by a specialized civilian bureaucracy, many of whose members were non-Muslim or of non-Muslim origin. Internal stability, the solicitude of an efficient bureaucracy concerned with promoting economic productivity, and a vigorous policy of trade expansion resulted in what one author has called "the Fatamid economic miracle": prosperous agriculture, an expanding handicrafts industry, and a flourishing foreign trade network extending from India to Spain.[1] All of this rebounded to the benefit of the Fatamid regime itself, allowing it to support a remarkably opulent court, to undertake the architectural glorification of its new capital, and to pursue an activist foreign policy.

At least initially, Fatamid ambitions were not confined to Egypt. In the late tenth century Fatamid armies carved out an Egyptian sphere of influence in Syria-Palestine and parts of Arabia as far south as the Yemen. Geography and the welter of local political forces which had emerged to the east of Egypt upon the collapse of centralized Abbasid rule prevented the extension of direct Fatamid authority beyond these regions.

Parallel to this military expansion, the early Fatamids pursued a vigorous propaganda effort to win adherents to their variant of Shi'ism. Fatamid missionaries versed in Isma'ili esoterics were dispatched to Arabia, the Gulf, and even to India, seeking to win adherents for the Fatamid cause. Their partial success in doing so both gave birth to some of the smaller Shi'ite communities in these regions, and served to consolidate commercial links between a flourishing Egypt and other Muslim lands. Egypt moved from the periphery to the center of Muslim political and economic life under the Fatamids, a position it was to hold for the rest of the medieval period.

Fatamid religious policy within Egypt itself presents something of a paradox. In contrast to their attempts to spread Shi'ism abroad, the Fatamids were less religiously aggressive in Egypt. Throughout the Fatamid era Shi'ism seems to have remained little more than the religion of the dominant elite living in Cairo. Shi'i law was introduced in the state-supported courts, and public cere-monies organized by the state took on a Shi'i coloring. Yet throughout the Fatamid period the population of the commercial center of Fustat, as well as the bulk of the rural Muslim popu-lation, are presumed to have remained Sunni and relatively unaf-fected by the official Fatamid version of Islam. With the notable exception of the eccentric if not unbalanced Caliph al-Hakim (996–1021), whose erratic policies included the persecution of Christians and the destruction of churches (as well as the prohi-bition of chess and the killing of dogs), the Fatamids are also credited with having been relatively tolerant of the still-sizable non-Muslim population of the country. Much of the civilian financial administration remained in Coptic hands, a situation which continued into later regimes.

The stability and prosperity Egypt had experienced under the early Fatamid Caliphs did not last. In the 1060s dual disasters struck Egypt. Several years of a low Nile flood led to famine throughout the country, and a decade of extended conflict occurred between different ethnic factions in the Fatamid military, in which the state treasury as well as much of the urban population were repeatedly pillaged. A measure of stability was restored in the 1070s. But the Fatamid state was never the same. Military strongmen dominated relatively weak Fatamid caliphs and competed for power among themselves through the second century of Fatamid rule; the previous efficient civilian administration which had fostered internal economic prosperity gave way to a more militarized and exploitative state. Externally the First Crusade's conquest of parts of Syria and Palestine, including Fatamid Jerusalem, in the 1090s meant the effective end of the Fatamid sphere of influence in the Fertile Crescent.

The end came in the 1160s, when conflict between rival strongmen prompted the main contenders for power to seek external support. A military force dispatched by the Muslim ruler of Damascus came to the aid of one faction; shortly thereafter a Crusader army entered the country at the behest of another. Egypt now became the scene of international rivalry between Christian Crusaders and Muslim counter-Crusaders; at one point in the struggle Egypt briefly became a Crusader protectorate. Ultimately Muslim arms prevailed. By 1169 the Crusaders had been repulsed and Egypt was in the hands of a military force now commanded by the Kurdish general Salah al-Din (Saladin). Two years later, as the last Fatamid Caliph lay on his deathbed, Egypt's new de facto strongman offered formal allegiance to the Abbasid Caliph at Baghdad. After two centuries, Egypt was again under Sunni – although still foreign – rule.

SALADIN AND THE AYYUBIDS

Saladin and his family ruled Egypt for nearly a century. Known in history as the Ayyubids (from Saladin's father Ayyub), they also exercised dominion over much of the Fertile Crescent. Saladin is the most famous and historically important of the Ayyubids. Operating from a solid base in Egypt, in the 1170s and 1180s he gradually brought much of greater Syria and northern Iraq under his authority. Now disposing of a larger military force than his predecessors in the counter-Crusade, in 1187–89 he destroyed the main Crusader army in the field and conquered much of the Latin Kingdom of Jerusalem. His assault on the main Crusader state set off the Third Crusade, involving the dispatch of several Latin Christian armies to Palestine to succour their co-religionists in the East. After three years of warfare centered on the Palestinian port of Acre, part of the territory of the Kingdom of Jerusalem was restored to Latin Christian rule. Nonetheless, Saladin's victories and conquests mark a turning-point in the contest between Muslims and Christians in the Fertile Crescent. With the Crusader states now largely restricted to the coastal strip, they were henceforth a much weaker force in the hurly-burly of eastern Mediterranean politics.

Saladin left his mark on Egypt as well. His termination of Fatamid Shi'ite rule in 1171 was followed by the restoration of Sunnism. Al-Azhar now became a Sunni institution; a Sunni chief judge replaced the Shi'ite appointee who had headed the Muslim legal establishment under the Fatamids. The *madrasa*, a new form of religious school developed in Western Asia to train Sunni scholar-jurists, was introduced to Egypt by Saladin; the madrasa in time became the dominant institution providing for Muslim higher education. Saladin's most visible mark on Egypt was beginning the construction of the Citadel, the massive fortress erected on a spur of the hills to the southeast of Cairo which henceforth became the seat of political power in Egypt.

Ayyubid rule over Egypt itself is generally regarded as having been beneficial for Egypt. The domestic economy prospered under the firm hand of Saladin and his immediate successors. Attention was paid to restoring irrigation works which had deteriorated in the strife of the later Fatamid years, and foreign trade both across the Mediterranean and to the Indian Ocean was encouraged by the regime. Culturally the country benefited from the turmoil produced by the Turkic migrations and Crusader invasions which were ravaging eastern Islamic lands. Migration to a more secure Egypt from turbulent eastern regions contributed to a shift in the balance of cultural leadership within the Muslim world from the east to the west, a shift which accelerated in the thirteenth century onwards as a result of the Mongol invasions.

When the Ayyubids fell, it was to internal challengers. In the face of continued external threats including two unsuccessful Crusader invasions of Egypt (1218–1221, 1249–1250), the later Ayyubids came to place greater reliance on highly trained mounted archers as their elite shock troops. Acquiring the skills demanded for the effective use of a recurved bow from horseback required great physical stamina and years of military training. To acquire suitable recruits, the regime relied more and more on the purchase of young Turkish slaves who could be subjected to the necessary discipline and rigor. By the 1240s such Turkish *mamluks* ("owned," "possessed") had become the core of the Ayyubid army. Eventually this elite force did as might have been expected: it took power into its own hands. The death of the last effective Ayyubid ruler, al-Malik al-Salih, in 1249, was followed by a decade of court intrigue, assassinations, several rulers, including the brief tenure of an Ayyubid princess as Sultan, and the eventual rise of the Mamluks to power. The definitive transition came in 1260 when one of their number, Baybars al-Bunduqdari, murdered the incumbent strongman (a fellow Mamluk) and consolidated power within Egypt. Thus began yet another alien regime in Egypt – the Mamluk "state of the Turks" [*dawlat al-atrak*] which was to rule Egypt for over two and a half centuries.

THE MAMLUKS

Even before assuming power, Baybars had been a field commander in the Mamluk army which had defeated an invading Mongol force at the battle of 'Ayn Jalut in Palestine in 1260, thereby preventing the extension of Mongol dominion from Iraq into Syria. Facing the Mongol menace and consolidating Mamluk control over Egypt's Syrian balcony absorbed much of Baybars' attention once in power. He did both with considerable success, checking Mongol probes from Iraq and subduing many of the smaller Muslim political units which had contested for territory in Syria upon the decline of the Ayyubids. From Baybars onwards, the Mamluk state included most of greater Syria as well as Egypt. Thanks in part to Baybars' adding to the new regime's Islamic legitimacy through giving refuge to a member of the Abbasid family after the Mongol conquest of Baghdad, the new regime was also able to exercise indirect authority over the Holy Cities of Mecca and Medina in western Arabia.

In the process of extending Mamluk authority in Syria, Baybars also reduced several of the remaining Crusader strongholds in Syria and Palestine. The final elimination of the Crusader presence in greater Syria was accomplished by his immediate successors Qalawun and al-Malik al-Ashraf. Thanks to their role in defending the Islamic west from the Mongols and their reduction of the remaining Crusader enclaves, the early Mamluk sultans occupy a place parallel to Saladin in the Egyptian historical memory – as champions of Sunni Islam against the infidel invaders who threatened the Muslim world in the twelfth and thirteenth centuries.

The Mamluk era from 1260 to 1517 is conventionally divided into two periods of almost equal length. From 1260 until 1382, the Mamluk sultans and their main military force of horse archers were primarily drawn from Kipchak Turks imported from the steppes of southern Russia and the Ukraine. This first phase of Mamluk rule is known as the Bahri period (from *bahr*, "river," due to the original barracks of the Kipchak Turk regiment being situated on an island in the Nile). After 1382, most sultans and their core military elite were drawn from Circassian slave recruits imported from the Caucasus. This is the Burji period (from *burj*, "tower," since the Circassion Mamluks were initially garrisoned in the tower of the Citadel).

The early Bahri decades were a period of relative stability and considerable prosperity. Both Baybars (1260–1277) and Qalawun (1279–1290) had relatively long and secure reigns by Mamluk standards. Although the 1290s were a decade of turbulence at the top, for most of the early fourteenth century the country benefited from the long reign of the able autocrat al-Nasir Muhammad (1298–1308, 1310–1341). Under the early Bahri sultans Egypt was the center of a large state disposing of complementary resources and controlling the trade routes from the east to the Mediterranean. Early Mamluk rulers encouraged foreign trade with India to the east and Europe to the north. The combination of internal prosperity and migration from abroad seems to have generated an appreciable increase in Egypt's population, which is estimated to have grown from under three million in the reign of Saladin to over four million in the early fourteenth century. Cairo in particular flourished under the early Mamluks. The city may have reached a population of half a million or more in the reign of al-Nasir Muhammad, a size it was not again to achieve until the late nineteenth century. Artistically the Mamluk era as a whole was one of lavish patronage of art and architecture by Egypt's ruling elite. It was under the Mamluks that many of the splendid mosques and *madrasas*, which still distinguish the medieval sections of Cairo, were erected.

The shift to a darker age occurred in the 1340s. The four decades after the death of al-Nasir Muhammad (d.1341) saw frequent civil war between different Mamluk factions. More important was the social disaster which struck in the 1340s. The Pan-Asian pandemic of bubonic plague known as the Black Death devastated Egypt just as it devastated Europe. Its initial visitation in 1347–1349 is estimated to have carried off one-quarter to one-third of the population of Egypt; perhaps two hundred thousand died in Cairo alone. The plague returned regularly throughout the later fourteenth and fifteenth centuries. By one count, there were fifty-five outbreaks of plague, twenty major ones, in Egypt from 1347 to the end of Mamluk rule in 1517. It is the immeasurable but undisputed decline of population produced by this repeated biological assault, with its attendant effects on workforce, productivity, and revenue, which lay at the root of many of the economic difficulties of the later Mamluk period.

The Burji period (1382–1517) was unquestionably a more troubled one than that of the Bahri sultans. Of twenty-one fifteenth-century sultans, only eight reigned for more than five years. In time, perpetual semi-civil war among different Mamluk factions led to a collapse of civic order. Outside the capital the erosion of central authority encouraged tribal revolts, particularly in Upper Egypt, against the rule of the alien and oppressive Mamluks. As the fifteenth century progressed, so did the vicious cycle of violence: "tribal disorder alternated with Mamluk frightfulness."[2]

Political instability was accompanied by economic decline. The drop in Egyptian productivity and tax-revenue due to the decline in population produced by recurrent bouts of plague and occasional low Niles led the regime to enact emergency measures which in the short term raised the desired revenue but had adverse long-term effects on the economy. Higher taxation and emergency financial levies imposed additional burdens on Egypt's now-smaller population. The expenditure of the bulk of what revenue was raised on foreign campaigns and inter-Mamluk strife reduced the consumption of luxury goods by the ruling elite and had deleterious effects on domestic handicrafts production. Extra-legal extortion by Mamluks and allied urban gangs plundered the urban economy and further accelerated its contraction. In the commercial sector, state monopolies of trade in particular products (sugar, pepper) eventually led to the disappearance of the class of private international merchants under whose initiative foreign trade had flourished. The depreciation of Egypt's previously solid currency further contributed to the erosion of Egypt's standing as a trade entrepôt. All was not darkness across the entire fifteenth century; the longer reigns of the Sultans Barsbay (1422–1438) and Qaitbay (1468–1496) were interludes of relative prosperity. But the overall trend was unmistakable – a decline in Egypt's agricultural base, its urban economy, and its commercial position.

The end of the Mamluk Sultanate came in the early sixteenth century. The regime faced major external threats from two directions after 1500. To the south and east Portuguese expansion into the Indian Ocean was immediately seen as a menace to what was left of Egypt's place in international trade. It prompted the Mamluk Sultan Qansawh al-Ghawri (1501–1516) to dispatch a fleet to contend – unsuccessfully – with the Portuguese for control of eastern waters. More serious was the threat from the north. Since the later fifteenth century Mamluk and Ottoman forces had skirmished over control of the borderlands between the two empires in northern Syria and southern Anatolia. A decisive clash might have been avoided save for the emergence of a militant Shi'ite dynasty in Iran which posed a serious challenge to Ottoman regional dominance. In the process of mounting a campaign against these heretics, the Ottoman Sultan Selim I decided to eliminate a potential Mamluk danger on his southern flank. Mamluk and Ottoman forces met in pitched battle at Marj Dabiq in northern Syria in August 1516. Thanks in part to a schism among the Mamluk leadership which eventually led to treachery, in part to the Ottoman possession of firearms (a weapon which the hidebound Mamluk elite had rejected as an unworthy device "with which even a woman could stop a number of men"[3]), Ottoman victory was complete. Thereafter Selim proceeded south through Syria to Egypt. Defeating what was left of Mamluk forces early in 1517, the Ottoman sultan entered Cairo, hung the last Mamluk Sultan Tumanbay (1516–1517) from the Zuwayla Gate, and had his own name read from the pulpits as new sovereign of Egypt. The long Ottoman era of Egyptian history was underway.

EGYPTIAN POLITICS AND SOCIETY UNDER THE MAMLUKS

Thanks to a large pool of contemporary chronicles and a rich legacy of physical remains, the Mamluk era has received more scholarly analysis than preceding periods of the Islamic epoch. It is in the Mamluk period that the characteristic institutions of Egyptian Muslim society can be clearly identified. Some of what applied in the Mamluk era had developed earlier; but it is only under the Mamluks that we can specify with precision the functional interrelationships among polity, economy, and society. The Mamluk era is where we see Islamic Egypt at its clearest.

Politically, Mamluk Egypt was dominated by an alien military elite. Originally mainly of Turkish ethnic origin, later primarily Circassian, there were never more than some tens of thousands of Mamluks living in Egypt and involved in politics at any one time. Captured by raiders or sold into slavery by their parents in youth, then purchased by Genoese slavers in the markets bordering the Black Sea and shipped to Egypt, the young men were enrolled in one or another Mamluk regiment. Converted to Islam and rigorously trained as mounted archers, Mamluks were emancipated upon completion of their military training. Describing the Mamluks as "slaves" is only partially correct. They were such early in their careers, but not once they entered active military service and moved on to assume positions of political leadership.

The key institution of Mamluk politics was the household. Foreign to Egypt, at first largely isolated from indigenous society, and undergoing intensive training with their regimental compatriots, Mamluks developed fierce attachments both to their regiments and their commanders. Regiments in time gave birth to what are known as households comprising a Mamluk commander, his loyal military followers, both slave and free, and associated civilian supporters (lawyers, scribes, merchants, toadies). Such households in effect became the political parties of the age. The internal political history of the Mamluk era was an incessant round of struggle between different Mamluk households for control of the sultanate. In most instances the death of the incumbent sultan immediately triggered a succession crisis. One scenario was for the leaders of the main households to maintain a son of the deceased ruler as puppet while parcelling out the spoils of office amongst themselves. Another, one which became the more prevalent pattern over time, was for the strongest commander to seize the sultanate himself and place his own Mamluks in key positions of power.

A remarkable feature of the Mamluk period was the relative marginalization of the children of Mamluks within the political system. Although there was no formal regulation excluding the sons of Mamluks from the military, throughout the Mamluk era army regiments drew the majority of their personnel from newly-imported slave recruits rather than from either the children of Mamluks or the indigenous population. On the one hand, Turko-Circassian youth, raised on the steppes or in the mountains, were believed to make the best warriors; on the other, slaves could most effectively be subjected to the rigorous training necessary to produce competent mounted archers. Exclusion of the *awlad al-nas* ("children of the people" i.e., the people who matter) was not total; some offspring of Mamluks entered the military and rose to positions of command, others served in auxiliary cavalry units. But the majority appear to have been absorbed into civilian society, becoming administrators, religious scholars, and occasionally literary figures of note. In effect they served as an intermediary stratum linking the largely alien ruling elite with their subjects.

The overall durability of this political system in which heridity mattered for little and a self-renewing alien elite engaged in a constant struggle for power demands analysis. The most plausible explanation is that Mamluk factionalism was a self-perpetuating zero-sum game. The division of the military elite into different regiments and households guaranteed continual strife. The victory of one household immediately generated winners and losers; the losers – if they remained alive – in turn soon banded together to renew the struggle. Since no sultan ever succeeded in replacing regiments and households with a more centralized military, there was no mechanism for breaking the endless cycle of factional strife.[4]

Equally intriguing is the question of how this alien military caste, which never amounted to more than a small percentage of the population of the lands they ruled, succeeded in dominating civilian society. Ultimately, Mamluk rule rested on force. The chronicles of the period are replete with examples of Mamluk violence directed against the indigenous population of Egypt and Syria. In theory only Mamluks could bear arms and ride horses. From horseback, they simply terrorized those lesser breeds who crossed their path. The sudden and arbitrary use of force both by the government and its dominant military elite; frequent resort to cruelty to make a point; ingenious methods of torture employed both for exemplary purposes and to extract wealth from others: all these measures were routine in the Mamluk era. Egypt under the Mamluks was not a very secure place to live.

There are also deeper structural reasons for the durability of Mamluk rule. The Mamluk system had an equally important basis in the military elite's appropriation of the bulk of the productive surplus of the country and their use of the revenues thereof to establish relations of clientage and dependency within civilian society. The institution of the *iqta'* – the grant of tax revenues from a specified agricultural area to a military officer in order for him to maintain a set number of troops – had developed in Western Asia under the Abbasids and been introduced into Egypt under the Fatamids and Ayyubids. Further refined under the Mamluks, the *iqta'* system was the financial basis of Mamluk rule, the mechanism assuring that the bulk of Egyptian (and Syrian) tax revenues fell into the hands of the military elite.

There were various grades and sizes of *iqta's*. The higher-ranking officers responsible for maintaining a hundred Mamluks from the revenue of their *iqta'* could have the tax revenues from an entire village or more at their disposal; lesser commanders of forty, or ten, or of five troopers would receive smaller grants. In time the *iqta'* system was extended to the urban economy. Even the granting of taxation-rights over such dubious enterprises as the sale of alcoholic drinks and prostitution were reported in the sources. The annual income of a high-level Mamluk commander in the more prosperous fourteenth century could reach a million dirhams, the equivalent of the annual wages of two thousand craftsmen. Mamluk *iqta's* were firmly centralized; heriditary succession to an *iqta'* was very rare and assignments were often short-term, particular *iqta's* frequently rotating among Mamluk commanders depending on the outcome of factional jockeying. The holders of *iqta's* were also assigned rural administrative functions relating to the maintenance of irrigation works and the supervision of the agricultural cycle. These obligations were exercised with varying degrees of effectiveness. In the more stable Bahri period Mamluk assignees of *iqta's* seem to have carried out these duties with relative efficiency. In the Burji period Mamluk concern for and attention to rural upkeep often lapsed due to the persistent inter-elite conflict of the era, further accelerating the agricultural decline which Egypt experienced in the fifteenth century.

The uses to which the Mamluks put the wealth obtained from the mechanism of the *iqta'* system are the key to their institutionalized dominance of civilian society. However turbulent at the top, Mamluk Egypt never saw the indigenous majority mount a serious internal threat to alien Mamluk rule. The rural majority, internally divided into hundreds of separate village communities and unable to combine for effective collective action, presented no serious threat to Mamluk domination. Tribal areas excepted, we hear little of sustained unrest or revolt in the Egyptian countryside after the early Abbasid period.

Urban Egypt saw more unrest: accounts of periodic bread riots in years of a low Nile, of the participation of urban gangs in inter-elite Mamluk conflict, even of occasional slave uprisings, pepper the chronicles of the Mamluk era. Yet none of this shook Mamluk rule over Egypt. Why not? The answer in large part lies in the ways in which the Mamluks linked key elements of Egypt's urban population to themselves and in effect bought collaboration through giving these groups a stake in the preservation of Mamluk rule.

There were three interrelated sectors of Egyptian urban society which had to be incorporated into the system to assure continued Mamluk dominance. The first was Egypt's commercial and merchant elite whose wealth gave them leverage within urban society. The second was Egypt's cultural elite composed of the Muslim religious class or *'ulama* ("learned men") whose moral authority gave them the ability to influence what, by the Mamluk period, had become Egypt's Muslim majority. The third were organized elements of the lower classes grouped together in an overlapping network of religious brotherhoods and neighborhood gangs, the potential of both of which for collective action had to be directed into channels where it would not threaten the regime itself.

Absorption of the merchant class was achieved primarily by economic means. Controlling the bulk of Egypt's agricultural surplus, Mamluk households were economic conglomerates. The economic viability of many members of the merchant elite was dependent on their access to the grain or other agricultural products which had been paid in kind as taxes, which had made their way into Mamluk-run granaries, and which Mamluk households subsequently sold through agents in urban markets. In time Mamluk households came to own much of the urban economy as well, accumulating workshops and markets in their economic portfolios. Thus much of Egypt's merchant and artisan population came to depend on good relations with one or another Mamluk household for their existence. As a consequence, they were in no position to rock the Mamluk ship of state. "The livelihood of everyone was attuned to the Mamluks ... ."[5]

The Mamluk-*'ulama* relationship was more complex. Much of the power and influence of the Muslim religious class in Mamluk Egypt came from the degree to which they permeated all levels of urban society. *'Ulama* served as preachers in the mosques, ministering to the spiritual needs of Muslim Egyptians. They were the teachers in the network of *madrasas* which had emerged in Egyptian cities by the Mamluk era, disseminating the principles of

Islam to the small minority of male Muslims who received formal education as well as to the occasional female who might informally audit their lectures. Perhaps where they touched urban society most profoundly was in their role as interpreters of Muslim religious law and as judges in the religious courts. 'Ulama administered the Islamic sacred law or *Shari'a*, the detailed body of legal norms based on Qur'anic injunctions and the example of the Prophet, which in theory governed all areas of life and was the primary definer of Muslim behavioral norms. The *'ulama* also sometimes served as the spiritual guides of the mystical Sufi brotherhoods (*tariqat*) whose prayers, rituals, and assemblies provided much of the personal and emotional content of religion for Egyptian Muslims. The influence of the *'ulama* reached all layers of urban society: rich and poor, educated and uneducated, male and (to a lesser degree) female, all looked for instruction and/or inspiration to this multicompetent religious elite.

The key to Mamluk influence over the *'ulama* was again economic. Although some *'ulama* had supplementary civilian occupations which generated independent incomes, as a body the religious class was dependent on the patronage of the Mamluks both for their individual well-being and for the support of the institutions they staffed. It was the patronage of Mamluk sultans and households which built the majority of the mosques and associated *madrasas* in which the *'ulama* worked, and which established permanent endowments to pay for the upkeep of these facilities and their employees. The Mamluk government itself recognized and supported the system of *Shari'a* courts staffed by *'ulama*. Similarly, some of the heads of Sufi orders were officially confirmed in their positions of leadership by the sultan. Sufi brotherhoods also received state support in the form of endowments supporting the convents or monasteries in which they pursued the inner way, as well as through gifts upon the occasion of religious festivals or the accession of a new sultan.

Despite its financial support of the religious class, the relationship between the Mamluk state and the *'ulama* was an ambivalent one. On the one hand the *'ulama* legitimized Mamluk rule through formally professing their loyalty to a new sultan upon his accession, through preaching obedience to the regime from their pulpits, and through calling upon the populace to support the

Mamluk defense of Islam against Christian Crusaders and infidel Mongols. On the other, the *'ulama* sometimes used their moral authority in an effort to mitigate the effects of interminable inter-elite strife, to petition the sultan or Mamluk households to reduce the scale of the financial demands they placed upon the populace, and occasionally to lead popular demonstrations protesting against high prices, grain shortages, or forced exactions. The *'ulama* were the lubricating oil of the system, the agent operating to reduce friction among its component parts.

Finally, how did the Mamluk state control Egypt's non-elite urban population? Mob action or violence in the form of riots over high grain prices, of assaults on lesser government functionaries associated with unpopular policies, and of crime pure and simple, were all persistent features of Mamluk Egypt. Yet none of this considerable urban unrest seriously imperilled Mamluk domination. The reason it did not do so was the regime's ability to divert popular frustrations onto easier and more appealing targets than the regime itself. Protest by the organized Sufi brotherhoods was constrained by their partial economic dependence on Mamluk largesse; it was also sometimes diverted into channels which did not threaten Mamluk dominance (e.g. attacks on wine shops, anti-Christian violence). The Mamluk relationship with the youth gangs (*zu'ar*) existing on the fringes of urban society was a symbiotic one. Urban toughs were sometimes enrolled as auxiliaries in inter-Mamluk factional struggles and in effect given a license to plunder the possessions of a rival faction. In other cases they were simply allocated a share of the spoils of state, being allowed to establish their own protection rackets similar to those operated by Mamluk households themselves over sectors of the urban economy. In effect, "Zu'ar violence was taken under the aegis of the Mamluks and turned back against the larger society... . What organized forces existed among the masses were thus contained within the existing political order."[6]

Especially in the fifteenth century, when Mamluk factional fighting became endemic and urban security largely collapsed, the power and exploitative role of organized elements of the urban underclass also increased. Both Mamluk viciousness and gang extortion ravaged civil society in the final years of the Mamluk era. Late Mamluk Egypt appears to have been experiencing institutional disintegration, the collapse of a functioning, if brutal, social order into a Hobbesian state-of-nature. Although never a land of idyllic bliss, at its best under the early Mamluk sultans Egypt had been considerably better than that. At least in urban areas, a routinized network of linkages had bound both civilian elites and popular classes to the regime. The institutional structure, while it unquestionably gave by far the most to the dominant Mamluks, met at least some of the needs of the organized sectors of civil society, giving them a stake in the system and thereby assuring the perpetuation of the Mamluk-dominated order until its defeat by an external force in 1517.

Ottoman Egypt

E gypt was a province of the Ottoman Empire from 1517 to 1914. The four centuries of Ottoman rule were not a uniform era of Egyptian history. This chapter covers the first three centuries of the Ottoman period (1517–1798), when substantially similar patterns existed equally in the country's political dynamics and in its social structure. The following chapter will address the course of Egyptian history over the long nineteenth century (1798–1914), when new developments in politics, economics, and society produced major transformations in the nature of Egyptian life.

EGYPT AS AN OTTOMAN PROVINCE

Egypt has been termed the "linchpin" of Ottoman dominion over the Middle East in the sixteenth and seventeenth centuries.[1] After its conquest Egypt served as a strategic base for Ottoman military operations in the eastern Mediterranean, the Red Sea, and western Asia; troops from the Egyptian garrison fought in Ottoman wars throughout the region. Of greater moment was Egypt's economic place within the Empire. Shortly after the conquest the annual remittance of surplus taxes from Egypt and Syria to the Ottoman treasury has been estimated as having provided fully one-third of imperial revenues. Egypt was also a major source of food (grain, sugar, rice) and other commodities for the gigantic market represented by the imperial capital of Istanbul. In the eighteenth century Egypt's political and economic significance within the empire gradually diminished, as both the erosion of Ottoman authority after

1700 and the internal turmoil that the country experienced served to limit what Egypt could provide in the way of manpower, revenue, and goods. The unruly Egyptian military was too out-of-control to be of use in foreign wars; budget surpluses shrank and in time dried up; the annual remittance to Istanbul was eventually replaced by a smaller tribute deriving from the sale of vacated Egyptian tax-farms.

An imperial decree (*Qanun-name*) of 1525 established the permanent format for Ottoman rule. It created a hybrid system of government and administration which differed significantly from other Ottoman provinces. It did so most specifically in its attempt to combine direct Ottoman supervision of Egyptian affairs with the adoption of the existing Mamluk military class as agents of Ottoman dominion.

Overall executive authority in Egypt was vested in an Ottoman governor variously referred to as *beylerbey*, *wali*, *wazir*, or *basha* ("pasha"). Governors were appointed for a term of one year; reappointment was possible. Until the nineteenth century appointees were drawn overwhelmingly from the Ottoman bureaucratic elite centered in Istanbul. Both their short term in office and their relative unfamiliarity with the province they were asssigned to govern often limited the effectiveness of governors in carrying out these tasks. Governors were advised in the conduct of their duties by a central council (*diwan*) comprising military commanders, top bureaucrats, and religious dignitaries. Several Ottoman regiments were stationed in Egypt as a permanent military garrison responsible for external defense and internal security. The civilian administration, the centerpiece of which was the treasury department, was staffed primarily by native Egyptians.

Actual Ottoman authority over the Egyptian countryside varied appreciably with geography and time. The districts in the more accessible Egyptian Delta were usually under central control save at their edges, where tribal elements sometimes exercised effective power. In Upper Egypt, geographically more remote from the center of Ottoman rule in Cairo, Ottoman dominion was often contested by powerful Arab tribes. Arab tribes were a frequent source of unrest early in the Ottoman period, until the combination of military repression and the appointment of leading tribal shaykhs as government agents in particular locales, worked to neutralize tribal resistance. Tribes continued to play a role in the political jockeying for power through much of the Ottoman period, their autonomy and power being significantly constrained only in the later eighteenth century.

A primary concern of the Ottoman regime governing Egypt was tapping the country's economic wealth. Taxes on the agricultural yield of the countryside are estimated to have comprised roughly two-thirds of all tax revenues collected from the late sixteenth through the late eighteenth centuries. Non-agricultural taxes (customs duties and other levies on commerce, license fees on urban crafts, fines imposed for violations of commercial regulations, the poll-tax collected from non-Muslims) generated the remaining one-third of tax revenue.

Methods of Ottoman tax collection within its Egyptian province varied in both character and effectiveness. Upon conquest the previous *iqta'* system of rural administration and tax-collection employed by the Mamluk Sultanate was abolished and replaced with the direct collection of taxes by salaried officials of the provincial administration. Through much of the sixteenth century a combination of effective governors and relative internal tranquillity did result in effective Ottoman tax collection. By the later sixteenth century, the financial difficulties which afflicted the Ottoman Empire as a whole from the 1580s onwards (inflation, depreciation of the currency, rising costs of defense), as well as pressure from local power groups, led to a gradual shift from direct tax collection to the practice of tax-farming as the prevalent mode of both rural and urban taxation. A tax-farm (*iltizam*) was the allocation of the right of tax collection over a specific locale or enterprise to a private individual who was obligated to return the stipulated tax to the central treasury, but could keep the surplus collected as personal profit. For the government tax-farming meant a more rapid receipt of revenue; for the tax-farmer (*multazim*) it meant an opportunity to get rich.

Sold at auction to the highest bidder, *iltizams* became the basis of most private fortunes in seventeenth- and eighteenth-century Egypt. They proliferated over time, coming to encompass not only tax rights over agricultural areas but also the right of tax collection over urban shops, commerce, and service occupations. Originally granted primarily to members of the military elite, tax-farms in time came to be held by a variety of people. In 1797, on the eve of the French invasion of Egypt, fifty-nine percent of existing tax-farms were in the hands of military men, nineteen percent were held by tribal shaykhs, thirteen percent by women, and seven percent by *'ulama*. By the eighteenth century many tax-farms had come to approximate private property, being sold, bought, and mortgaged, and their holders receiving the right to pass them on to their heirs. Tax-farming proved a counterproductive practice for the central government. Statistics gathered by the French indicate that the central treasury was receiving only one-fifth of the land tax collected from rural areas, most of the rest remaining in the hands of tax-farmers.

GOVERNORS, REGIMENTS, AND MAMLUKS

The contest for the control of tax-farms and the revenue they generated was the central dynamic of Egyptian politics from the sixteenth through the eighteenth centuries. On one level this involved a perennial struggle between the central administration of the province headed by the pasha and more locally-based constellations of power. By far the most important of the latter were the military forces stationed in Egypt. What complicated the contest was the co-existence and competition of two rival military cadres – the Ottoman regiments permanently garrisoned in Egypt, and the Mamluk military class which continued to perpetuate itself through the first three centuries of Ottoman rule. Ottoman Egyptian politics were a triangular struggle among Ottoman governors, Ottoman regiments, and Mamluks, an endless tussle in which each of the three parties emerged dominant at particular points in time but none succeeded in totally eliminating their rivals and thus in changing the nature of the game.

Four Ottoman regiments were permanently stationed in Egypt upon its conquest. Three additional regiments, in part created to incorporate Mamluks into the Ottoman military, were formed between the 1520s and the 1550s. These regiments provided external security, policed (with varying degrees of commitment) the major cities, and furnished the personnel for local garrisons in the countryside. Over time, Mamluks and other residents of Egypt entered Ottoman ranks. Their officers obtained control of tax-farms and, as more and more urban guilds affiliated with particular units for protection, a considerable civilianization of the originally Ottoman regiments occurred.

Ottoman regiments were not the only military force in Ottoman Egypt. In part because of their perceived military utility, in part because they were viewed as a counterweight to insurrection on the part of the local garrison, the preexisting Mamluk military elite was soon incorporated into the fabric of Ottoman rule. The *Qanun-name* of 1525 gave formal recognition to the Mamluks, creating the first Mamluk regiment and appropriating many of the administrative techniques developed under the Mamluk Sultanate as part of the Ottoman system. Slaves destined for training as Mamluks continued to be imported to Egypt throughout the first three centuries of Ottoman rule. In place of the dominance of first Kipchak Turks and later Circassians under the Mamluk Sultanate, Mamluk recruits under the Ottomans came from a variety of ethnic groups both within and outside the Empire. In time Georgians and other peoples of the Caucasus, Anatolian Turks, Greeks, Bosnians, Albanians, even western European captives, could be found among the ranks of the Mamluks.

Mamluk commanders appointed to Ottoman military or civilian posts were known as beys. As time progressed, Mamluk beys played an increasingly prominent role in the Ottoman government of Egypt. Because of their familiarity with local conditions they were often appointed as district administrators. When tax-farming replaced direct tax collection, beys received many of the tax-farms. From the later sixteenth through the eighteenth centuries, Mamluk beys and their military retainers were a central, and frequently the dominant, force in Egyptian politics.

The agency through which Ottoman regimental officers and Mamluk beys conducted their struggle for office and power was the household. Households of the Ottoman period in many ways resembled those which had dominated political life under the Mamluk Sultanate. The basis of a household was a patron-client relationship between a powerful army commander and his military slaves, free soldiers, and civilian retainers. The physical center of the household was the "house" (*bayt*) of the master, which variously served as his palatial residence, assembly-point for clients, and fortress in time of need. Households in turn allied with one another in coalitions or factions which competed – sometimes through financial and other forms of influence, sometimes by force – for control of high office, tax-farms, and political dominance.

There were also differences between the households of the Mamluk and Ottoman eras. Whereas previously the leadership of households had been monopolized by the Mamluk military elite, under the Ottomans high civilian officials and regimental officers were sometimes able to construct networks of retainers. Households of the Ottoman period included a wider range of members – Ottoman functionaries resident in Egypt, migrants from elsewhere in the Empire who came to Egypt as soldiers, native Egyptians who had succeeded in infiltrating the ranks of the military. Households of this nature were not unique to Ottoman Egypt; they have been analyzed as "the fundamental assimilative structure of Ottoman elite society," the mechanism through which a mobile and multi-ethnic cohort of governmental functionaries, military slaves and mercenaries, and other ambitious men moving through the sprawling territories of the Ottoman Empire, were absorbed and integrated into local structures of power.[2]

The balance of power among governors, Ottoman regiments, and Mamluk beys of course varied over time. The overall efficiency of the imperial apparatus in the early and mid-sixteenth century allowed Ottoman pashas to retain local dominance for the first several decades of Ottoman rule. After 1580 financial pressures and the consequent resort to tax-farming strengthened the hand of Mamluk beys and their households in particular. Save for occasional interludes of regimental resurgence or successful manipulation of factional rivalries by governors, coalitions of Mamluk households were the preeminent force in Egyptian politics for most of the seventeenth and eighteenth centuries.

A serious attempt to transcend the structural limits of factional struggle came only in the later eighteenth century, during the brief ascendancy of the military strongman 'Ali Bey "al-Kabir" ("the Great"). 'Ali Bey controlled Egypt for only a few years in the later 1760s and early 1770s. Yet in that short time he undertook major new initiatives which, although transitory, nonetheless anticipate the more permanent changes effected by the viceroy Muhammad 'Ali early in the next century. One such precedent was his ruthless attempt at both political and economic centralization. Politically his reign combined an attempt to place his own retainers in the key posts of state with a sweeping purge of rival military households in Cairo; he also mounted a systematic campaign of repression of the tribal elements in Upper Egypt which had been a thorn in the side of the provincial government throughout the Ottoman period. The economic counterpart of these policies was his effort to assert control of tax-farms and other sources of state revenue, such as customs duties, for the benefit of himself and his followers, and his imposition of onerous new forced extractions on the urban economy to support the expansion of his military machine and the territory under his control. Externally 'Ali Bey's military forces invaded both the Hijaz and Syria, bringing the Holy Cities under his sway and at one point reaching as far north as Damascus. 'Ali Bey also entered into diplomatic contact with a European power (in his case Russia, involved in war with the Ottoman Empire in the early 1770s), and brought European military experts to Egypt to advise and improve the capabilities of his military forces. Deposing two Ottoman appointees as pasha and inserting his own name into the Friday sermon (a traditional Muslim symbol of sovereignty), 'Ali Bey seems to have been on the verge of moving towards formal independence prior to the abrupt crumbling of his rule in the face of a challenge from an ambitious subordinate in 1772–73.

Despite parallels with his nineteenth-century counterpart, 'Ali Bey the Great did not effect a permanent structural change in the nature of Egyptian politics and administration. After his fall, Mamluk factions and factionalism remained the essential feature of politics; tax-farming continued as the main method of taxation, and his external initiatives proved ephemeral. Bitter factional strife persisted through most of the 1770s; in the 1780s and 1790s Egyptian politics were dominated by the uneasy alliance of two Mamluk household leaders, Ibrahim and Murad Beys. They were still effectively the dominant political figures in the country in July 1798, when a French military force commanded by Napoleon Bonaparte disembarked at Alexandria.

TURKS AND PEASANTS, MUSLIMS AND NON-MUSLIMS

The Ottoman and Mamluk elite dominating Egyptian politics formed only a small proportion of the country's population under

Ottoman rule. The bulk of the populace was made up of native-born Egyptians, by now overwhelmingly Arabic-speaking and primarily Muslim in religion. Population estimates are highly speculative prior to the nineteenth century. The total population may have increased early in the Ottoman period, in the more stable and prosperous sixteenth century; it may have contracted somewhat in the later eighteenth century due to a combination of plague, famine, and political turmoil. The savants of the French expedition estimated a total sedentary population of around 2.5 million in 1798; recent scholarship has suggested a significantly higher population of about 3.8 million. Cairo remained the country's metropole, its population rising from perhaps 150,000 at the time of the Ottoman conquest to over 200,000 (263,000 according to French estimates, 210,000 in a recent recalculation) at the close of the eighteenth century. No other Egyptian city of the Ottoman era exceeded 20,000 before the early nineteenth century.

In the social hierarchy there were clear distinctions of status and power between "Turks" (*atrak*), the term usually applied by native Egyptian writers to both Ottomans and Mamluks, and the Arabic-speaking indigenous population whom those in power often lumped together as "peasants" (*fallahin*) regardless of occupation or residence. Whereas Egyptian writers sometimes castigated the "Turks" as bad Muslims due to the often unruly behavior of the Ottoman forces garrisoning Egypt, the "Turks" in turn regarded native Egyptians as a servile population unfit for politics or war. In the contemptuous words of one Ottoman governor, "I will not give [military] salaries to *fallahin*. Salaries are for the Turks."[3] From the Egyptian side literary works from both the Mamluk and Ottoman eras indicate that literate Egyptians had not totally submerged their identity within Islam, but retained an awareness of Egypt's distinctiveness as a uniquely fertile region of the Muslim world, as a land of great historical antiquity and splendor, and more recently as a citadel of Islam against external assault. At least for some Egyptians, "the land of Egypt" (*al-diyar al-misriyya*) was an identifiable and emotionally meaningful entity within the larger Muslim polity of which it was now a province.

On the whole, the gap between the foreign Ottoman-Mamluk ruling class and the indigenous population appears to have been less rigid than in the preceding era of the Mamluk Sultanate. The dominant households of the Ottoman period had an integrating tendency which at least economically brought together the alien ruling class and segments of the indigenous population. Native merchants were associated with regimental or Mamluk households, serving as business agents and making loans (not always voluntarily) to the latter. Wealthy merchants sometimes imitated the ostentatious lifestyle of Mamluk beys, surrounding themselves with a similar cluster of wives and concubines, slaves and retainers. Although the relationship between a military grandee and a wealthy merchant was not symmetrical, shared economic interests to some degree linked merchants and Mamluks, and served as a practical bridge between the alien political elite and the indigenous commercial elite.

Whereas politics were dominated by non-Egyptians, Egypt's religious institutions of Ottoman Egypt were largely in the hands of native Egyptians. The bulk of the *'ulama* were Egyptians. Many were of rural origin, formal education serving in Egypt as elsewhere in the premodern world as a vehicle of social mobility. Thanks in large part to official patronage, it was in the Ottoman period that al-Azhar eclipsed other educational institutions and became the premier Muslim religious center in Egypt, a university of several thousand students in which the bulk of Egyptian *'ulama* henceforth received their higher education.

The Ottomans had inherited an elaborate system of Muslim religious courts. Other than appointing an Ottoman chief judge (*qadi*) to supervise the overall functioning of the system, they did little to tinker with it. The *Shari'a* courts staffed overwhelmingly by native Egyptian *'ulama*, were vital both to the smooth operation of commercial life (business contracts and partnerships were regularly registered in the courts, and many commercial disputes were adjudicated there) and to the regulation of personal matters (disputes over issues such as marriage, divorce, inheritance and child custody were often resolved by the judge of one of the many Muslim courts found both in Cairo and in provincial towns). Even the legal affairs of Egypt's non-Muslim minorities sometimes came under the sway of the *Shari'a* courts; disputes between Muslims and non-Muslims were routinely heard in the Muslim court, and non-Muslims sometimes chose to take personal cases between non-Muslims to the *qadi* because of a greater prospect of effective enforcement.

'*Ulama* also played a role, although a more subsidiary one, in Egyptian political life under the Ottomans. The '*ulama* frequently served as intermediaries in factional strife; in some instances factions called on the '*ulama* to legitimize their rule or to condemn that of their rivals. Less frequently but nonetheless occasionally, the leadership of the religious hierarchy also served as tribunes of the indigenous population, denouncing the abuses and extortions of the military elite and attempting to moderate the level of exploitation of the native population endemic in Ottoman Egypt. The political role of Egypt's '*ulama* increased over time. The high point of their political influence came in the late eighteenth century when incessant inter-elite factionalism drew them deeper into political life as intermediaries, and their protestations against Mamluk extortion and oppression became more frequent.

Whereas the classically-educated '*ulama* were those who defined and disseminated normative Islam, Sufi adepts and the brotherhoods they led were the carriers of popular Islam. The Sufi brotherhoods appear to have proliferated and to have become more central to popular Muslim religious practice during the early Ottoman centuries. Their passionate and sometimes unorthodox rituals and ceremonies supplemented the more formal behavioral guidance provided by schools and courts, in the process serving to fill out the emotional dimensions of religious life. Living Sufi shaykhs were an infallible source of guidance along the mystical path for their disciples; the tombs of deceased Sufi shaykhs were places of pilgrimage and prayer for followers of their order. Although there was considerable overlap between '*ulama* and Sufis, there was also a degree of tension and rivalry between the more austere and formalist version of religion promoted by the '*ulama* and the ecstatic and often dubiously "Islamic" rituals of the brotherhoods. Official and popular Islam were far from a seamless web.

Egypt's non-Muslim minorities appear to have fared relatively well under Ottoman rule. By the time of the conquest of Egypt the Empire itself had developed a tradition of tolerance of its large non-Muslim population, and the same benign attitude was applied in Egypt when it was incorporated into the Ottoman fold. There is only occasional evidence of official or popular persecution of religious minorities in the Ottoman period (e.g. new decrees restricting minority dress; the ad hoc closure of individual non-Muslim places of worship; infrequent mob attacks on minority quarters or churches), and little indication of significant non-Muslim conversion to Islam. Copts and Jews often served the state as financial specialists (tax-collectors and customs agents). There was appreciable economic interaction between Muslims and minority groups. The general level of prosperity of the non-Muslim minority communities as a whole was in all probability no lower than that of the Muslim majority with its larger peasant base.

To be sure, Muslims and non-Muslims were not equal in Ottoman Egypt. Christians and Jews continued to pay a head-tax in exchange for their religious and communal autonomy, as well as to be theoretically subject to various restrictions on public behavior and dress (the latter often neither enforced by one side nor observed by the other). Such interaction as there was between Muslims and non-Muslims occurred overwhelmingly in the public rather than the private domain. In Cairo minorities tended to reside in primarily but not exclusively minority residential quarters and to socialize mainly with co-religionists. Egypt's Christian clergy played a role similar to that of Muslim *'ulama* in the social and cultural, although possibly less in the economic and political, life of Egypt's Coptic minority. They served as the source of religious instruction and guidance, and as the arbiters of much personal law which was defined by church teaching and administered in church tribunals.

ECONOMIC EXPANSION, CONTRACTION, AND STRUCTURAL CHANGE

The state of the Egyptian economy under Ottoman rule largely paralleled the country's political evolution. The sixteenth century was one of relative economic stability, of agricultural prosperity and even expansion, thanks to the restoration and extension of irrigation works, and of commercial vitality. Despite the post-1500 European presence in the Indian Ocean, through the sixteenth and seventeenth centuries Egypt continued to occupy an important place in regional and world trade. Egyptian sugar, rice, and flax were major Egyptian exports to Ottoman markets as well as to southern Europe. Internally a well-developed textile industry continued to supply most of the needs of the domestic market for textiles until well into the eighteenth century. A new foreign product, coffee, was introduced

into Egypt from Yemen in the sixteenth century and rapidly became
an item of mass consumption. The new institution of the coffee house
where it was consumed soon became a popular place of socialization
and recreation. Coffee and the coffee house proved to be a mixed
blessing. Whereas on the one hand the latter allowed "early-rising
worshippers and pious men" a place where they could "drink a cup
of coffee adding life to their life," on the other, the coffee house also
served as a meeting-place for "dissolute persons and opium-eaters"[4]

Politics eventually took its toll on the initially flourishing
economy of Ottoman Egypt. The practice of tax-farming is
generally estimated to have been injurious to economic life, the
short-term nature of many tax-farms both discouraging
investment and leading to increasing exploitation of peasant cultivators by tax-farmers whose main interest in their tax-farm was in
extracting the maximum immediate benefit. The late eighteenth
century in particular was a period of increasing economic travail.
Much of the blame for economic deterioration is laid at the feet of
'Ali Bey al-Kabir, whose ruthless drive to garner more revenue in
support of his political ambitions both oppressed peasant cultivators and led to the despoliation of merchants. The decades
between his fall (1773) and the French invasion (1798) saw a
continued high level of political extortion, the plunder of shops
and sometimes even towns by marauding troops, and a string of
famines and plagues.

Despite this deterioration at the close of the eighteenth century,
the economy of pre-1800 Egypt also witnessed important developments pointing towards the more "modern" economy which came
to prevail in the nineteenth century. Although technically most agricultural land was the property of the state under the Ottomans,
recent research in court records has indicated the gradual extension
of what amounted to private property rights by cultivators. By the
eighteenth century in particular, peasants were renting land to
others, pawning land to meet debt obligations, and selling if not the
land itself at least the right to cultivate the land in transactions
which were recognized in the courts. The older assumption that the
development of agricultural private property rights was a post-
1800 development needs considerable qualification.

The same is true for the assumption of an exclusively subsistence economy in the rural sector. Again recent examinations of

the Egyptian economy under the Ottomans indicate substantial commercialization of both production and distribution in the agricultural sector. Nelly Hanna's research on the life of a Cairo merchant at the turn of the seventeenth century has demonstrated "widespread" agricultural production for sale in local or national markets, the presence of "fairly large" agricultural holdings by peasants which clearly exceeded the area needed for subsistence farming, and the existence of urban merchant investment in agricultural production and food processing.[5] Kenneth Cuno's research on the eighteenth century, beyond documenting the development of what approximated to private property rights over land, has also shown the presence of flourishing market towns dependent on agricultural production. Numerous weekly markets were held in which goods circulated both among villages and into the urban sector, and there also existed legally acceptable forms of investment and moneylending designed to mobilize capital for financing the production of cash crops.[6] The commercialization of Egyptian agriculture was an evolutionary process extending over much of the Ottoman era, rather than a revolution achieved only by Muhammad 'Ali and his successors in the nineteenth century.

The existence of a well-developed network of guilds governing the functioning of the urban economy has been demonstrated only for the Ottoman period. A mid-seventeenth-century Ottoman traveller enumerated 262 guilds in Cairo; the French Expedition counted 193 at the close of the eighteenth century. In some cases guilds were religiously or ethnically distinct (Nubian servants, Coptic goldsmiths, Jewish button-makers). Not all were of equal status; some were regarded as "moral" (physicians, druggists, booksellers), others as "immoral" (prostitutes, beggars, dealers in black slaves). As elsewhere in the Ottoman Empire, guilds were essentially a state-supported institution for regulating urban economic production and distribution. Guilds were closely linked to the state, which had to approve the leadership selected by guild members and whose courts were responsible for upholding guild rules. In many cases the guild served as the mechanism of urban tax collection, taxes being levied on guilds as collective bodies. Guilds managed a variety of important economic functions: allocation of materials to members, setting prices and standards, regulating dealings between guild members. In time they became main social as well as economic agencies. Guilds had elaborate ceremonies of initiation as well as distinctive symbols and banners; guild members participated as a group in the processions which marked major holidays. Along with the residential quarters into which cities were subdivided, the guild formed a key institution for the smooth functioning of urban society.

"Class" is always a problematic category of analysis for premodern societies, where the most clearly-defined social divisions were vertical rather than horizontal. Its limitations noted, the monumental description of Egypt produced by the scholars of the French expedition provides a useful analysis of social stratification in urban Egypt at the close of the eighteenth century. The total workforce in the metropole of Cairo was estimated at about ninety thousand. At the top of the pyramid stood the dominant military elite which numbered in the range of ten thousand, a total which included the opulent heads of military household as well as their rank-and-file retainers. Among civilians, the highest category in terms of wealth were several hundred affluent international merchants. Some five to six thousand better-off merchants involved in domestic commerce came next, followed by a civilian middle class of perhaps fifteen thousand lesser merchants and artisans engaged in handicraft production. The rest of the urban workforce comprised an undifferentiated lower-class mass of sixty thousand day laborers, those in menial occupations, and the unemployed. Beneath this massive lower class was a slave population of uncertain size. Other calculations indicate that disparities in wealth between the top strata and those at the bottom increased in the turmoil of the later eighteenth century, and the standard of living of the weakest and most vulnerable segments of urban society – the poorest of whom never ate meat and whose children went naked – had declined over the eighteenth century.

GENDER RELATIONSHIPS AND REALITIES

The same court records which do so much to clarify the nature of economic activity in Ottoman Egypt also present us with considerable information about gender relationships in what was now a predominantly Muslim society. Court records are most illuminating on family relationships and on the economic activities of women. Muslim marriage was a contract between husband and wife specifying the obligations assumed by the former and the rights granted to the latter. Marriage contracts also often specified that a husband had to maintain his wife at a level of support appropriate to her social standing. When husbands did not fulfill these obligations, women went to court to obtain their stipulated rights. Women were often autonomous agents in court proceedings, appearing in court in person and testifying on their own behalf (although it took the testimony of two women to equal that of one man). In some cases the court imprisoned husbands for failure to meet their financial obligations to their spouses. Women could also sue for divorce in the courts; the frequency with which they did so is unclear.

All schools of Islamic law gave women well-defined property rights. Women were legal persons with the right to possess, to inherit (although not in equal portions with men), and to dispose of property. Between thirty and forty per cent of all property deeds registered at the registry office in Cairo from 1749 to 1789 were made out in the name of women. Although formal ownership does not establish that women actually controlled the property registered in their name, other court data indicate active involvement in the economy by women. The character of that involvement varied considerably by class. Lower-class women of course worked – in the fields in the countryside, as servants in the domestic economy, sometimes as artisans in commercial enterprises. As a result of both inheritance and marriage, upper-class women of both the alien Mamluk ruling caste and of the indigenous Egyptian merchant/religious elite accumulated sizable estates sometimes composed of multiple urban or rural properties. Court records show elite women holding tax-farms, entering into business partnerships, engaging in trade and commerce, sometimes by using hired managers or slaves as their business agents, and lending money from their own resources to their husbands to finance economic activities. "In spite of the fact that society was ostensibly divided into a public sphere for men and a private one for women, elite women developed networks in much the same fashion as did their men and penetrated the public sphere with ease."[7]

Due to practical imperatives, the normative restrictions placed upon women's physical mobility in Muslim theoretical writings did not operate for many lower-class women. Lower-class urban and rural peasant women of necessity went out in public to work. The strict seclusion of women was a luxury which could be afforded only by families of the upper and higher middle classes. Even among the upper-classes, where wealth allowed men more physical restriction of women, the womens' quarters or harem was not hermetically sealed from the outside. Peddlers, masseuses, and musicians entered the harem to sell, to serve, or to entertain; female religious teachers came to recite the Qur'an on Fridays; women of the elite visited each other and sallied forth to visit the shrines of prominent, particularly female, saints. Recent research has suggested that the town quarter, rather than the individual house, was the meaningful social space for urban women, the domain within which they could circulate and socialize with relative freedom.

Women of the Mamluk ruling elite played various roles in the political life of Ottoman Egypt. As among the ruling families of dynastic Europe in the same period, women were sometimes used as objects in establishing or cementing relationships among powerful men. Daughters or concubines of Mamluk grandees would be given in marriage to a subordinate as a way of formalizing and consolidating the bond between patron and client. The marriage of the widow of a deceased Mamluk commander to his chief lieutenant seems to have been a fairly common practice, serving as a mechanism for maintaining continuity within Mamluk households. In effect, elite women became heritable property within the framework of household politics.

The treatment of women as objects in intra-elite politics did not preclude a more autonomous role for some. Through marriage women obtained access to the wealth of their husbands. In the case of her husband's death – clearly not an atypical occurrence given the endemic strife among the military elite – the wife stood to inherit part of his estate. Given the rapid turnover among the heads of Mamluk households due to the same strife, wives sometimes served as household matriarchs maintaining a sense of continuity within a household. Through marriage to trusted lieutenants they kept the household intact; when the men were otherwise occupied in internal conflict or foreign wars the wives managed and guarded the wealth of the household; when husbands were killed, property remained under the effective control of their widows. Overall, "the harem represented relative stability in the midst of a turbulent, changing society. Here the usurping strongman might hesitate to tread; here his vanquished foe would stash his wealth in the hope of better days to come … . The women of the household were thus not mere accessories to a household's power, prestige, and longevity but were vital elements of them."[8] As we shall see, the presumptive "modernization" of Egypt in the nineteenth century had ambiguous implications for the opportunities available to Egyptian women.

Modernizing Egypt/Colonizing Egypt

THE FRENCH OCCUPATION OF EGYPT, 1798–1801

The "modern" era of Egyptian history is conventionally (and with dubious specificity) dated as having commenced on 1 July 1798, when a French military expedition commanded by General Napoleon Bonaparte disembarked near Alexandria. Moving inland from the coast, the French rapidly seized control of the northern reaches of the country. Within a month of their arrival the French defeated the Mamluk military elite in the Battle of the Pyramids near Cairo and occupied Egypt's main city. French control of Egypt was never complete; remnants of the Mamluks withdrew into Upper Egypt, which French flying columns never brought fully under French authority.

The French occupation of Egypt lasted only three years. Napoleon's fleet was destroyed by the British and his forces were repulsed in an effort to advance by land into Ottoman Palestine. In August 1799 Napoleon himself abandoned his troops in the field and left Egypt to return to greater things in France. By 1801 a coordinated Ottoman-British expeditionary force had entered Egypt and forced French evacuation. Little more than three years after the French had arrived with visions of Eastern empire, the first European occupation of Egypt of the modern era came to an end.

The emphasis upon things European characteristic of much of the modern historiography of Egypt has sometimes led to unwarranted assumptions about the significance of France's Egyptian adventure. The French certainly attempted to work significant changes in

Egyptian life. Bold Napoleonic proclamations asserted French respect for Islam, denounced the tyranny of the alien Mamluks, and declared the sympathy of France for Egypt's oppressed indigenous population. New central and provincial councils designed to involve the native religious class and local notables in the French administration of Egypt were established. The French introduced the printing press to Egypt and published Egypt's first newspaper, an official journal intended for French consumption.

All of this had but a limited impact upon Egyptians. The dominant Egyptian response to the French presence was one of hostility and resistance. Opposition to the French presence was encouraged by Egypt's Ottoman sovereign, which declared war on France and whose propaganda emphasized the incongruity of revolutionary France's self-proclaimed sympathy for Islam. Within a few months of the French occupation of Cairo, French financial exactions and punitive security measures kindled an urban uprising, which was suppressed only by the French bombarding parts of the city. The center of indigenous resistance was al-Azhar. Its leaders were many of the same shaykhs and notables whom Napoleon had hoped to involve in the French administration of the country. Lesser forms of Egyptian anti-French agitation and localized calls to resistance in provincial areas continued for the duration of the occupation. On the intellectual level, other than a grudging admiration for the learning and skills of the French savants who accompanied the expedition, found in Egyptian chronicles of the period, there is little evidence of a positive French impact upon educated Egyptian opinion.

Nonetheless, France's brief occupation of Egypt was not historically inconsequential. Its cultural impact may have been greater for France than for Egypt. The massive weight of the Egyptian historical legacy left an indelible impression upon the French sons of the Enlightenment who came to Egypt with Napoleon. The monumental catalog of Egypt's ecology, economy, and society, the *Déscription de l'Egypte,* produced by the scholars and scientists who accompanied the French expedition, was one of the main sources of nineteenth-century European infatuation with things Egyptian and still serves as the basis for much of our knowledge of Egyptian conditions at the close of the eighteenth century. For France the occupation of Egypt, however brief, left a permanent perception that France was destined to play a significant role in the affairs of the eastern Mediterranean in general, and Egypt in particular. Within Egypt itself, the main consequence of the French occupation was political. The French military defeat of the Mamluks, themselves a divided and declining force by the late eighteenth century, paved the way for the establishment of a new political order after the departure of the French.

MUHAMMAD/MEHMED 'ALI PASHA, 1805–48

The withdrawal of French forces from Egypt in 1801 was followed by several years of political turmoil, as various Mamluk factions and Ottoman military contingents contested for ascendancy within the country. The struggle was eventually won by an ambitious Ottoman officer of Albanian extraction, Muhammad or Mehmed 'Ali (Arabic "Muhammad," Turkish "Mehmed"). At first skillfully maneuvering among rival factions to gain allies and to extend the area under the control of his forces, later appealing to Egyptian civilian society as the champion of stability, Muhammad 'Ali was able to win the support of the Egyptian religious establishment which in May 1805 acclaimed him as governor of Egypt. Eventually the Ottoman government recognized Muhammad 'Ali's *fait accompli* and confirmed his appointment to the post.

Muhammad 'Ali served as Ottoman governor of Egypt from 1805 until 1848. Also sometimes referred to by his Ottoman rank of Pasha, Muhammad 'Ali is often called "the founder of modern Egypt." The appellation is apt. Equally in the spheres of politics, in economics, and in regard to Egypt's cultural orientation, his long reign witnessed major new initiatives which transformed the face of the country and set Egypt on the road of precocious modernization which was to distinguish it from most of its Middle Eastern neighbors through the nineteenth century.

Muhammad 'Ali's initial preoccupation was the consolidation of his personal power in Egypt. This took several years. A Cairene movement of resistance to the reassertion of Ottoman rule was soon crushed. In 1807 a British expeditionary force sent to occupy Alexandria was contained and repulsed. In 1809 Muhammad 'Ali subjected previously tax-exempt religious foundations to state control and taxation in a move against the autonomous position and power of the religious class; when the leader of the religious establishment protested, he was exiled. The most serious threat to his position was posed by those Mamluk households which had survived the vicissitudes of the past few years. Military expeditions sent to Upper Egypt gradually subdued the Mamluk clusters which had made that region their base since the French occupation. The symbolic end of Mamluk power came in March 1811, when Muhammad 'Ali invited many of the surviving Mamluk beys to a ceremony at the Citadel, and loyal forces massacred the unsuspecting guests as they exited the reception. Their leaders killed, their households subsequently sacked, the Mamluks were finished as an independent military force. Individual Mamluks served as officers in the Pasha's new army throughout his reign; but the basis of autonomous Mamluk power was broken by 1811.

Parallel to the elimination of potential rivals, Muhammad 'Ali erected an alternative apparatus of centralized authority. At its core Muhammad 'Ali's government was a household regime in many respects similar to those of the previous Ottoman era. Sons, nephews, and other relations filled many of the most prominent offices of state both military and civilian. Beyond this inner circle of relatives, Ottoman administrators and soldiers of different ethnic origins (Turks, Albanians, Greeks, and others) who had sought their fortunes in Egypt, and Mamluks often of Circassian background who chose to serve the Pasha, held the bulk of high and middle-level positions of responsibility. Together, this "Turko-Circassian" elite dominated Egyptian politics for much of the nineteenth century. A pragmatic rather than ideologically oriented ruler, Muhammmad 'Ali also used the skills of men of talent of diverse backgrounds – Armenian migrants, Coptic financial experts, French and Italian advisors – in his new bureaucracy and military. All were directly responsible to the Pasha himself, the "Great Benefactor" who at least until the last years of his reign worked long hours in directly supervising his subordinates.

Yet Muhammad 'Ali's reign also witnessed the development of more bureaucratic and formalized institutions of government. Provincial administration was systematically reorganized in a set of nested boxes staffed by appointees whose duties were clearly defined and whose lines of accountability flowed back to the center. Within the central administration Muhammad 'Ali initially governed through a large number of bureaus, or departments, responsible for different areas of administration. In the later 1830s these various agencies were consolidated into a smaller number of distinct ministries (Foreign Affairs, War, Marine, Civil Affairs, Finance, Education, Industry). A structurally modern Egyptian bureaucratic apparatus dates from the reign of Muhammad 'Ali.

Parallel to the creation of a more modern administration at the service of the Pasha came the construction of a new military machine. The composite military force, comprising Albanians, other Ottoman mercenaries, and former Mamluks upon which Muhammad 'Ali had been compelled to rely in his early years in power, was an unruly and unreliable instrument of power. In 1815 the Pasha embarked on an ambitious program of military modernization, the creation of a military "New Order" (*nizam jadid*), similar to that attempted shortly before by the Ottoman ruler Selim III. The main model was France. Advised by a French adventurer by the name of "Colonel" Seve (later Sulayman) Pasha, military schools training officers in the modern arts of war were established. New infantry units composed of companies, battalions, and regiments on the French model, and supported by field artillery, now replaced the undisciplined cavalry forces of the Mamluk era. At the same time the Pasha's dockyards at Alexandria and Bulak undertook the construction of a new Egyptian fleet. Departments of War and Marine organized the necessary logistical support.

Muhammad 'Ali's military machine combined old and new features. In its command structure it was a household army in some ways similar to that of preceding regimes. Many of its top commands were entrusted to the Pasha's sons or other relatives, newcomers to Egypt; its officer ranks were often staffed by former Mamluks also of alien origin. Its lower ranks were different. Muhammad 'Ali at first looked to the Sudan to find the necessary manpower for his new army. When Sudanese slaves proved susceptible to disease, in 1823 the Pasha turned to the mass conscription of Egyptians. Henceforth most of the enlisted personnel, and in time much of the lower officer ranks of the Egyptian military, were staffed by native Egyptians. It was certainly not a "national" army in its ethos – its commanders were non-Egyptians who despised their Egyptian subordinates, conditions of service were dreadful, desertion was always a persistent problem. But the Egyptian character of much of its personnel was a major departure from previous "Egyptian" armies.

The modernity of Muhammad 'Ali's military lay primarily in its approach to warfare. The Pasha's new army relied primarily on infantry, closely supported by artillery, rather than upon cavalry. Its personnel was subject to rigid discipline and training, and was designed as a military *machine* whose individual parts would behave in unison in response to the commands of their officers. Although it often did not function with the precision and efficiency intended – recent research has indicated multiple problems of defective equipment, failures of provisioning and supply, and overly optimistic operational plans which collapsed when their implementation was attempted in the field – it was closer to the armies of nineteenth-century Europe than to its Middle Eastern predecessors. At least in theory, "the warrior had become an extinct species and was replaced by the disciplined, trained soldier."[1]

Muhammad 'Ali's military was modern and efficient enough to make possible a far-reaching program of Egyptian expansion in the middle decades of the Pasha's long reign. Over the thirty years between 1811 and 1841, Muhammad 'Ali's army or navy saw extended service in four neighboring regions. In the 1810s units of the Pasha's (still largely traditional) army were dispatched to central Arabia at the behest of the Ottoman Sultan to deal with the Wahhabi threat to Ottoman suzerainty over Arabia. Egyptian forces were initially successful in their Arabian campaigns, defeating the Wahhabis and thereafter garrisoning parts of the Peninsula. This was a shortlived Egyptian presence; some areas were abandoned in the 1820s, others at the close of the 1830s.

Egyptian forces saw action in both Europe and Africa in the 1820s. One arena was Greece, where Muhammad 'Ali's new army and navy were called upon by the Ottoman Sultan to counter Greek insurrection. The defeat of the Egyptian navy by the British and French at Navarino in 1827 effectively ended Egypt's involvement in Greece; land forces were withdrawn in 1828. Acting on his own initiative, in 1820 Muhammad 'Ali sent military forces south into the Sudan in the first of several expeditions aimed at obtaining Sudanese slaves and gold. Although the use of Sudanese as soldiers failed and little gold was found, these Sudanese expeditions had more permanent results. Much of what is today the Sudan came under Egyptian control beginning in the reign of Muhammad 'Ali.

The Pasha's most ambitious military expansion was undertaken in the 1830s. Now possessing the most powerful military in the Middle East, in 1831 Muhammad 'Ali sent his forces to conquer Ottoman Syria. They did so with relative ease. For most of the 1830s Muhammad 'Ali effectively ruled much of Palestine, Lebanon, and Syria. When in 1839 his forces defeated an Ottoman army and menaced the empire's Anatolian heartland, Muhammad 'Ali seemed poised to supplant the Ottomans as master of the Eastern Mediterranean. Such was not to be. The British forged a European coalition committed to the preservation of Ottoman integrity against the Egyptian threat. In the face of revolt in greater Syria, produced by overtaxation and conscription, and encouraged by British agents, Muhammad 'Ali was forced to retreat. When he became the object of a combined Austro-British military operation directed first against Egyptian forces in the field and later against Alexandria, he buckled and ordered Egyptian withdrawal from greater Syria. By 1841 diplomacy produced a compromise of sorts; the Pasha received the heriditary governorship of Egypt and his conquered territory in the Sudan, but was forced to abandon any hope of empire in Ottoman Asia. Egypt worked out its destiny within the narrower confines of the Nile Valley from 1841 onwards.

A new bureaucracy and military required new men. To obtain the same, Muhammad 'Ali undertook important initiatives in Egyptian educational and cultural life. The dispatch of Egyptians to Europe to learn useful skills such as printing, shipbuilding, or modern military techniques commenced in 1809; numerous other student missions were sent abroad over the next forty years. A parallel process was encouraging European military men and technical experts to come to Egypt to educate Egyptians in the same applied sciences. Within Egypt itself a network of new state-run military schools was inaugurated. An effective modern army required support services such as medical treatment or engineering expertise; educational reform thus led to the establishment of the first specialized medical, engineering, and other technical schools in Egypt. Parallel cultural initiatives of Muhammad 'Ali's reign included printing presses producing works in Arabic and Turkish, the first newspapers in indigenous languages (official gazettes written in Arabic and Turkish), and in 1835 the creation of a School of Languages to provide foreign language training for young Egyptians responsible for translating works from European languages. Although training in Muhammad 'Ali's new schools remained overwhelmingly technical during his reign, and translation and publication concentrated on the dissemination of "practical" knowledge which would enhance the power of the state, nonetheless these cultural initiatives laid the necessary foundation for the development of new ideas about politics, society, and culture in subsequent generations.

The Pasha's bureaucratic, military, and cultural innovations were in large part made possible by the sweeping changes in the Egyptian economy which occurred under his regime. Early in his reign Muhammad 'Ali imposed a government monopoly over the sale of agricultural goods. Private transactions first in grains, later in other agricultural products, were forbidden; instead the government purchased agricultural commodities from the cultivator at a state-determined price well below the free market level and in turn took charge of marketing. Until the later 1830s, when economic and political pressures led to a liberalization of the trade regime, the state was the primary beneficiary of Egypt's share in the great growth in regional trade which occurred after the close of the Napoleonic wars.

Parallel to the control of trade came state domination of agriculture. In his first decade in power Muhammad 'Ali succeeded in working three major changes in the way agricultural land was held and administered in Egypt. One reform was to make the lands and properties of previously tax-exempt religious foundations subject to state taxation. The second was to confiscate existing tax-farms, thereby bringing the bulk of agricultural land under state control. The third was to carry out a cadastral survey which provided the state with up-to-date information on the details of Egyptian agricultural cultivation. Collectively, these measures in effect nationalized agricultural land in Egypt and laid the basis for state direction of agricultural production as well as for state appropriation of the profits from agriculture. Actual cultivation was still largely conducted on a family basis; but the family unit now farmed subject to tighter state supervision than had been the case previously, and saw more of the benefits of its labors flow into the coffers of the state.

Muhammad 'Ali's reign witnessed significant alterations in the character of Egyptian agriculture. Under state direction and using the forced labor of the peasantry, considerable effort was put into the repair and deepening of existing canals as well as into the further extension of irrigation works. The cultivated area is estimated to have increased by roughly one-third under Muhammad 'Ali. Deeper canals and larger reservoirs facilitated a gradual shift from "basin" irrigation, where the summer inundation of the Nile was allowed to flood the land and permitted the growing of one winter crop after the recession of the flood, to a more intensive system of "perennial" irrigation in which water was available for year-round use and consequently more than one crop a year could be grown.

The best-known of Muhammad 'Ali's agricultural reforms came after 1820, when the chance discovery of a new strain of long-staple cotton led the Pasha to promote the growth of cotton for export to the expanding cotton factories of Europe. Egypt's export of raw cotton nearly doubled between 1821–25 and 1845–49. The march on the road to cotton dependency began under Muhammad 'Ali. Yet his agricultural innovations were not limited to cotton; the Pasha's government also encouraged the cultivation of other cash crops intended for export (sugar-cane, indigo, rice), and promoted the growth of a wide range of new fruits and vegetables in Egypt.

The benefits of this agricultural expansion flowed primarily to the state. Muhammad 'Ali's years in power were difficult ones for Egypt's peasant majority. Some males were now subject to military conscription and long periods of onerous military service from which some men never returned. A larger number of men and women alike – hundreds of thousands in some years according to contemporary estimates – were compelled to work for the state on irrigation works and other public service projects. The slack summer season of relative leisure evaporated as the extension of perennial irrigation and the cultivation of summer crops necessitated year-round work in the fields on the part of the peasantry. In place of approximately 150 days of agricultural labor a year under the ancient agricultural regime of basin irrigation, the shift to perennial irrigation extended the peasant's work-year to roughly 250 days a year.

At the same time as the state demanded more labor from Egypt's peasantry, it also deprived cultivators of much of the benefits of their labors. Taxation and the state monopoly of trade operated in tandem to funnel the agricultural surplus to the state. Overtaxation, in the sense of the state imposing a tax burden in excess of the peasant cultivator's ability to pay, is a repeated theme in accounts of Egyptian agriculture in the later decades of Muhammad 'Ali's reign. It led to peasant loss of land due to non-payment of taxes, to peasant flight, and in some cases to peasant revolt against the rapacious demands of the centralizing state.

The state also deprived many peasants of their customary rights over agricultural land. Several processes initiated particularly from the 1820s onwards operated to pave the way for the emergence of a new landed elite in the countryside. In exchange for supervising cultivation and tax collection, village shaykhs were exempted from taxation and sometimes awarded control of idle village lands. As peasant flight due to overtaxation resulted in areas being lost to cultivation, the government resorted to tax-free assignments of blocks of untilled land to high officials in the hope that they would be able to return these areas to cultivation. Finally, large chunks of land were simply given to members of the royal family as land grants under their control and supervision. A recent calculation estimates that peasants controlled slightly less than half (forty-seven per cent) of surveyed agricultural land by the close of the Pasha'a reign; in contrast, thirty-seven per cent was under the control of notables and twelve per cent had been given to members of the ruling family.[2] The process of concentrating land holdings in the hands of a small minority of Egyptians had its genesis under Muhammad 'Ali.

Together, the combination of forced labor, of a longer growing season, of overtaxation, and of loss of rights over land meant that "the majority of the producers put in more work for less benefits."[3] They did not accept increased exploitation passively. Accounts of self-mutilation to avoid conscription and of desertion, once conscripted, are frequent, as are reports of peasant flight in an effort to escape the accelerating demands of the state. Armed revolt was the peasantry's ultimate form of protest. Uprisings involving thousands of peasants in prolonged struggle against the regime are reported in Upper Egypt, in particular from the 1820s through the 1840s. Most forms of resistance were futile. The formation of a one-eyed regiment presumably discouraged self-mutilation; fleeing peasants were hunted down and returned to their estates; rebellion was repressed by force. These forms of protest indicate the darker side of Egypt's modernization under Muhammad 'Ali; it was achieved largely at the expense of the Egyptian peasantry.

Muhammad 'Ali's projects of economic modernization extended beyond Egypt's agricultural economy. Ruling at the cusp of the Industrial Revolution and familiar with new trends in the world economy through his European advisors, Muhammad 'Ali's economic vision encompassed the industrial sphere. From the 1810s through the 1830s the Egyptian state attempted a sweeping program of industrialization. Some thirty textile factories, most intended to process the cotton now being grown in increasing volume in Egypt, were opened by the early 1830s; numerous other installations – for the manufacture of war materials (gunpowder, muskets, a foundry casting artillery), for shipbuilding, and for processing other commodities (sugar, silk, paper, glass) – were also established. Muhammad 'Ali's factories represented an attempt to insure that Egypt was included in the emerging industrial economy of the nineteenth century.

Unlike the initiatives in agriculture which largely achieved their aims, Muhammad 'Ali's program of industrialization was a failure. By the 1840s most factories were either closed or abandoned by the state. The reasons behind the failure of the Pasha's effort at creating an Egyptian industrial sector is a contentious issue in modern Egyptian historiography. Egyptian historians give greatest weight to an external factor, specifically the Treaty of Balta Liman of 1838, between the Ottoman Empire and Great Britain, in which the Ottoman government agreed to severe limitations on the tariffs which could be imposed on imported goods. Thus deprived of tariff protection similar to that afforded to nascent efforts at industrialization elsewhere, Egypt's fledgling industries could not compete sucessfully with British exports to the region. Non-Egyptian historians generally question the presumed negative impact of Balta Liman upon

Egypt's domestic market, and give more weight to the internal shortcomings of the factories which according to contemporary reports were plagued by problems of inadequate power (some had to rely on turbines driven by animals), by wastage and sabotage on the part of their coerced and mistreated workforce, and by the inefficiency of the Pasha's overly centralized administration. Whatever the precise blend of reasons, the result was that Egypt did not succeed in building an industrial sector at the start of the Industrial Revolution.

The definitive destruction of the Mamluk political system which had dominated Egypt for several centuries; the gaining of substantial independence from external imperial control; the establishment of a structurally modern bureaucracy and a military now partially staffed by the indigenous population; the creation of a new educational system; the fostering of agricultural growth and commercially-oriented export agriculture; and a redistribution of control of land which in time grew into a new landed elite in the countryside: these are the most obvious ways in which Muhammad 'Ali left a permanent mark upon the country he ruled for so long. At a deeper level, Muhammad 'Ali's reign represented a new kind of state in Egypt. The government was relating to the people of Egypt in a radically different way by the early nineteenth century. It now attempted to control and to direct, as well as to profit from the benefits deriving from the Egyptian economy. Equally, it made unprecedented efforts to organize the life and the work of the indigenous population (conscription into the military, forced labor on a massive scale on public work projects, the use of new techniques of population control and management such as draft registers, medical examinations, and desertion lists). Muhammad 'Ali's reign marked the beginning of "a new conception of government which was essentially *interventionist* rather than merely *preservationist* in nature."[4]

Whether the new kind of state created by Muhammad 'Ali was a "nation", in the sense of being a community of sentiment with which the Egyptians who now served it identified in a positive sense, is more problematic. At least within the central instrument of the regime's power, the army, there were profound cleavages between the Egyptian conscripts who made up the bulk of the army and the Turko-Circassian officers who commanded them.

Muhammad 'Ali certainly created an Egyptian state; the creation of an Egyptian nation lay in the future.

THE SUCCESSORS OF MUHAMMAD 'ALI, 1848–79

Upon his own infirmity and surrender of the reigns of power in 1848 (he died in the following year), Muhammad 'Ali was succeeded as Ottoman governor of Egypt by several of his descendants: briefly by his son Ibrahim (1848), then by a grandson 'Abbas Hilmi I (1848–54), another son Muhammad Sa'id (1854–63), and another grandson Isma'il (1863–79). In general terms, the reigns of 'Abbas Hilmi I, Muhammad Sa'id, and Isma'il, from 1848 to 1879, form a distinct period in the history of nineteenth century Egypt, one marked by a consolidation of many of the initiatives of Muhammad 'Ali, as well as by further movement along the economic and social path of Westernization upon which Egypt had been placed by the great Pasha.

A feature of the diplomatic settlement of the Egyptian-Ottoman crisis of 1839–41 had been Ottoman recognition of Muhammad 'Ali's family as heridatary governors of Egypt and the Sudan. Isma'il carried the process of dynasty-building further. In 1866 he was able to obtain an Ottoman decree giving him the right to mint coinage and to bestow decorations; the decree also limited succession to the governorship of Egypt to Isma'il's direct descendants. Several years later additional bribery in Constantinople gained him the title of "Khedive", or Viceroy, from the Ottoman government, thus giving the governor of Egypt a unique status among Ottoman provincial officials. In practical terms these imperial concessions did not amount to much; Isma'il's reign as Khedive ended with his abrupt dismissal by the Ottoman Sultan in 1879. Symbolically, however, the special place Egypt came to assume within the Ottoman fold in the mid-nineteenth century served to reinforce the sentiments of Egyptian distinctiveness and national identity set in motion by the country's precocious modernization.

The reigns of 'Abbas, Sa'id, and Isma'il witnessed the further development of a modern bureaucratic apparatus in Egypt. It was in the middle decades of the nineteenth century that both a hierarchical administrative structure and a corps of trained bureaucrats capable of staffing them took definite form. By 1872 there were a dozen ministries of state. An appointed Privy Council and a Council of Justice assisted the ruler in the task of supervising his expanded administrative machine. In terms of personnel, formal ranks and a corresponding pay scale were created within the bureaucracy. To a considerable degree this rationalization of the machinery of government existed more on paper than in reality; from the top the ruler constantly manipulated the bureaucracy through special appointments, clientage, and other forms of personal favoritism.

The apparatus of government refined by Muhammad 'Ali's successors resulted in a more intrusive Egyptian state. By the time of Isma'il, the government was interfering in the lives of its subjects more than it had in the past: there were higher and more efficiently collected taxes, now sometimes gathered by means of public whipping; formal police forces were created in urban areas, relying on techniques of intimidation to maintain order; guild officials were appointed to regulate in minute detail the productive activities of crafts which formerly had enjoyed more autonomy; an attempt to regulate the country's intellectual life was conducted through state censorship. All this increased the weight of the state upon its subjects.

One other development of the reign of Isma'il pointed in the opposite direction. In 1866, Isma'il created an indirectly elected Chamber of Notables to serve as an advisory body for the government. Composed of 75 notables indirectly elected from across Egypt, it debated issues of state policy and passed advisory resolutions for the Khedive and his administration. It was certainly less than an Egyptian parliament; "elections" were reportedly managed by provincial officials, it convened irregularly, and the Khedive was free to disregard its advice. Nonetheless, in the years of turmoil which ensued in the late 1870s the Chamber of Notables became the forum for demands for constitutional government.

Egypt's economic and cultural course of development under the successors of Muhammad 'Ali largely unfolded within the parameters set down by the great Pasha. The middle decades of the century were a period of rapid agricultural growth. The expansion of the agricultural area and of perennial irrigation continued. Over half of Egypt's cultivated land was producing two crops a year by the mid-1870s. The expansion of cotton cultivation led the way.

Egyptian exports of raw cotton more than quadrupled between the early 1840s and the late 1870s. The fertile Delta became Egypt's primary area of cotton cultivation. Although cotton was unquestionably Egypt's agricultural mainstay from the 1860s onwards, it was not the only crop grown for the world market; sugar cultivated primarily in Upper Egypt also became a significant export crop.

The mid-nineteenth century was the decisive period of transition to a monetarized and commercialized economy in Egypt. Economic exchange and the payment of taxes was now overwhelmingly conducted on a cash basis. In the wake of the abolition of Muhammad 'Ali's monopoly of trade in 1838, merchants both native and foreign traversed the Nile Valley as far south as the Sudan purchasing agricultural commodities, and in turn peddling manufactured goods in the countryside. The transition to a fully commercialized economy was greatly facilitated by new steamship services on the Nile, by the construction of a network of railway lines beginning in the 1850s, and by the introduction of a telegraph system and a national postal service from the 1860s onwards. The expansion and commercialization of agriculture meant that peasant cultivators had to obtain better varieties of seed, had to buy draft animals and water lifting devices, and in some cases had to hire labor. To facilitate all this, credit and money-lending operations grew apace: "almost every village now had its shopkeeper/money-lender."[5] The texture of Egyptian rural life had changed appreciably by the 1870s.

In several respects, monetarization and commercialization operated to the detriment of Egyptian cultivators. The vagaries of the international market for agricultural products introduced great volatility into Egyptian agriculture. Egypt boomed in the early 1860s when the American Civil War produced a seller's market for raw cotton. It suffered an abrupt depression in 1866–67, when American cotton reentered the world market and cultivators who had rushed to expand production were faced with severely reduced prices for their crop. At the same time the peasant's growing resort to borrowing to meet the requirements of producing for a commercial market led to peasant indebtedness and land alienation.

The latter process dovetailed with the acceleration of the trend towards the concentration of landholding which had commenced under Muhammad 'Ali. New land laws in 1847 and 1858 confirmed notable possession of lands which they had acquired under Muhammad 'Ali. The final step towards consolidating the concentration of landholding came in 1871, when a desperate need for funds prompted Isma'il to offer landholders the opportunity to obtain full private property rights over their holdings in exchange for advance payment of six years of land taxes.

Partial estimates for the 1870s demonstrate the degree to which the process of concentration of landholding had occurred over the previous half-century. An estimated one-fifth of all of Egypt's culti-vated land – almost one million feddans (one feddan equals 1.038 acres) – belonged to the Khedive and other members of the ruling family, in estates sometimes running to tens of thousands of acres. Palace registers, probably incomplete, list another 145 high offi-cials outside the ruling family who had estates of over five hundred acres. In contrast, peasant holders lost an estimated three hundred thousand acres of land to large landholders during the reign of Isma'il, mainly as a result of debt and consequent land alienation. Much of Egypt's most productive land thus passed into the hands of a small elite.

In contrast to the quickening pace of economic life, the 1850s and early 1860s saw little of note in the cultural sphere. Few significant educational or cultural initiatives date from the reigns of 'Abbas or Sa'id. It was quite a different story under Isma'il: an enthusiast of European civilization whose proud boast was that "my country is no longer in Africa, it is in Europe."[6] Isma'il's years in power saw major developments in the further Westernization of Egyptian elite education, learning, and social life.

The state educational system was a major beneficiary of Isma'il's largesse. Thanks to state sponsorship, dozens of new specialized schools were opened in the 1860s and 1870s. Two particularly important educational institutions were the School of Languages (closed by 'Abbas in 1850 but reopened in 1866), which later became the secular School of Law in which many of Egypt's leading politicians received their training, and a teacher's college for Arabic, *Dar al-'Ulum*, which played a similar educational role for many of Egypt's intellectual luminaries of the late nineteenth and early twen-tieth centuries. It was also under Isma'il that the first state-supported school for women was opened (1873). In 1875, prior to the severe financial crisis of the late 1870s which caused educational retrenchment by the government, there were an estimated five thousand students in the specialized advanced schools and institutes of the reinvigorated state-school system.

A parallel expansion of privately-funded education occurred in the 1860s and 1870s. Scores of European missionary schools, some offering education to men, others to women, opened in Egypt in the pro-Western atmosphere of the Khedive's Egypt. By 1875 perhaps as many as nine thousand students were enrolled in missionary and minority community schools. Although al-Azhar was still the largest educational institution in Egypt (some eleven thousand students in 1875), it was mainly the new Western-oriented professional elite educated in the secular state and the missionary and minority community school systems who shaped the tenor of Egyptian public life from the late nineteenth century onwards.

Isma'il's patronage of learning and science extended beyond formal education. His reign witnessed the opening, usually with state support, of several of the seminal cultural institutions of modern Egypt: a Society of Knowledge, to sponsor the translation and publication of scientific works; the Khedivial Geographical Society, to promote geographical exploration and the study of landuse, irrigation, and the like; the Khedivial Library, later the National Library of Egypt; a museum for the preservation and display of Egyptian antiquities, now the Egyptian Museum; and the Cairo Opera House, built by the state to celebrate the opening of the Suez Canal in 1869: all date from the reign of Isma'il. Much of the institutional infrastructure which supported the cultural activities of Egypt's new Westernized elite took tangible shape in the 1860s and 1870s.

A particularly important area of innovation under Isma'il was that of journalism. Although printed periodical publications appeared under the French administration and in the reign of Muhammad 'Ali, journalism in Egypt remained a state-sponsored venture until the 1860s. Specialized Arabic journals addressed to particular professions began to appear early in the reign of Isma'il, as did foreign-language periodical publications designed to serve the growing foreign communities now resident in Egypt. An independent political press took shape only in the 1870s. Many of Egypt's early newspapers were established by immigrants from greater Syria who found the atmosphere of the Khedive's Egypt a more liberal one than that of their Ottoman-controlled homeland. One such periodical was *al-Ahram (The Pyramids)*, founded by the Syrian Taqla brothers in 1875 and arguably Egypt's most important newspaper of the twentieth century. Political journalism exploded in the later 1870s, when financial crisis led to political ferment and a loosening of the ability of the state to control political opinion. By the end of Isma'il's reign in 1879, Egypt's periodical press was solidly established as the dominant forum of cultural expression and political debate in Egypt.

The Europeanization of Egyptian culture was in part driven by a growing European physical presence in Egypt. In 1848, Egypt may have had ten thousand European residents. By the start of the British occupation in 1882, the number had grown to perhaps ninety thousand. The magnet drawing Europeans to Egypt was the country's economic boom of the mid-nineteenth century and the opportunities available in its increasingly commercialized and export-oriented economy. Most lived in Egypt's main cities (nearly fifty thousand in Alexandria, over twenty thousand in Cairo, another seven thousand in Port Said in 1882). The largest colonies were the Greek (more than thirty-seven thousand), the Italian (over eighteen thousand), and the French (almost sixteen thousand), followed by smaller Austrian and British communities.

Egypt's European residents had an impact disproportionate to their numbers. Economically much of the cotton trade was dominated by European merchants who provided seeds and credit to rural cultivators, who purchased the crop, and who arranged for its export to Europe. Greek traders penetrated the length of the Nile Valley, hawking the products of the Industrial Revolution. European merchants were even more visible in Egypt's main cities, where much of an expanding retail trade in imported goods was funnelled through Greek or Italian shops and where European-run banks played a pivotal role in facilitating commercial transactions. Socially this European resident population was the initiator and a good part of the market for the new European-style apartments, hotels, and restaurants which gave Alexandria, Cairo, and Port Said their distinctive flavor. The European intellectual impact was equally significant. Christian missionary schools educated upper-class Egyptians as well as European residents of Egypt, and newspapers in European languages were a parallel source, alongside the expanding Arabic-language press, for the dissemination of European ideas to Egypt's expanding literate elite.

The growing European presence in Egypt was far from an unmitigated blessing. Their prominent place in the expanding commercial economy and the higher wages which skilled European workers received all served as irritants and causes of resentment for less advantaged Egyptians. Similar to the American Wild West at the same time, Egypt's "Klondike on the Nile" often attracted an adventurous and unruly sort of immigrant. Especially in the port cities, ethnic tension and conflict grew from the 1860s onwards. Juan Cole has noted twelve incidents of urban violence between native Egyptians and members of different European communities from 1863 to 1875.[7] Similar tensions developed in the countryside; resentment against the sharp business practices of Greek peddlers was one element fuelling a nativist rebellion in the Sudan in the early 1880s.

The most obvious negative feature of the European penetration of Egypt came in the area of finance. Driven by a need for capital to finance infrastructure improvements, Muhammad 'Ali's successors resorted to loans from abroad. The Egyptian government arranged its first foreign loan under 'Abbas in 1852. Continuing financial pressures led his successor Sa'id to commit to two further and larger foreign loans. Isma'il arranged for seven major foreign loans between 1864 and 1873.

By today's standards, the international money market of the mid-nineteenth century was a shady operation at best. Major European merchant banks arranged the terms of most of Egypt's foreign loans. As far as historians can reconstruct their terms, "the amount taken in commission and other hidden charges was enormous."[8] Most of the major loans were floated on European bourses, where their speculative nature usually led to undersubscription and thus to Egypt receiving considerably less than the face value of the loan. Of Isma'il's seven major loans with a total face value of roughly sixty-five million pounds sterling, it is estimated that Egypt actually received about forty-four million pounds. Annual interest on these loans ranged from eight per cent to 11.5%.

The results were disastrous. By 1875, Egypt had a total debt of ninety million pounds sterling (domestic as well as foreign loans).

The situation proved unbearable for the regime; in April 1876, Egypt announced it was going to have to postpone payment of its debt obligations. The successors of Muhammad 'Ali, Isma'il in particular, had bankrupted Egypt.

BANKRUPTCY, NATIONALISM, AND OCCUPATION, 1876–82

Egypt's indebtedness to Europeans and its declaration of bankruptcy set off a prolonged political crisis within the country. The concern of foreign creditors about the solvency of the Egyptian government led to increasing European interference in Egypt's financial affairs in the late 1870s. In 1876, European pressure resulted in the appointment of foreign controllers to oversee Egyptian finances. By 1878, the Egyptian government had been forced to appoint Europeans as Ministers of Finance and Public Works.

Isma'il's financial mismanagement, his weakened position, and the growing European involvement in Egyptian affairs in turn produced an Egyptian backlash. Various sectors of society within the country now emerged to challenge Khedive and foreigner: rural magnates, represented in the Chamber of Notables, wishing to restrain the exactions of an increasingly rapacious state; members of the bureaucracy and military, whose position was being placed in jeopardy by financial retrenchment, cutbacks in the bureaucracy and army, and the hiring of European officials; and Egyptian intellectuals and journalists desirous of limiting both domestic autocracy and foreign penetration. Antipathy to European domination and to the political absolutism of the Muhammad 'Ali dynasty produced Egypt's first organized political parties as well as its first expressions of modern nationalism asserting the right of Egyptians to rule themselves.

Three rival forces contested for power in Egypt from 1876 to 1882. One was the regime itself, seeking to maintain as much authority as possible in the face of European pressure and nationalist opposition. Another was the European powers and their local representatives, anxious about debt repayment, desirous of more control over Egyptian affairs, and apprehensive about both the stability of the Khedivial regime and the intentions of its domestic opposition. The third was an unstable nationalist coalition whose slogan "Egypt for the Egyptians" expressed its shared goals of placing restrictions upon an autocratic regime and of checking European penetration into Egypt.

The regime was the first loser. Isma'il's attempts to navigate between the Scylla of European pressure and the Charybdis of domestic opposition within the Chamber of Notables failed. When in early 1879 he suddenly endorsed the Chamber's program of constitutional reform, European representations to the Ottoman government produced a curt missive from the Sultan addressed to the "ex-Khedive" which deposed Isma'il and installed his son Muhammad Tawfiq (1879–92) as Khedive of Egypt.

From this point onwards the primary struggle was between Tawfiq's collaborationist government, increasingly reliant upon and supported by the European powers, and various opposition groups opposed to Khedivial autocracy and European domination. Over time Egyptian army officers became the most prominent component of the opposition. The Egyptian nationalist movement of the early 1880s is often referred to by the name of the leader of the army faction, Colonel Ahmad 'Urabi, as the 'Urabi movement.

Through much of 1880–81 a combination of elite pressure within the Chamber of Notables and periodic demonstrations by army officers forced a weakened Khedivial regime in the direction of constitutional and parliamentary government. By early 1882 'Urabi was Minister of War in a ministry dominated by nationalists. Egypt seemed well on its way to an Egyptian-run parliamentary regime. At this point the third force in the triangular struggle became decisive. The nationalist ministry's populist tenor and its policy of dismissing European employees of the Egyptian government, as well as urban tension and rioting between Egyptians and Europeans, led to a confrontation with the European powers. Great Britain and France mounted a joint naval demonstration off Alexandria in support of the increasingly marginalized Khedive in May 1882. When in July the nationalist ministry rejected a British ultimatum demanding that they stop fortifying shore defenses, the British fleet bombarded the city (the French abstained). The die was cast by July 1882; while Khedive Tawfiq took refuge on a British warship and declared 'Urabi a rebel, an 'Urabist national congress in effect deposed the Khedive and formed an emergency administration to govern Egypt.

Precisely what drove a reluctant and divided British Cabinet to intervene with force in Egypt is still debated. The conventional explanation of the British occupation of Egypt emphasizes British concern for the safety and security of the Suez Canal, which since its opening in 1869 had become Britain's major lifeline to its eastern possessions. Recent research has shown another factor as being of equal or greater importance; alarmist and exaggerated warnings by the British men on the spot that Egypt faced "anarchy" and that the entire European position of privilege which had developed in recent years was menaced by the new nationalist regime. The result is what matters: in the summer of 1882 Great Britain dispatched naval and land forces to occupy Egypt. The Egyptian army was decisively defeated at the battle of Tel al-Kabir in September; shortly thereafter, British troops entered Cairo and eliminated the nationalist government. Eighty-one years after the French had left Egypt, a second and longer foreign occupation was underway.

THE BRITISH OCCUPATION OF EGYPT, 1882–1914

Great Britain's domination of Egyptian affairs from 1882 to 1914 is a classic example of indirect colonial rule. Technically, Egypt remained an Ottoman province until World War I. The family of Muhammad 'Ali continued to serve as Viceroys, or Khedives, of Egypt: Muhammad Tawfiq during the first decade of the British occupation and his son 'Abbas Hilmi II, from 1892 to 1914. Ministries sometimes headed by members of the polyglot elite which had emerged earlier in the nineteenth century, and sometimes headed by native Egyptians, administered the day-to-day affairs of the country.

They did so, however, under British supervision and in accord with British directives. The ultimate sanction of British power was military. The Egyptian army was disbanded immediately upon the British conquest of the country; a new and smaller army commanded by British officers was established thereafter. Only a small permanent British military force – initially in the range of twelve thousand troops, five thousand or less after the Anglo-Egyptian reconquest of the Sudan in 1898 – was stationed in Egypt to garrison the frontiers and to assert British control in case of domestic disturbance.

The key British civilian official in Egypt was the British Consul-General. He was officially only the equal of the consular representatives of the other European powers in what was still a province of the Ottoman Empire but in reality the British Consul-General was the de facto overlord of Egypt. For the first quarter-century of the British occupation (1883–1907) the post was held by one individual, Sir Evelyn Baring, later Lord Cromer. More than anyone else, British policy in Egypt was shaped by Lord Cromer. The briefer tenures of his successors – Sir Eldon Gorst from 1907 to 1911, Sir Herbert Kitchener from 1911 to 1914 – left less of a mark upon Egypt.

Particularly in the early years of the occupation, the British position was constrained by European, especially French, resentment over Great Britain's unilateral occupation of Egypt, and by the existence of the Caisse de la Dette, an international commission dominated by representatives of the European powers which had been established to supervise Egyptian finances after Egypt's bankruptcy in 1876. Prosperity and financial solvency gradually reduced the blocking-power of the Caisse. By the time of the conclusion of the Anglo-French Entente Cordiale (1904) in which France finally acknowledged British primacy in Egypt, British control of Egyptian affairs no longer faced significant international constraints.

Cosseted within the security blanket of the British Empire, Egypt played no independent role in international politics from 1882 to 1914. The country's only extended external crisis of the period related to Egypt's position in the Sudan. Egyptian domination over the Sudan was thrown off in the early 1880s, when a native revolt with a messianic thrust defeated Egyptian forces and created an independent Sudan. Operating under great financial pressures and seeing no great danger to their own position in Egypt from the south, Egypt's new British overlords let the Sudan sit. Their attitude towards Egypt's ex-colony shifted by the late 1890s when the French, now ensconced in west Africa, appeared to be moving towards extending their influence to east Africa. A combined Anglo-Egyptian military expedition (paid for by Egyptian state revenues) reconquered the Sudan, nominally for Egypt, in 1896–98; by 1899 an Anglo-Egyptian "condominium", in which Egypt and Great Britain theoretically shared power in the Sudan, was established. In reality, after 1899 British officials ran the Sudan with minimal Egyptian influence over policy or its implementation. The issue of Egypt's claim to the Sudan was not a major issue up to World War I; it became a huge irritant in Anglo-Egyptian relations upon Egypt's attainment of formal independence after the war.

British influence over Egyptian affairs increased over time. In the first decade of the occupation the Khedive Tawfiq, who had only retained his position in 1882 through the force of British arms, generally proved a compliant ruler willing to follow British instructions. His ministers were at first sometimes more recalcitrant. When one Prime Minister declined to comply with a British suggestion in 1884, a letter from Foreign Secretary Lord Granville made it clear that Egyptian ministers "must, on important matters, do what they were told" or face dismissal from office.[9] In 1893, when 'Abbas Hilmi II attempted to shuffle his ministry without seeking prior British approval, he was rebuked and compelled to promise that henceforth he would seek British advice on all important matters. A year later, when 'Abbas criticized the British-run Egyptian army, he was publicly humiliated by the Consul-General. Cromer's put-down of the young Khedive put an end to any pretence of Egyptian administrative autonomy. A docile Prime Minister (Mustafa Fahmi) remained at the head of the Egyptian government almost uninterruptedly for the reminder of Cromer's tenure in Egypt. Through the assignment of British advisors to Egyptian ministries and the appointment of Britishers as middle-level officials in the bureaucracy, the influence of the British on the determination of Egyptian policy was extended further down the administrative chain. Increasingly, operational control of the formally-Ottoman government of Egypt passed into British hands.

The British presence within the Egyptian government gradually expanded. In 1896 there were 286 British officials in the Egyptian administration; by 1906 the number had grown to 662. The British presence was particularly pronounced at the upper levels of government. In 1905, forty-two per cent of higher posts in the administration were held by Britishers. British officials eventually came to dominate the Ministries of Justice and the Interior, both concerned with security matters, and the Ministry of Public Works which supervised agriculture and irrigation. Drawn primarily from the upper classes, most British officials in Egypt were "amateurs in government", with "only a modicum of training" in Egyptian history and culture.[10] As a group they led an isolated existence in Egypt, associating mainly with each other and leading their personal lives largely within their own network of residences, clubs, and schools catering to their needs. Imbued with late nineteenth-century European views about superior and inferior "races," they also tended to regard Egyptians as a lesser breed incapable of governing themselves.

British purposes in Egypt were fundamentally conservative; primarily to maintain stability and order in a strategically situated country in which a vital artery of imperial communications (the Suez Canal) was located, secondarily to preserve and promote the prosperity of the European-oriented Egyptian economy which in the British view represented "progress" and which also (not incidentally) was a source of raw materials for Great Britain as well as a market for British manufactured goods. In practical terms, this meant doing things which fostered Egyptian prosperity and consequently the domestic tranquillity of the country, while not doing things which might challenge their own position, such as encouraging Egyptian institutions of self-government which could serve as the seat of a challenge to the British position, or promoting higher education which would have the effect of producing a larger nationalist cadre opposed to foreign dominance. British priorities are captured in government expenditures on security versus those on education a decade into the occupation; whereas seven hundred and forty-nine thousand pounds sterling was spent on public security in 1892, only ninety-one thousand pounds was expended on public education.

British India, where Cromer had served before coming to Egypt, was the model for many of his policies as Consul-General. Under Cromer the greatest emphasis was placed on furthering the political stability and enhancing the economic prosperity of the country. To Cromer, good government involved the following: overcoming the financial problems of excessive expenditure and debt which had led to British intervention; correcting some of the worst abuses of the arbitrary Khedivial administration; expanding Egypt's agricultural base through new irrigation works; and lightening the tax burden upon the cultivator.

Within these conservative parameters, the British effected several major changes in Egypt's political and economic life from

1882 onwards. New civil and criminal codes were drafted shortly after the occupation. Use of the whip, or *kurbaj*, to compel peasant services was abolished, and the *corvee*, or resort to compulsory peasant labor on public works projects, was discontinued and replaced by voluntary labor. British supervision of the Ministries of Justice and the Interior is sometimes credited with bringing a greater level of probity in the administration of justice, and with eliminating at least some of the capriciousness previously characteristic of Khedivial rule. (An improved administration of justice was not initially the case; judicial abuses including the torture of suspects committed by local Commissions of Brigandage, established to deal with a rise in rural crime, eventually generated a scandal and indeed served as the occasion for greater British involvement in judicial matters.) In the financial realm, accounting procedures were regularized and state expenditures gradually brought in line with revenue. Diplomatic negotiations with the European powers resulted in a revision of the originally burdensome terms of debt repayment and in Egypt gaining a larger share of its own revenue for internal use. By 1891, the Egyptian government was running a budgetary surplus. This greater degree of financial flexibility, as well as the economic prosperity of the era, in turn permitted a modest reduction in land taxes. To some degree, the rough edges of the more powerful state which had emerged in nineteenth-century Egypt were sanded and smoothed under British influence.

The greatest impact of British domination was felt in the Egyptian economy. Seeing the stability of their position in Egypt as dependent on Egyptian prosperity, the British oversaw major additions to Egypt's irrigation network and a further extension of the country's cultivated area. A British advisor was assigned to the Ministry of Public Works as early as 1884. Under British direction, existing canals and barrages were reconstructed; new subsidiary canals increased the area suited for perennial irrigation; and in 1902 a major dam spanning the Nile at Aswan which would store much of the summer flood for irrigation purposes in Upper Egypt was completed. British experts, many with previous experience in India, now supervised cultivation in the field. Whatever the prevailing philosophy in Britain itself, the role of the state in the economy of Britain's Egyptian semi-colony did not shrink.

With more water available for agricultural use, Egypt experienced a second agricultural boom during the British occupation. Agricultural output was augmented by the fact that much agricultural land was now receiving a year-round supply of water and thus growing more than one crop a year. The total value of Egyptian crops is estimated to have nearly doubled in real terms between 1886–87 and 1912–13. Cotton remained king, accounting for ninety per cent of Egyptian exports by the eve of World War I.

There was a darker side to Egypt's agricultural expansion under British domination. With much of its cultivated area now devoted to growing cotton, the country which had been the granary of the Roman and subsequent empires became a net importer of food products by 1900. The commercialized nature of the economy in most of the country meant that cultivators were dependent on the market for credit and vulnerable to swings in the world price of their products. As a result, the processes of peasant indebtedness and land alienation continued under the British. Perhaps most ominous for the future was the gradual decline in cotton yields from the turn of the century onwards as a result of the extension of cultivation to marginal lands, of an influx of new pests attacking the crop, and of the over-watering of fields which led to a rise in the underground water table. Dependence on imported food supplies, peasant land alienation, and declining cotton yields continued to be serious problems in Egypt for much of the twentieth century.

Growth, yes; structural change, no. In the countryside the processes of the concentration of landownership in large estates and the corresponding loss of control of land by the actual cultivator which had begun under Muhammad 'Ali and his successors was not reversed after 1882. According to official estimates, whereas twelve thousand, five hundred families possessed forty-four per cent of Egypt's cultivated land in plots of fifty acres or more in 1913, at the other end of the scale the vast majority of the rural population – 1.4 million families – owned twenty-six per cent of the cultivated area in plots of five acres or less. Only an estimated nine per cent of all rural families owned enough land to support themselves in 1907; fully seventy per cent of rural families were land-poor and had to rely on the sale of their labor to supplement what their land could produce; and twenty-one per cent of rural families were landless. Egypt's stratified rural society, if anything, became more stratified under British hegemony.

Beyond the agricultural sector, the main outlines of the Egyptian economy also remained substantially unchanged after 1882. The rapidly growing commercial sector of the economy retained its foreign-dominated character under the British occupation. Foreign capital whether brought by European immigrants or invested directly from abroad flowed into Egypt; foreign investment in the Egyptian economy stood at ninety-two million pounds sterling by 1914. Foreigners continued to dominate much of the commercial economy of Egypt. Banks, land and mortgage companies, and export-import houses, many founded by foreign speculators or owned by foreign capital, mushroomed in the economic boom of the 1890s (although many went broke in a wave of bankruptcies when world depression took its toll on Egypt from 1907 onwards).

A more controversial area is the fate of Egyptian industry under British domination. The traditional nationalist narrative of British policy systematically stifling Egyptian efforts at industrialization may be overstated. While in some instances the British-dominated government adopted measures clearly designed to hamper Egyptian industrialization (the classic example is the imposition of an eight per cent excise tax on domestic textiles in order to deprive two new local factories of any competitive advantage vis-à-vis manufactured imports), there are also cases where the administration provided occasional temporary tariff support for other efforts at industrialization. Perhaps more important than any action to discourage industry was the lack of any British desire or commitment to promote industry as a supplement to Egypt's overwhelming and increasingly problematic dependence on agriculture.[11]

British policy aside, the profits being generated in the agriculture sector as well as the flow of foreign capital into Egypt did result in some investment in industry and the emergence of a modest industrial sector concentrated in textiles and food processing. Cotton spinning and weaving enterprises, sugar refineries, cement plants, and tobacco factories had all appeared in Egypt by World War I. Yet factory production remained a minor component of the Egyptian economy. Of an estimated half a million workers in "industry" in the early twentieth century, only a small minority – possibly thirty to thirty-five thousand – worked in modern factories. An ethnic hierarchy similar to that found in the commercial sector also developed in industry. Skilled positions were often held by European or other immigrants, native Egyptians being relegated to more menial tasks.

The period of the British occupation is also notable for what the British chose not to do in Egypt. One clear area of relative neglect was that of Egyptian self-government. Shortly after their occupation of Egypt the British sponsored the creation of provincial councils and a partially elected, partially appointed, Legislative Council to advise the Khedivial government. In practice, these bodies, of course representing only the upper stratum of Egyptian society, were regarded as irrelevant by Lord Cromer and appear to have had no significant impact on policy during his tenure as Consul-General. Sir Eldon Gorst was more sympathetic to notable input into administration, expanding the authority of the provincial councils and encouraging the members of the Legislative Council to take a more active role in policy-making. Sir Herbert Kitchener continued the process, in 1913 establishing a larger and more powerful Legislative Assembly with an elected majority. These belated initiatives notwithstanding, both the Khedivial government and its British overlords operated for the bulk of the British occupation mostly unrestrained by representative institutions.

The other great area of British neglect was education. Lord Cromer viewed the purpose of public education to be little more than that of training a suitable number of civil servants; he also feared that, as had been the case in India, too large an educated population would contribute to nationalist agitation. In addition, particularly in the early years of the occupation the government of Egypt faced severe financial constraints. Thus British self-interest and Egyptian financial necessity led in the same direction – to limit government support for public education. State support for education was severely reduced early in the occupation. Some higher schools were consolidated, others eliminated; an attempt was made to limit enrollment in state schools to the number of students which could be absorbed in the economy and administration; financial aid for students was cut. State support for education amounted to less than one per cent of government expenditure over the period from 1882 to 1902, and until 1914 never exceeded 3.4% of annual expenditure. British neglect of Egyptian education was a central grievance of Egyptian nationalists when a visible nationalist movement coalesced in the early decades of the twentieth century.

Educational stagnation notwithstanding, the years of British occupation witnessed significant cultural change in Egypt. For most of the period the press remained relatively free. Numerous newspapers and periodical publications appeared, serving as a forum for the discussion of social and cultural issues. Debate was not confined to men; a lively women's press took shape from the 1890s onwards, adding the voices of educated women to public discourse. The late nineteenth and early twentieth centuries were the era when many of the ideas characteristic of modern European thought – belief in individual autonomy and freedom; adherence to secular principles of social organization; faith in the power of science to realize progress – circulated among Egypt's Westernized elite.

Religious life was not immune from these currents of change. The seminal Muslim figure of the era was Shaykh Muhammad 'Abduh, an ex-'Urabist and sometime-exile who eventually rose to the leadership of the Egyptian religious establishment. Intellectually, 'Abduh formulated many of the central concepts of the modernist or reformist interpretation of Islam which in time took hold among many educated Egyptians. He called for the purification of the faith from medieval corruptions; advocated the need to adjust the ethical injunctions of religion to changing circumstances; and insisted on the ability of contemporary Muslims to use their God-given reason in interpreting scripture rather than being bound by the precedents of the past. Institutionally, 'Abduh presided over the first significant reform of the curriculum of al-Azhar, beginning a slow process of change within Egypt's previously neglected religious educational system.

The direction of Egyptian nationalism under the British occupation is one of gradually accelerating discontent and activism, but also one of little effective impact on the British hold on Egypt prior to World War I. Egypt saw little organized opposition to British dominance during the first decade of the occupation. Shock at the ease of British conquest seems to have encouraged political passivity. A collaborationist Khedive in office from 1882 to 1892

(Tawfiq) provided no lead for nationalist activism. British confirmation of the position and privileges of the existing elite meant there was no specific incentive to fuel anti-British sentiment among the leading sectors of society. Unrest in the early years of the occupation was most visible outside of urban areas. Something like a rural crime wave, in some cases individual instances of theft or assault, in others the work of peasant bands, struck the Egyptian countryside after 1882. The degree to which this violence was an expression of anti-British sentiment, or had deeper roots in the disintegration of rural society due to commercialization, land alienation, and social stratification, remains an open question.

Parallel to the growth of the British presence within the Egyptian government, overt resistance to British occupation increased over time. Although his challenge to British authority in 1893–94 failed, the new Khedive 'Abbas Hilmi II did his best thereafter to encourage nationalist opposition to the British. Financial support for newspapers critical of Cromer and British policy was one avenue of opposition. Another was establishing links with younger Egyptians, by temperament less wedded to the existing order than their elders and also beginning to realize that the growing British presence in the state bureaucracy was a threat to their own career opportunities. Several anti-British secret societies, most rooted in the higher schools or appealing primarily to students, emerged in the 1890s. One recent graduate of the secular Law School who had links with the Khedive, Mustafa Kamil, was the key figure in the student activism of the 1890s. Involved in the creation of a secret nationalist society formed with Khedivial support in 1893, Kamil first became prominent when propagandizing against the British occupation on a trip to France in the mid-1890s. Speaking publicly against the occupation upon his return to Egypt, by the late 1890s Mustafa Kamil had emerged as the youthful tribune of Egyptian nationalist sentiment.

Nationalist opposition to the British occupation became appreciable only in the early twentieth century. The catalyst for increased nationalist activism was an incident of 1906. In June a hunting party of British soldiers became involved in an altercation with peasants near the Delta village of Dinshawai; one soldier died as a result. The British reaction was draconian. A special military tribunal tried fifty-two villagers, of whom four were sentenced to death, twelve given prison sentences, and others condemned to be publicly whipped. The hangings and whippings were carried out in front of the rest of the village. British brutality at Dinshawai galvanized Egyptian opposition to the British occupation. The faith of educated Egyptians in British civility was shaken; poets wrote odes of commemoration; a folk-ballad expressed the popular reaction in its lament of how "They fell upon Dinshawai/And spared neither man nor his brother."[12]

Largely as a result of the turn of Egyptian feeling in the wake of Dinshawai, several formal political parties emerged in Egypt in 1907. All were overwhelmingly bodies based in and appealing to urban Egypt. The most important at the time was the Nationalist Party [*al-hizb al-watani*] led initially by Mustafa Kamil until his premature death in 1908, thereafter by the lawyer Muhammad Farid. The Watani Party was the most popular movement among now-politicized younger Egyptians. The more elitist Party of the Nation [*hizb al-umma*], founded by a cohort of Egyptian notables also in 1907, was the main vehicle for the expression of moderate Egyptian nationalism.

The two parties reflected quite different nationalist perspectives. The speeches and writings of Mustafa Kamil, founder and immortal hero of the Watani Party, combined a deep emotional attachment to Egypt ("If I had not been born an Egyptian, I would have wished to become one"[13]) with a more instrumental orientation towards the Ottoman Empire. The Watani Party was the more vehemently anti-occupation group, having as its main political goal the immediate evacuation of the British from Egypt. Perceiving Egypt's Ottoman connection as a potential lever to force the British out, it articulated both a local Egyptian patriotism and loyalty to the Ottoman Sultan/Caliph. The rhetoric of its spokesmen was also more populist as well as more Islamically colored, voicing resentment against the prominent foreign presence in the Egyptian economy. It also sometimes expressed similar resentment over the presumed privileged position of Egyptian Copts under the British umbrella. The general orientation of the Watani Party (minus its Ottoman inclination, which became meaningless with the destruction of the Ottoman Empire after World War I) became the historical reference for later populist and Islamically oriented Egyptian nationalism.

The outlook of Ahmad Lutfi al-Sayyid, chief ideologue of the Umma Party, was less strident in tone and more exclusively Egyptianist in substance. Lutfi's statement of purpose, published in *al-Jaridah* newspaper, captured the party's overall orientation: "*Al-Jaridah* is a purely Egyptian paper which aims to defend Egyptian interests of all kinds."[14] For Lutfi Egypt was a distinct and unique national community whose historical development as a separate state over the course of the nineteenth century had severed any meaningful connection with its technical Ottoman sovereign. Lutfi was also less hostile to the British presence in Egypt, seeing positive benefits from British rule and arguing that internal reform and revival needed to take precedence over agitation against external domination. In contrast with the anti-foreign and occasionally anti-Coptic tone of Watanist propaganda, Lutfi was the great advocate of a secular nationalist outlook which saw all residents of Egypt as partners in one national community which he envisaged as developing along the same primarily secular lines as the nations of contemporary Europe. Lutfi's elegant prewar writings articulating this Egyptianist and largely Western-derived form of nationalism served as the inspiration for the secular trend within Egyptian nationalism in the era of independence.

These pre-World War I nationalist parties achieved little prior to the regional transformations wrought by World War I. The Umma Party was an explicitly elitist movement seeking little more than the education of public opinion in a gradualist and secularist mode. The more populist Watani Party was the main opponent of British domination in the years before the war. Although it had some success at the popular level, winning considerable student support, establishing branch committees and night schools, and establishing links with the nascent Egyptian labor movement, the more radical and Islamic tone of its propaganda after the death of Mustafa Kamil in 1908 also lost it the backing of more cautious Egyptians. The assassination of a collaborationist Prime Minister by a young Watanist supporter in 1910 brought down state repression against the party. New press laws suppressed Watanist journals; its spokesmen were placed on trial for sedition; its leader Muhammad Farid eventually fled Egypt and took sanctuary in Constantinople. Muffled within Egypt itself, the Watani Party was reduced to an exile movement in the years immediately before the outbreak of the Great War. Although there was unquestionably more anti-British sentiment in Egypt than there had been a decade earlier, Great Britain's dominant position in the country had not been seriously affected by nationalist activism up to 1914.

EGYPT OVER THE LONG NINETEENTH CENTURY

There are several features of Egypt's development over the long nineteenth century which need to be discussed before moving on to the twentieth century. One is population growth. Egypt's population around 1800 is now estimated to have been close to four million. The census of 1907 calculated a total population of 11.3 million. Growth was accompanied by shifts in the distribution of population. The cotton boom in the Egyptian Delta acted as a magnet for migration from Upper to Lower Egypt, and the growth of an export economy generated explosive growth in Egypt's port cities along the Mediterranean and Suez Canal. The proportion of the population living in cities increased from something in the range of ten per cent in 1800 to about fifteen per cent at the end of the century.

Political stability and economic expansion seem to have been the main factors behind population growth; where the former reduced the man-made constraints on population growth resulting from political turmoil and endemic violence, the latter provided the material support for a larger population and also may have stimulated growth (children were functional in Egypt's expanding agricultural economy). Medical improvements seem to have played a lesser role. Although limited efforts at improved sanitation at least in urban areas were undertaken by the government from the 1830s onward, epidemics (plague, later cholera) continued to strike Egypt throughout the century and infant mortality rates remained high. Since the rate of expansion of Egypt's productive base kept pace with or exceeded the rate of population growth until roughly 1900, population growth was not yet the major problem it has since become in the twentieth century.

Less quantifiable but equally profound shifts occurred in Egyptian community structures. Much of the tribally organized nomadic population living along the fringes of the Nile Valley or in the Eastern and Western Deserts gradually became sedentary over the course of the century. The growth of the power of the centralized state and the expansion of the agricultural sector of the economy worked in tandem to constrain tribal autonomy and encourage pastoral nomads to shift to settled agricultural pursuits. Within once-tribal communities a process of social differentiation also set in. Tribal shaykhs became government officials and/or large landlords while their tribal retainers in many respects became indistinguishable from the peasant majority.

The nature of Egyptian village life also changed. While the village remained the home of most Egyptians, both the political and economic autonomy of the village community eroded as a result of political centralization and economic commercialization. From Muhammad 'Ali onwards, the government brought villages more firmly under state control and supervision than had been the case in the past. Simultaneously the expansion and intensification of commercial linkages between countryside and city linked villages to a wider world economy. Like tribal communities, villages experienced a process of social stratification as village headmen became government functionaries and/or large landowners while the majority of villagers lost control of land and became tenants or landless laborers. By the early twentieth century, sharp social cleavages divided village society. The remark of an Egyptian notable to a British guest when the latter inquired why the former did not sit outdoors and read in the evening indicates the contemporary perception: "You don't really think that a landlord in the districts could sit out on the veranda after dinner, with a bright light over his head, do you, and not get shot?"[15]

Social change was greatest in Egyptian cities. Again largely as a result of the growth of state power and the emergence of an externally oriented and dominated economy, older urban social structures lost part of their function and significance in the nineteenth century. The quarters of Egyptian cities ceased to be important social units as the role of quarter headmen and watchmen in maintaining order and security was taken over by new agencies of the central government. Urban guilds were once thought to have been largely eliminated as a result of the surge in manufactured imports which was assumed to have eliminated the handicrafts industry upon which the guild system was based. We now know that both handicraft production and guilds were more resilient than previously believed. While some guilds ceased to operate and most had part of their regulatory function assumed by the centralizing state, other guilds continued to exist and to play a part, although reduced in scope, in the organization of urban economic industry and commerce.

The most visible change in urban life was the emergence of a new kind of city alongside older, more traditional, urban precincts. With a burgeoning population of European residents attracted by Egypt's economic boom from the middle decades of the century onwards, and with the gradual emergence of an indigenous Westernized elite, the texture of life in at least Egypt's main cities now took on a European veneer. New urban areas designed in imitation of Paris, built on a grid pattern and criss-crossed by broad boulevards to accommodate the passage of the carriages of the affluent, emerged outside the walled quarters and winding lanes of older quarters. The buildings which lined the streets of these new districts now resembled the monumental architecture of nineteenth-century European cities – arcades, grillwork balconies, windows looking to the street. Like their European models, these westernized urban areas featured new amenities such as gas lighting, piped water, and by the 1880s the first telephones. Some of their buildings offered novel forms of social experience; European-style hotel accommodations for the parties of tourists Thomas Cook was bringing to Egypt, restaurants serving *coq au vin*, travelling companies performing *Aida* or *Rigoletto* at the Cairo Opera House. *Palace Walk*, Najib Mahfuz's marvelous fictional portrait of urban life set in Cairo during and after World War I, is peppered with references to the prominence of foreigners and foreign institutions in the life of the city; the tobacco shop of Matoussian, the Suares omnibus, Costaki's bar.

The new westernized districts were the center of Egyptian political and economic vitality from the late nineteenth century onwards. Although mosques and Sufi centers continued as the focus of urban social and religious activity for many urban dwellers (Cairo still had 264 of the former and 225 of the latter in the 1870s, according to a contemporary enumeration), public affairs and high finance were conducted in the Viceroy's palaces and the government bureaus, and in the banks and commercial houses, now overwhelmingly located in the new city. As elsewhere in the nineteenth-century Middle East, "the new cities gradually drained the life away from the old ones."[16]

The eclipse of older urban areas and the prominence of new districts was accompanied by the decline of older elites and the emergence of new ones. In the centuries before 1800, three groups had been most important in Egypt's politics, economy, and society. The foreign-born Mamluks formed Egypt's ruling elite; a partially-native, partially-Ottoman, class of wealthy international merchants stood at the top of the commercial sector; and the religiously-trained Muslim *'ulama* and the Coptic clergy were the arbiters of the cultural life of Egypt's Muslim majority and Christian minority. All three groups declined after 1800. The Mamluk households which had dominated politics were eliminated by Muhammad 'Ali, and the Mamluk institution itself died a natural death upon the formal abolition of the trade in slaves within the Ottoman Empire in the 1870s. Egypt's indigenous merchant class initially was reduced to the status of state employees by Muhammad 'Ali's system of commercial monopolies, and later was gradually supplanted as the country's commercial elite by merchants of European background who were better connected to the world economy. Both *'ulama* and priests were progressively marginalized by the emergence of an alternative educational system with a largely non-religious content as well as by the spread of Western ideas and customs among a new educated elite oriented towards Europe and European ways. With some individual exceptions, the tone of Egyptian cultural and intellectual life from the middle decades of the nineteenth century onwards was largely set by men educated largely outside the older religious educational systems. Modernization produced a deep cultural schism in Egypt by the early twentieth century, a gap between the Europeanized orientation and lifestyle of the dominant elite and the more traditional outlook and values of religious classes who had been shunted to the sidelines.

What of new elites? Egyptian politics for most of the nineteenth century was dominated by the composite Turko-Circassian aristocracy of former Mamluks, Ottoman immigrants, and Armenian or European advisors who had formed the basis of Muhammad 'Ali's administration. In time this group also became the core of a new landlord class which had acquired land under Muhammad

'Ali and had their position consolidated under his successors. The cultural identity of the Turko-Circassian cohort is a more complex story. Although they and their descendants retained a heavy Ottoman orientation throughout the period (Turkish was still spoken in some aristocratic households in the early twentieth century, and personal connections with Constantinople through frequent visits, summer homes, and intermarriage, remained strong) in other respects the Turko-Circassian elite was gradually Egyptianized. Ehud Toledano's research on the character of the elite in the 1850s finds them to be "gradually acquiring an Egyptian tinge" by mid-century.[17] Language indicates the shift; whereas Ottoman Turkish was the language of administration under Muhammad 'Ali and his immediate successors, it was largely supplanted by Arabic by the 1870s.

More important in the long run was the emergence of a new Egyptian elite. Muhammad 'Ali began the process of empowering (some) Egyptians. He established new state schools teaching useful skills to state servants; conscripted rural Egyptians as soldiers and eventually as junior-grade officers in the army; and employed village headmen as government agents who were rewarded for their services by being given control of tracts of land. His successors continued to draw upon Egyptians for service in the bureaucracy, to use Egyptians as officers, and to privilege the position of the new rural elite through the grant of full private property rights over land. As we have seen, Egyptian intellectuals and journalists, Egyptian army officers, and the indigenous landed elite formed much of the leadership of the Egyptian nationalist movement which challenged Khedivial autocracy in the late 1870s and early 1880s. Although their political aspirations were stifled by the British occupation, the economic and social position of the indigenous elite was not eroded in any serious way by British hegemony.

There were several components to the Egyptian elite by the early decades of the twentieth century. The Turko-Circassian cohort of the ruling family, its many relatives, and propertied aristocrats of Ottoman descent formed the top layer. They still staffed many of the high offices of state and enjoyed a luxurious lifestyle thanks to their possession of large landed estates. A relatively distinct class was Egypt's foreign merchant community controlling the bulk of commerce and finance. This community lived mainly in the Westernized districts of Alexandria and Cairo, or in the new cities along the Suez Canal, and was served by its own network of non-Egyptian schools and social facilities modelled on those of Europe. Often speaking imperfect or no Arabic, this foreign *haute bourgeoisie* was both socially and emotionally disengaged from the country which had made them rich. Somewhat lower on the economic and social pyramid was Egypt's new indigenous elite of native landowners, educated civil servants and teachers, and members of the liberal professions. To a considerable degree the top stratum of the indigenous cohort was merging with the previously distinct Turko-Circassian elite through the gradual Egyptianization of the latter and their own growing economic and cultural prominence. It was the composite upper class of ex-Ottoman aristocrats and landed families, Egyptian civil servants and educated professionals, which provided the political and cultural leadership of Egypt for much of the twentieth century.

The uneven and ambiguous consequences of Egypt's modernization are best exemplified by the changing position of women over the course of the long nineteenth century. Judith Tucker has documented a significant erosion in the economic position of both rural and urban women over the course of the century. In the countryside the sexual division of labor was accentuated as a result of peasant land alienation and the emergence of large estates. "Men filled the ranks of day laborers, whether as service tenants or hired wage workers, while women tended the family plot."[18] New land laws resulted in men more often than women becoming the formal owners of agricultural plots which previously had been the possession of the family unit. In the cities women continued to work in petty trade, in handicrafts production, and in service occupations, and women were occasionally employed in the few factories which emerged in nineteenth-century Egypt. Yet in the new urban economy in which handicrafts counted for less and commerce bulked larger, women assumed a lesser place than men; "all skilled work went to men" while women were relegated to the "world of casual services and informal networks."[19] The overall result of the wider disparities in the economic roles of men and women in nineteenth-century Egypt was an "accentuation of female dependence" upon males.[20]

Social change similarly operated to increase rather than to reduce the differential between men and women. What might be termed the knowledge gap between the sexes widened as more men received formal education in the new state school system. While some girls did gain access to the primary school network run by the religious establishment, no state secondary school admitted girls up to World War I. The small percentage of (upper-class) women who received post-primary education did so mainly in the network of private, often foreign, schools which had emerged in nineteenth-century Egypt. While their exactitude is questionable, nonetheless official figures for Egyptian literacy demonstrate the scale of the gap: the census of 1907 estimated eleven per cent of males over the age of seven, but only 0.3% of females, to be literate.

Shifts in social patterns which affected women were largely limited to a small minority of upper-class women. Foreign and missionary education produced the same effect of a Europeanization of outlook and manners as was occurring among upper-class men. By the later decades of the century the women of the elite were learning French, the language of international culture, in the schools run by this or that order of sisters. In their adult years they lived largely isolated lives in European-style villas removed from the hustle and bustle of the old city. When they did venture out to visit one another or to attend theatrical perform-ances at the Opera House they wore modified European dress and rode in European-style horse-drawn carriages. More significantly, Afaf Lutfi al-Sayyid Marsot suggests there was an overall reduction in the social role and place of elite women as Victorian values spread among the westernized Egyptian upper and middle classes: "women were transformed into children guided by their rational menfolk, for they could only be emotional and senti-mental. Even the roles assigned to women – the realm of morality and child-rearing – became trivialized" in the new nineteenth-century framework which separated the world of men and power from the domestic arena to which women of the upper and middle classes were increasingly confined.[21]

Egyptian women were not the only social group who lost power, wealth, status, or more generally the ability to shape the course of their own lives over the course of the long nineteenth century. *'Ulama* losing their cultural hegemony; native merchants reduced to a subordinate position in the expanded and foreign-dominated commercial economy; urban handicrafts workers deprived of their livelihoods because of competition from European manufactured imports; and most importantly the bulk of the rural peasantry who lost control of land and ended up as tenants or landless wage laborers: many Egyptians were victimized by the growth of the powerful centralized state and the internally stratified, externally oriented, economy which emerged in Egypt over the long nineteenth century.

SIX

Liberal Egypt

WAR, REVOLUTION, AND INDEPENDENCE, 1914–22

World War I was a watershed for Egypt. Shortly after the
Ottoman Empire's entry into the war in the fall of 1914,
Great Britain declared a formal British Protectorate over the
country. Simultaneously the British deposed the pro-Ottoman
Khedive 'Abbas Hilmi II, then in Constantinople, and appointed
his uncle Husayn Kamil as titular ruler of Egypt with the new title
of Sultan. Upon the latter's death in October 1917, he was
succeeded by his brother Ahmad Fuad.

Four long years of war proved massively unsettling for Egypt. In
the countryside the forced sale of grain and animals to support
British military operations, accompanied by the dragooning of tens
of thousands of Egyptian peasants to serve in a British Labour Corps
that was created to construct military facilities in Europe and the
Middle East, generated rural deprivation and discontent with British
rule. In the cities wartime inflation and the rampages of British and
Imperial troops garrisoned in Egypt generated similar pressures and
resentment among the urban population. Egypt's politically articulate elite had been demonstrating increased opposition to the
British presence in Egypt before the war; wartime difficulties reinforced their desire to end the British occupation of Egypt. By the last
year of the war President Wilson's Fourteen Points em--¹
self-determination of peoples, with its intimation ۱
order after the war to end all wars, raised hopes tha
British domination of Egypt might indeed be in sight.

Two days after the armistice of November 11, 1918, ended hostilities in Europe, a delegation of Egyptian notables led by a former Minister of Education, Sa'd Zaghlul, visited High Commissioner Sir Reginald Wingate to request an end to the British Protectorate and Egyptian representation at the forth-coming peace conference in Paris. While the British pondered the issue through the winter of 1918–19, Zaghlul and his associates took the initiative in organizing a mass movement to work for Egyptian independence. The Wafd ("Delegation") was a broadly-based political front supported by much of the indigenous Egyptian rural landed elite and professional middle class which had emerged over the course of the nineteenth century. A general congress in January 1919 brought several hundred notables into the movement. At the same time Wafdist emissaries, often educated youth, gathered signatures in towns and villages on a deposition authorizing the movement's leaders to make the case for the "complete independence" of Egypt. From 1919 onwards, the Wafd was Egypt's premier political organization.

Faced with a burgeoning independence movement emerging in their Egyptian Protectorate, the British in March 1919 arrested Zaghlul and two of his colleagues and exiled them to Malta. The result was revolution. In March/April 1919, Egypt was convulsed with political protests and violence. Virtually daily demonstrations and strikes – by students, by civil servants and merchants, by groups of workers and unions, by Egyptian Copts as well as Muslims led by their respective religious establishments, and by Egyptian women – called for the release of the Wafd and demanded complete independence. Normal life was brought to a standstill in Egyptian cities. The uprising in the countryside was more violent and sometimes anarchic, involving attacks on British military and civilian personnel, installations, and communications facilities.

Although it was eventually controlled by British military rein-forcements sent to Egypt, the uprising of March/April 1919 marked the beginning of an extended period of Anglo-Egyptian political confrontation which in time did lead to formal Egyptian independence. From early 1919 to early 1922 Egypt underwent a three-sided political struggle. One force was the Wafd, whose leaders were released from detention as a result of the uprising. Continuing to demand complete independence for Egypt, Wafdist spokesmen conducted intermittent and ultimately inconclusive negotiations with the British in 1919–21. Regarding themselves as the will of the nation rather than one of many political forces ("we are a nation and not a party," as Zaghlul put it), the Wafd denied the legitimacy of the second force in the struggle. This was made up of various Egyptian ministries appointed by Sultan Fuad, often from remnants of the dwindling Turko-Circassian elite, who also attempted to negotiate Egypt's future status with the British. Much of the substance of Egyptian politics in the turbulent years after World War I was taken up by the competition between an ascendant Wafd and impotent ministries whose authority to speak on behalf of Egypt was constantly being undercut by Zaghlul.

The third actor in the struggle was of course the British. Rebellion in 1919 and sustained protest thereafter gradually wore the British down. By early 1921 a Royal Commission of Inquiry conceded that a protectorate over Egypt could not be maintained and would have to be replaced by an alternative relationship. When initial negotiations aimed at defining the terms of the latter failed, High Commissioner General Sir Edmund Allenby in February 1922 cut the Gordian Knot by demanding that his home government accept the inevitable and declare the independence of Egypt. On February 22, 1922 London did so, issuing a unilateral declaration of Egyptian independence. It was a qualified form of independence, however. The declaration reserved four areas – Egyptian defense, the security of Imperial communications through Egypt, the protection of foreign minorities, and the Sudan – as matters of British concern until such time as a treaty regulating their status should be concluded. At last Egypt had independence – of a sort.

THE PARLIAMENTARY MONARCHY, 1922–52

The political institutions of a formally independent Egyptian parliamentary monarchy took shape in 1922–23. Sultan Ahmad Fuad took the title of King Fuad I. Over the protests of the Wafd, which wished an elected constituent assembly, an appointed commission was established to draft a constitution. Adopting a constitution proved a contentious process; the Wafd boycotted its proceedings, and initial drafts proved unacceptable to either the King or the British. The end result, promulgated in April 1923, was a document which established a parliamentary form of government but which gave significant constitutional authority to the monarchy. Appointing and dismissing the Prime Minister and Cabinet were the prerogative of the King, as was the power to prorogue or dismiss parliament by decree. Whereas the parallel Electoral Law of 1923 provided for a Chamber of Deputies elected by universal male suffrage, two-fifths of the membership of the upper house of parliament was to be selected by the King. Largely as a result of the powers vested in the monarchy, no elected parliament in the thirty-year history of the parliamentary regime ever went full-term.

A second inhibiting factor in independent Egypt was the continuing British position in the country. Physically, this was much diminished upon the formal grant of independence in 1922. Some sixteen hundred British officials had been employed by the government of Egypt in 1919–20; most left their posts upon independence. Nonetheless, British officials continued to serve in key security posts (the Cairo Chief of Police until 1946 was Thomas Russell Pasha), and a new Department of European Affairs created in the Ministry of the Interior in 1924 in effect operated as a British intelligence bureau within the Egyptian government. The chief British official in Egypt (from 1914 a High Commissioner; an Ambassador after the conclusion of the Anglo-Egyptian Treaty of 1936) met regularly with Egyptian Prime Ministers, tendering frequent "advice" which the latter ignored at the risk of incurring British opposition to their continued tenure in office. The ultimate British sanction in a formally independent Egypt was the presence of British military forces in the country. The British maintained military garrisons on Egypt's main cities until after World War II. Even when British forces were relocated out of urban areas in the late 1940s, the large British military installation in the Canal Zone was a constant reminder of British power and a continuing irritant in Anglo-Egyptian relations until its withdrawal after the Revolution of 1952.

Egyptian politics in the three decades from 1922 to 1952 is often described as a triangular struggle for power among the Wafd, the King, and the British. The Wafd's insistence on "complete independence" for Egypt at least through the interwar period made it the great opponent of Great Britain; its commitment to parliamentary ascendancy similarly earned it the hostility of the Palace. The King (Fuad to 1936; his son Faruq thereafter) and the monarchy's civilian allies were the second force. Both Fuad and Faruq wished to rule rather than merely reign. They did so in part through the agency of what are known as "minority" parties, elitist groupings of Wafdist opponents or Wafdist dissidents who were willing to ally with the monarch in order to attain office. The third actor was Great Britain, committed to preserving what it regarded as vital imperial interests in Egypt. In normal times it attempted to do so through the medium of the advice being given by the British High Commissioner or Ambassador; in times of crisis it used the threat of military force to work its will.

The triangular contest among the Wafd, the King, and the British was not an equal one. Whereas the Wafd possessed wide popular support, the King held crucial constitutional powers. British power lay in the almost unchallenged assumption of Egyptian politicians that British interests needed to be taken into account, and consequently their frequent deference to British advice. Ultimately power resided in the presence of British military forces in the country and the threat of the use of them to insure the protection of those interests.

This unequal distribution of resources among the contestants usually operated to the detriment of the Wafd. Although the Wafd won every relatively free election in Egyptian history (no election was totally open), it held ministerial office for only roughly eight of the twenty-eight and a half years between the first parliamentary election in January 1924 and the military coup of July 1952. The first Wafdist ministry, that headed by Sa'd Zaghlul in 1924, was forced to resign by British pressure; subsequent Wafdist ministries headed by Zaghlul's successor as leader of the Wafd, Mustafa al-Nahhas, held office in 1928, 1930, 1936–37, 1942–44, and 1950–52, but were all dismissed by the King short of their full term. The ministries holding office in Egypt for most of the liberal era were usually non-Wafdist coalitions of minority parties which had been placed in power by the monarch and which ruled with his overt or covert backing.

Egyptian politics under the monarchy were elite politics. Throughout the parliamentary period Egypt's formal political parties competing for office were led by men of property whether urban or rurally based. Landowner representation in parliament was particularly pronounced; between 1924 and 1952, forty-three per cent of parliamentary deputies and fifty-eight per cent of cabinet ministers are estimated to have been large landowners. Over time, the elitist nature of parties and parliament produced disillusionment with the system itself, and was a major factor encouraging the emergence and growth of other forces with an alternative vision of what Egyptian public life needed to become.

The continuing British presence in Egypt throughout the parliamentary era also skewed Egyptian political development. Ending the British occupation and attaining "complete independence" was the transcendant issue of Egyptian politics under the parliamentary regime. Although there is no reason to doubt that most Egyptians did resent, and wished to terminate, the British occupation, the issue also became a political football among rival parties, an issue over which to revile the inadequate patriotism of one's opponents. As such, it contributed to the political instability of the period. At a deeper level, the obsession with the question of the British presence combined with the upper-class dominance of Egypt's political institutions to divert attention from socio-economic issues. Except partially for the Wafd in its final turn in office in 1950–52, none of Egypt's notable-dominated governments either gave significant attention to, or undertook major initiatives aimed at, resolving questions of growing class inequality and accelerating mass impoverishment. Preoccupation with the issue of national independence served to allow a self-serving elite to push more divisive internal problems under the rug. As was the case with the notable-dominated nature of the political system, this neglect of increasingly serious socio-economic issues by the political establishment contributed to the eventual delegitimization of the parliamentary system.

The course of Egyptian politics from the grant of formal Egyptian independence in 1922 to the military seizure of power in 1952 was a descending spiral. Egypt's first national election in early 1924 produced a sweeping Wafdist victory. Sa'd Zaghlul and his colleagues held ministerial office for most of 1924, until the harsh terms of a British ultimatum, delivered after the assassination of a high British official, led to Wafdist resignation. Zaghlul never held ministerial office again. For most of the rest of the decade Egypt was governed by cabinets of non-Wafdist politicians aligned to one degree or another with the Palace. From the start Egyptian parliamentary politics were never very decorous. Mutual accusations of political favoritism, administrative incompetence, and financial embezzlement formed much of the content of the highly partisan press, and served to discredit all parties involved. A good deal of this seems to have had a basis in fact. From the first Wafdist ministry of 1924 onwards nepotism, a spoils system in appointments, and purges of the supporters of the opposition, were regular features of governmental practice. Yet, in comparison to what was to follow, the 1920s were a period of great freedom of expression and only occasional public turmoil or violence.

The 1930s were a darker era. Internationally the early years of the decade saw a severe world depression which had an appreciable economic impact upon Egypt. Domestic political trends were also discouraging. Palace maneuvering in mid-1930 succeeded in installing a pro-Palace ministry led by the "strongman" of Egyptian politics, Isma'il Sidqi. Sidqi's premiership from mid-1930 to late 1933 was a period of authoritarian Palace-inclined rule. The Wafdist parliament was dismissed; the Constitution of 1923 was replaced by a more autocratic one which gave the king the right to veto legislation; the electoral law was amended to limit eligibility for public office to a smaller and more elitist, and thus presumably a less Wafdist, pool of candidates; new laws attempted to muzzle the press. Autocracy generated resistance. The early 1930s witnessed considerable public protest sometimes spilling over into violence, including instances of sabotage directed at government installations and assassination attempts upon Sidqi himself. The Sidqi years are regarded as having set ominous precedents for government coercion as well as for the resort to violence by the opposition.

There was a gradual return to what passed for normalcy in Egyptian politics from 1933 onwards. Sidqi's massive unpopularity eventually led King Fuad to replace him with less controversial, although still pro-Palace, Prime Ministers who moderated some of the harsher features of Sidqi rule. Student demonstrations in late 1935 helped produce the reinstallation of the Constitution of 1923. King Fuad died in April 1936, to be replaced by his young and initially quite popular son Faruq. A relatively free election in May

1936 returned the Wafd to office. It was this Wafdist government which in 1936 presided over what was the major political achievement of the decade, the conclusion of the Anglo-Egyptian Treaty of 1936 which established a formal alliance between Great Britain and Egypt and in the process regularized, but did not eliminate, the previously undefined British presence on Egyptian soil. The Wafd remained in power until late 1937, when a serious internal schism within the party and a wave of street violence between pro- and anti-Wafdist elements provided the occasion for the new King to dismiss it from office. From early 1938 until the eve of World War II, Egypt was again governed by coalitions of anti-Wafdist parties operating under strong royal influence.

Egypt also witnessed the emergence of new forces in the 1930s. Important new socio-political movements emerged with the erosion of the legitimacy of the elite-dominated parliamentary order. The two most important were the Muslim Brotherhood, an explicitly Islamist organization begun in the later 1920s which combined the demand for a more Islamic structuring of state and society with a call for greater social justice, and Young Egypt (1933–), a youth-oriented paramilitary movement influenced by European fascism which denounced the shortcomings of parliamentary government and advocated more efficient models of rule. The Brotherhood and Young Egypt were only the start of the process of radicalization; they were joined by other, more anti-establishment extraparliamentary movements in the 1940s.

World War II temporarily interrupted normal political life. As Allied and Axis military forces dashed back and forth across the desert to the west of the Nile Valley, the country became a major theater of military operations during the early years of the war. The security of Egypt was a vital British wartime concern, and as such generated more overt British interference in Egyptian domestic politics. In June 1940 British pressure forced the ousting of a ministry believed to hold Axis sympathies. A more momentous British intervention occurred in February 1942, when British tanks surrounded the royal palace and threatened King Faruq with forced abdication unless he complied with a British ultimatum to install the Wafd in office which by then was more pro-British.

The incident of February 4, 1942, is treated as a crucial pivot in Egyptian domestic politics in most narratives of modern Egyptian history. It is credited with simultaneously discrediting both the Wafd, a declining popular movement now revealed as willing to collaborate with the occupier in order to attain power, and the King who bowed to British force. The Wafd never fully recovered its nationalist aura, already damaged by previous internal schisms and financial scandals, after February 4, 1942. The incident also contributed to Faruq's eroding image, itself increasingly tarnished by the Egyptian monarch's sybaritic personal behavior from the mid-1940s onwards.

The circumstances of world war effectively prevented significant internal initiatives in the early 1940s. The main achievement of the Wafdist government of 1942–44 came in foreign affairs, where it took the lead in beginning negotiations with the leaders of other technically independent Arab countries towards the formation of an organization linking the Arab states in a new regional body. Although the League of Arab States came into existence only in March 1945, after the Wafd's ouster from office, the process of the league's establishment had been inaugurated by the Wafd. As war receded from the Middle East, so did British concern for its Egyptian base. By October 1944 the King felt sufficiently comfortable to dismiss the Wafdist ministry.

The downward spiral of Egyptian parliamentary politics reached its nadir in the later 1940s. From the dismissal of the Wafd in late 1944 until the start of 1950, Egypt was governed by coalition minority-party ministries possessing even less popular legitimacy than the Wafd. The massive British presence during the war had muzzled most forms of political activism. With the end of the war previously suppressed tensions exploded. Much of the discontent was socio-economic in origin. Long-term social tensions, produced by the growing impoverishment of much of the population and the widening gap between classes, were reinforced by more short-term problems such as wartime inflation and postwar urban unemployment as British installations and workshops closed and dismissed most of their Egyptian labor force. Both generated mass anger and popular activism. Issues of foreign policy fed into the postwar turbulence. From late 1945 through mid-1947, the efforts of successive Egyptian ministries to renegotiate the terms of the Anglo-Egyptian Treaty of Alliance sparked massive anti-British demonstrations. The question of Palestine, where many Egyptians supported the Palestinian Arab cause after 1945 and where the government became involved in a losing war effort against Israel in 1948–49, further roiled the political waters.

The net result of these overlapping sources of tension was a level of sustained political turmoil and violence unparalleled earlier in the history of the parliamentary monarchy. Nationalist protest against the lingering British presence was a repeated feature of the immediate postwar years, leading to clashes between demonstrators and police and literally scores of deaths in street confrontations. This overlapped with a wave of labor strikes and factory sit-ins, industrial unrest which itself sometimes escalated into violence between workers and the authorities. Nor was the countryside immune from class conflict. Incidents of peasant collective action – mainly the seizure of land or the destruction of estate property – that was directed against landlords, their agents, or the authorities, paralleled urban protest. Political assassination was the tip of the iceberg of violence. Among other victims, two Prime Ministers died at the hands of assassins between 1945 and 1948 (Ahmad Mahir and Mahmud Fahmi al-Nuqrashi, both of the Sa'dist Party), and the murder of the latter is generally believed to have prompted agencies within the government to sponsor the 1949 assassination of the charismatic leader of the Muslim Brotherhood, Hasan al-Banna.

Initially, the early 1950s were an intermezzo of sorts. Relatively free elections in January 1950 returned the Wafd – however tarnished, still the most popular political party in Egypt – to office. The Wafdist ministry of 1950–52 included some reformist figures and introduced several modest initiatives aimed at alleviating socio-economic disparities within the country. But its longstanding preoccupation with the nationalist issue of the British occupation remained the primary concern of its leaders. Late in 1951, the Wafdist ministry provoked a confrontation with the British by unilaterally abrogating the Anglo-Egyptian Treaty of 1936. Simultaneously, it inaugurated a low-key guerrilla campaign designed to harry the British out of their remaining military base along the Suez Canal. The latter set in motion a chain of events which eventually led to the fall of the ministry itself. On January 25, 1952, British troops killed over fifty Egyptian police in an assault on their barracks in the city of Isma'iliyya. The following day, January 26, was "Black Saturday." While angry crowds surged through Cairo protesting against this British massacre of Egyptians, organized bands of incendiaries ("organized" by whom is still an open question) undertook the systematic torching of commercial, primarily Western-owned, establishments in the city. Several hundred buildings including a leading symbol of the European presence in Cairo, Shepheard's Hotel, were destroyed; more than thirty people, mostly non-Egyptians, died.

It may also be argued that liberal Egypt died on Black Saturday. The collapse of law and order in the capital provided the excuse for King Faruq, who himself has been accused of having been implicated in paying for the incendiary bands, to dismiss the Wafd from office. The king himself did not last much longer. After six months marked by the tenure of four different prime ministers, a group of younger army officers seized power in Egypt on July 22–23, 1952 . On July 26 – exactly six months after he permitted and perhaps colluded in the destruction of his capital – they sent King Faruq into exile. The era of the monarchy and of parliamentary government was over in Egypt.

ECONOMY AND SOCIETY, 1922–52

Egypt experienced growing economic problems and widening social cleavages between the early 1920s and the early 1950s. Together, economic difficulties and social disparities appear to have meant a deteriorating quality of life for the bulk of Egyptians. They also played a major role in generating the political turmoil which became more frequent and sustained under the *ancien régime* as time passed, and eventually in producing the demise of the parliamentary monarchy.

Agriculture accounted for roughly two-thirds of gross Egyptian domestic product in the early twentieth century. Save for the growing use of chemical fertilizers, agricultural methods of production remained largely traditional. Humans and animals did the work, using tools and techniques which had been employed for centuries if not millennia. The geography of the country did not allow for the indefinite continuation of the impressive rate of expansion of the cultivated and cropped area as had occurred over the nineteenth century. The total cultivated area increased only slightly under the parliamentary monarchy; its rate of expansion now fell well behind the country's rate of population growth. Equally ominous were the productivity problems of Egyptian agriculture. Due primarily to overwatering and inadequate drainage, average crop yields per acre declined by about fifteen per cent between 1900 and the 1920s. Only in the 1930s, thanks to government investment in drainage and irrigation, did average yields return to their 1900 levels before declining again in the 1940s due to wartime shortages of fertilizer.

An imbalanced distribution of landownership and thus of the benefits of agriculture was one of Egypt's main legacies from the nineteenth century. If anything, patterns of landholding became more skewed after World War I. The number of small landowners holding plots of five acres or less increased by over a million (1.4 million to 2.5 million) between 1913 and 1948. Whereas over two and a half million small landholders owned a total of just over two million feddans of cultivated land in plots averaging less than an acre each in the late 1940s, twelve thousand large landholders possessed a slightly larger total in estates averaging nearly 200 feddans. Estimates of the landless population are more imprecise than figures for landholding, but range at between one and two million landless rural families by the 1940s. Agronomists calculate three acres of agricultural land to be the minimum required to support a family in the fertile Nile Valley; by World War II, over ninety per cent of rural families are estimated to have held less than this amount of land or to have been totally landless.

The poor, a steadily growing proportion of the rural population, appear to have become poorer over the three decades of the parliamentary era. The rural standard of living remained stable during the relatively prosperous 1920s. Due to world depression, falling prices which also led to falling wages, and problems of indebtedness, the standard of living declined appreciably during the 1930s. Per capita consumption of food products such as cereals, pulses, and sugar, are estimated to have decreased over the 1930s and to have remained depressed into the early years of World War II. In the early 1930s, 150 days of agricultural labor earned a total wage of about five Egyptian pounds; "at such rates, the labour of the workman or small peasant verges on the symbolic."[1] Living conditions may have improved in the more prosperous postwar period, but not before contributing to the wave of protest and violence which shook the Egyptian countryside in the years immediately preceding the Revolution of 1952.

Egypt's problems within the agricultural sector were partially, but only partially, offset by developments in the urban economy. By World War I, Egyptian business leaders were becoming alarmed concerning what the combination of a stagnating agriculture and a growing population would mean for the country's future prosperity. The obvious answer seemed to be an expansion of industry. The years during and after the war witnessed various projects designed to foster a greater degree of industrialization in Egypt. The boldest was the creation in 1920, in the midst of the postwar nationalist ferment, of Bank Misr ("misr" is the Arabic word for Egypt). "An Egyptian bank for Egyptians only," Bank Misr restricted shareholding to native Egyptians. Its explicit purpose was the financing of indigenously owned Egyptian industrial and commercial enterprises. In the years between the two world wars, Bank Misr led the way in the establishment of various new Egyptian-owned businesses including textile factories, publishing, insurance, and tourism companies, and Egypt's national airline Misr Air. Economic nationalism thus paralleled political nationalism.

A constraint upon industrialization in Egypt was the limitation upon tariff duties to which the country had been subject since the mid-nineteenth century. In 1930 the government of Isma'il Sidqi was able to impose higher tariffs which provided some advantage for domestic industries. Thanks in part to this tariff protection, major new industrial enterprises, especially in textiles and food processing, were founded in the 1930s. World War II also served as a boost to Egyptian industrialization, as wartime difficulties of transport reduced the flow of manufactured goods into Egypt and as the sizable British war machine based in the country demanded food, clothing, and other supplies which had to be met by local production.

The result of new industrial initiatives, tariff protection, and the stimulus of war was the emergence of an appreciable Egyptian industrial sector. Since official figures included everything from large mechanized enterprises to small workshops and repair facilities under the category of "industry," precise statistics on Egyptian industrialization during the parliamentary era are meaningless. What can be said is that local industry was meeting the bulk of domestic demand for textile products as well as for shoes, soap, furniture, tobacco, and alcoholic beverages by the 1940s. Egyptian industry was bi-polar; whereas the vast majority of enterprises were small-scale operations with only a few workers each (over ninety-five per cent of "industrial" firms employed ten or fewer workers in 1947), at the other end of the scale a few massive industrial ventures, especially in textiles, employed thousands of workers in large factories clustered in the vicinity of Cairo and in industrial centers in the cotton-producing Delta.

The expansion of Egypt's industrial sector over the parliamentary period needs to be set in perspective. Industry's contribution to national product was undoubtedly larger, possibly approaching fifteen per cent by one estimate for 1950, but was still considerably less than that generated by agriculture. The aspiration of making industry a significant counterweight to agriculture still had a considerable way to go.

The economic nationalism manifested in the creation of Bank Misr and in the drive to industrialize had its commercial parallel in a movement to Egyptianize the economy. This took some time to materialize. The foreign presence in commerce, finance, and industry remained appreciable for most of the interwar period. On the eve of World War I, over ninety per cent of joint-stock capital in Egypt – substantially the modern sector of the economy – was held by foreign investors; the percentage had decreased, but only to eighty-six per cent, by 1933. Nor was Bank Misr as hostile to collaboration with foreign capital in practice as in theory. Foreigners served as members of the board of some of the Bank's enterprises, and the Bank undertook joint ventures with foreign firms in the 1930s.

Significant Egyptianization of the economy occurred only gradually. Many of the new industries founded in the 1930s and 1940s were created by Egyptian capital. By 1948 the share of foreign capital in joint stock companies had fallen to sixty-one per cent. A post-war law of 1947 mandated that forty per cent of the membership of the boards of companies be Egyptian, that fifty-one per cent of the stock of new enterprises be held by Egyptians, and that ninety per cent of the workforce of new companies be Egyptian nationals. As a result, the percentage of Egyptian company directors and employees accelerated in the late 1940s and early 1950s. Like the drive to industrialize Egypt, the effort to Egyptianize the commanding heights of the economy was underway before the Revolution of 1952. It would be substantially completed in the first decade of the Revolution.

* * *

Underlying many of the economic difficulties of the parliamentary era was population growth. According to census figures, Egypt's population increased from 12.7 million in 1917 to 19 million in 1947 (the 1947 figure may be inflated). Given that the rate of expansion of the cultivated area slowed appreciably over the same period, continuing population growth generated a burgeoning imbalance between population and available resources in the countryside. The depressing conclusion of an economic survey written in the early 1950s was that "about half the present rural population is 'surplus' in the sense that there is no adequate employment for it within the present agricultural framework."[2]

With limited and diminishing prospects in agriculture, more and more Egyptians flocked to the cities. Cairo's population grew from 790,939 in 1917 to over two million thirty years later; Alexandria increased from 444,617 in 1917 to nearly a million in 1947. Similar rates of growth occurred in some of the new centers of industry in the Delta and in the commercial centers along the Suez Canal. Urbanization had major consequences for Egypt's political culture as well as its social structure. As more and more Egyptians came to live in cities they were exposed to educational opportunities, social pressures, and political stimuli which were largely absent or attenuated in the countryside.

In general the elite-dominated governments of the parliamentary period had a poor record in terms of encouraging meaningful social change. One notable exception is the area of education. Primary education was made compulsory by law early in the parliamentary era (1925). The number of Egyptians enrolled in all levels of public schooling increased nearly fivefold in the first two decades of independence (from 230,470 in 1925–26 to 1,128,200 in 1945–46). Although most of the educational increase was at the elementary level, there were over seventy-five thousand students in Egyptian state secondary schools and another fourteen thousand in state universities by the end of World War II. Heavily politicized as a consequence of their education which stressed national values and commitment, and gradually radicalized as a result of deteriorating economic conditions and constricted job opportunities, secondary school and university students were an essential component of the new non-parliamentary movements of right and left, as well as of the growing political turbulence of the 1930s and 1940s.

A new social geography, one reflecting a century of economic modernization and cultural Westernization, was taking shape in Egypt by the interwar period. At the top levels of society the Turko-Circassian elite who had dominated politics for much of the nineteenth century were a vanishing breed. No longer augmented by Ottoman migration to Egypt and gradually integrated into local society through intermarriage and shared patterns of education and socialization, the twentieth-century descendants of Egypt's former masters gradually blended into a new composite elite. Egyptian society and politics under the parliamentary monarchy were dominated by a newly formed Egyptian upper class composed partially of remnants of the old Turko-Circassian aristocracy, but in greater numbers by a new indigenous elite of wealthy landowners, prosperous merchants, industrial entrepreneurs, senior government bureaucrats, and an emerging professional class of doctors, lawyers, and engineers.

Despite their now largely local origins, "Egyptian" is a problematic adjective for the country's upper class. Heavily Europeanized by education, by frequent travel to France or Britain, and by association with and emulation of the practices of Egypt's foreign *haute bourgeoisie*, the values and lifestyle of the elite mirrored those of Europe. English or, more usually, French were the languages of polite discourse; upper class costume and consumables were luxuries imported from Europe; salons, soirées, and galas were modelled on those of European high society. In the words of one member of the cohort, "... we're so English, it's nauseating. We have no culture of our own."[3] This alienation from their own society eventually doomed Egypt's upper class to social extinction.

Equally significant shifts were occurring at the middle and lower levels of urban society. As a result of urbanization, expanding formal education, and a wider range of occupational niches within a more modernized economy, new middle strata were taking shape in the early decades of the twentieth century. "Effendi/effendiyya," formerly an Ottoman term for state servants, is the descriptor used to denote the core elements of Egypt's modern middle class. The ever-expanding body of students and teachers, government functionaries, merchants and clerks in Egyptian-staffed businesses and firms, part of the industrial workforce such as technical school graduates whose education set them apart from unskilled labor: effendi encompassed most members of these sizable social groups. A degree of Western education was the main hallmark of an effendi; Western-style dress (trousers, jacket, and fez/tarbush) were his visual marker. In the social hierarchy the effendiyya stood below the even more Europeanized upper class for whom the Ottoman term "pasha" was still employed, but above the urban working population and the peasantry of the countryside.

The cultural complexion of the effendiyya is a complex issue. On the one hand, their formal education in a heavily Westernized school system, as well as the political rhetoric of the era with its emphasis on parliamentary government and secular social patterns, worked to inculcate and reinforce Western and liberal values among Egypt's effendiyya population. At the same time resentment over the prominent position of foreigners in the Egyptian economy, as well as constricted employment opportunities as the effendiyya cohort grew in size, and disillusionment with the corrupt political establishment that was dominated by the upper classes, all combined to generate anti-European sentiment. A political system which could not satisfy effendiyya aspirations was rejected, and a call made for a more authentic and efficient structuring of state and society. These contradictory impulses existed side-by-side; a linear portrayal of the outlook of a social formation which was as buffeted by change as the effendiyya is impossible.

Effendis were at the center of Egyptian public life under the parliamentary monarchy. They formed much of the activist following of the Wafd during the hectic years of nationalist uprising after World War I, as well as much of the party's support in its subsequent struggle against the monarchy and the British. As a newspaper of 1930 summarized the importance of the urban educated middle class in Egyptian political culture during the interwar era, it was the effendiyya who "moulded public opinion and led the nation in times of crisis, set up its ideals and stamped it with its particular character."[4] The political inclinations of the cohort shifted over time. In the 1930s segments of the educated middle class turned to the anti-establishment movements such as the Muslim Brotherhood or Young Egypt which were voicing their grievances in more nativist language. After 1945 radicalized students, teachers, and government employees were, along with industrial workers, at the heart of the political protest of the postwar period.

Social and economic modernization also forged a new working class. The concomitant of a larger and more mechanized industrial sector was a more cohesive and self-conscious labor force. Due to ambiguities in the definition of "industry," estimates of the number of industrial workers by the post-World War II period are problematic. An industrial workforce of approximately half a million workers, most employed in small shops but a sizable percentage of perhaps as much as one-third or more working in large-scale enterprises, is probably a reasonable estimate for the later 1940s. The concentration of sizable numbers of workers in large enterprises, such as the textile factories in Shubra al-Khaymah on the outskirts of Cairo or the Delta industrial town of al-Mahalla al-Kubra, had important political consequences. It was the workers and unions in these new industrial centers who formed the core of Egypt's autonomous and militant postwar labor movement, and who combined with the movements based within the effendiyya to radicalize Egyptian politics and to pave the way for revolution in the 1950s.

Perhaps the most fundamental social process occurring in Egypt over the three decades of the parliamentary monarchy was the widening of the gap between Egypt's small but politically ascendant upper class and the rest of the population. The differential between elite and mass grew equally in regard to economic position, social patterns, and political outlook. Thanks to commercial and industrial diversification and Egyptianization, the assets of Egypt's small upper class may have increased; more certain is the deterioration of living conditions for the mass of the rural population. Socially the lifestyle of the Egyptian upper class became if anything more "irredeemably coloured by life north of Marseilles"[5] and as such more distinct and disassociated from the mores and values of the mass of Egyptians. Politically the upper-class leadership of the established parties, which controlled the levers of power throughout the parliamentary era, were intent upon the preservation of elite privilege. It was the disinclination of the upper-class dominated political establishment to meaningful change that generated the political protest of the 1930s and 1940s, and which eventually allowed the rapid destruction of the old order after the Egyptian military seized power in 1952.

CULTURAL LIFE IN LIBERAL EGYPT

The era of the parliamentary monarchy was one of exuberant intellectual expression. The necessary infrastructure for a vibrant life of the mind – a cosmopolitan literate minority, an extensive network of press outlets and periodical publications, a tradition of relative freedom of expression in cultural affairs – had taken shape in Egypt in the decades immediately preceding formal independence. Competition for office among rival political parties and frequent alteration in power among competitors prevented any one force from permanently stifling cultural expression. The result was an explosion of speculation on political, social, and cultural issues. Under the parliamentary monarchy Egypt's intellectual life was unquestionably more open, and perhaps richer in content, than at any previous point in Egyptian history.

The 1920s were an exceptional period for Egyptian cultural expression. Scores of daily newspapers and hundreds of weekly or monthly publications appeared on a regular or semi-regular basis. Cultural debate centered on the respective merits of "old" versus "new" (*qadim/jadid*), synonyms for Arabo-Islamic versus Western ideas; passionate diatribes by the proponents of each outlook filled the pages of literary journals. The most striking position in the cultural wars of the 1920s was articulated by a cohort of prominent native Egyptian intellectuals born in the late nineteenth century, many of whom had received at least part of their education in Europe. Advocates of a liberal outlook in the widest sense of the term, men such as Muhammad Husayn Haykal, Taha Husayn, 'Abbas Mahmud al-'Aqqad, Ibrahim 'Abd al-Qadir al-Mazini, and Salama Musa set the intellectual tone of the new Egypt. Their writings of the 1920s promoted many of the seminal concepts which had defined the nineteenth-century liberal perspective: a commitment to individual freedom of thought and behavior, the advocacy of secular social patterns, an evolutionary view of the natural world, faith in the power of modern science to bring progress. Correspondingly, their commitment to secularism and freedom of expression led them to question the validity of traditional beliefs and institutions, especially those associated with Islam which in their view had sometimes acted historically as a barrier to individual liberty and collective progress.

A similar Westernizing current expressed itself in Egyptian associational life. On the left, small Egyptian socialist parties appeared early in the decade, until crushed in 1924 by a Wafdist government which, however committed to political liberalism, was no friend of social radicalism. The decade witnessed the formation of the most durable of Egyptian feminist organizations, the Egyptian Womens' Union. Formed in 1923, its activities reflected the Westernized outlook of the Egyptian upper- and middle-class women who formed its base. Reforms such as universal suffrage, greater legal equality through the revision of laws relating to marriage and divorce, and expanded access to education for women, were the principal goals advocated in its journal *L'Egyptienne* (originally published in French, but not in Arabic until the late 1930s). Both the agitation of the Egyptian Women's Union and the fact that much of the male political elite shared a similar secular perspective did result in some incremental reform legislation relating to women: raising the legal age of marriage, introducing limits on male prerogatives in divorce, and by the late 1920s opening university education to women.

In the realm of the arts theatrical productions, many either presenting Western plays or indigenous takeoffs on similar themes, flourished. The decade also witnessed the birth of the Egyptian film industry. Egyptian visual artists experimented with the latest trends of avant-garde art. The most famous single artistic artifact of the decade was Mahmud Mukhtar's "The Revival of Egypt" (*Nahdat Misr*), a monumental sculpture created with official support and erected with great fanfare in 1928 in front of the Cairo train station (since then, moved to the square in front of Cairo University). Its two main elements symbolized the hopes of the decade. One was a sphinx-like figure slowly arising from the ground, just as Egypt was arising and reviving with independence;

the other was a peasant woman removing her veil to gaze into a more liberated future.

Two books of the mid-1920s reflect the Westernizing outlook of the decade. One was a short tract on Islamic history, *Islam and the Bases of Rule*, published by the Azharite Shaykh 'Ali 'Abd al-Raziq in 1925. Sparked by the 1924 abolition of the office of the Caliphate by the government of Turkey, its essential thesis was that the Caliphate had no scriptural legitimacy and indeed had been a pernicious institution historically. The second work was a literary study, *On Pre-Islamic Poetry*, published by the Sorbonne-trained literary critic Taha Husayn in 1926, which subjected Islam's sacred scripture, the Qur'an, to critical analysis and treated some of its prophetic narratives as myth rather than as revealed truth.

Together, the works of 'Ali 'Abd al-Raziq and Taha Husayn represent the cutting edge of the modernist outlook of the 1920s. Whereas the broader point of the former was that the political arrangements of the Muslim world, Egypt included, did not need to be constrained by past precedents but could develop along modern lines, the latter asserted the necessity of rational inquiry into the contents of sacred scripture. The fate of both authors upon expressing such views also needs to be noted. 'Ali 'Abd al-Raziq was subjected to a disciplinary hearing by the religious hierarchy of al-Azhar and dismissed from the corps of *'ulama*. Public furore compelled Taha Husayn to withdraw the original version of his work and to reissue a sanitized text under a new title. While the liberal outlook may have prevailed in intellectual circles, it was not embraced by the totality of the articulate public.

Although never totally eliminated, the liberal perspective so visible in Egyptian cultural expression in the 1920s receded from 1930 onwards. Economic and political circumstances – world depression and a declining standard of living domestically, state repression and growing political violence – had a great deal to do with eroding the earlier expectations of the 1920s. The overall mood of the 1930s was certainly not one of optimism. Terms such as "anxiety," "crisis," and "chaos" pepper the discourse of the decade. A diminution of enthusiasm for things Western was visible in the literary arena, where the post-1930 writings of several notable authors who earlier had dealt with European historical figures or social themes now turned to address subjects drawn from the Arabo-Islamic historical reservoir. Biographies of the Prophet Muhammad and of the leaders of the early Muslim community became a growth industry in Egypt in the 1930s; works on Islamic history generally remained a major literary genre through the 1940s.

The anti-establishment movements of the effendiyya which became prominent in the 1930s also rejected much of the Western-influenced liberal outlook which had been so prominent in the 1920s. In its place their spokesmen propounded alternative ideas drawn either from the Islamic legacy (the Muslim Brotherhood) or influenced by contemporary European Fascism (Young Egypt) as better models for Egypt's political, economic, and social organization. Advocating specific proposals which would have changed both the political institutions and the socio-economic structure of Egypt in a more populist and egalitarian direction, the propaganda of the new anti-establishment movements cannot be pigeonholed as "reactionary." But their rhetoric certainly rejected much of the secularism and the emphasis on the rights of the individual versus the collectivity which had characterized the liberalism of the 1920s.

The drift away from the values of the 1920s accelerated in the 1940s. The most prominent feature of the postwar years, when relative freedom of speech returned after several years of wartime censorship, was the flourishing of social as well as political radicalism of both the right and the left. From one side of the spectrum the reassertion of the contemporary relevance of indigenous Arab and Islamic models continued to be articulated in the literary output of numerous Egyptian authors. The postwar years were the heyday of the Muslim Brotherhood and similar socio-religious organizations calling for a more Islamically-informed order in Egypt. With a postwar membership estimated at anywhere from in the range of two hundred thousand to over half a million, the Muslim Brotherhood was Egypt's premier public organization after World War II. It was not alone; a contemporary enumeration claimed to have identified some 135 societies of an Islamist character existing in Egypt by the late 1940s.

The postwar period also witnessed the flourishing of radicalism influenced by contemporary socialism and Marxism. With fascist models discredited by military defeat, Young Egypt reconfigured its alienation from the existing order by renaming itself the

Socialist Party of Egypt and articulating its substantially unchanged proposals for populist political and economic reform in more acceptable language. The postwar years witnessed the formation of several more genuinely socialist and communist parties in Egypt. With much of their intellectual leadership drawn from resident foreign communities, and usually fragmented by ideological disputes, Egyptian socialism never acquired a mass base. Its greatest influence was upon the expanding and more autonomous labor movement centered in large industrial firms, many of whose leaders framed their struggle for better conditions in socialist terms. The political growth of the left was paralleled by new trends of social realism in literature and the visual arts, as a new generation of Egyptian social critics and creative artists such as Muhammad Mandur, Rushdi Salih, Louis 'Awad, and 'Abd al-Rahman al-Sharqawi voiced their criticisms of an unequal social order and called for greater social justice in the lexicon of European Marxism. If one literary work had to be isolated to represent the new radical mood of the postwar era, it might be Sharqawi's novel *The Earth* (1954), a searing indictment of social cleavages and official oppression in an Egyptian village.

New currents within the Egyptian womens' movement in the 1930s and 1940s also demonstrate the drift away from liberal values. A womens' adjunct to the Muslim Brotherhood, the Society of Muslim Sisters, had been formed in the 1930s. With only a few thousand members in the late 1940s, it never demonstrated the mass appeal of its male counterpart. More significant was leftist involvement and radical activism by educated Egyptian women. A political party appealing explicitly to women, the Egyptian Feminist Party, was formed in 1944; its program included the advocacy of birth control and abortion. University-trained women were a minority, but nonetheless active participants, in several of the leftist movements of the postwar era. The *Bint al-Nil* [Daughter of the Nile] Union, formed by Durriya Shafiq in 1948, had a distinctly sharper edge than its upper-class predecessor, the Egyptian Womens' Union, had had in the 1920s. Its name was selected to express its more populist and Egyptian indigenous character, in contrast to the elitist upper-class aura of the Egyptian Womens' Union. Its tactics were also more militant than the latter; in 1951 Shafiq led a womens' sit-in in parliament to demand the vote for women.

The overall tenor of Egyptian intellectual life changed significantly over the three decades of the parliamentary monarchy. In the wake of the Revolution of 1919 and the realization of formal independence, the complex of liberal political conceptions and secular social values which Egypt's indigenous elite had absorbed since the late nineteenth century were the dominant current in public discourse. A generation later, the shortcomings of the political system and the alienation of that elite from the bulk of the rest of the population had given birth to a range of alternative visions of political and social organization. From one side the Muslim Brotherhood and similar groups denounced the European-derived laws and institutions of the parliamentary regime and called for a more authentically Egyptian order. From the other side groups such as the socialist movements and labor unions propounded largely Western, but hardly liberal, solutions for Egypt's problems. The radicalism of "right" and "left" were not polar opposites. Although Islamically oriented and Marxist social critics might present their views in different conceptual frames, their main grievances and some of their specific proposals for ameliorating them were similar. What united them most was their belief that the parliamentary monarchy dominated by the upper-class had failed in addressing Egypt's social problems and economic difficulties.

The intellectual discontents of the 1930s and 1940s notwithstanding, an account of Egypt in the liberal age should not conclude without noting the positive legacy of the era. The thirty years of the independent Egyptian monarchy was a period of great intellectual freedom in which a wide range of ideas found expression and elaboration. Substantively, many of the alternative visions of a better polity and society which Egyptians have voiced in the decades since the overthrow of the *ancien régime* echo those first propounded between 1922 and 1952. Emotionally, many Egyptians look with fondness on an era in which there was so much freedom of opinion and interplay of ideas. However transitory, the period of the parliamentary monarchy left a rich intellectual residue for contemporary Egyptians to draw upon.

Revolutionary Egypt

MILITARY COUP, REPUBLIC, AUTHORITARIAN RULE

The liberal era of Egyptian history effectively came to an end in July 1952, when elements of the Egyptian armed forces executed a successful military coup. Disillusioned with governmental corruption and with the deepening economic problems which remained unaddressed by the parliamentary establishment, in 1949 junior officers in the Egyptian military had formed a secret organization known as the "Free Officers." Their discontents resonated with others; over the next few years the Free Officers won the support of numerous other junior- and middle-rank officers. The leaders of the group originally envisaged being strong enough to make a bid for power in the mid-1950s. Forced to accelerate their plans for a coup upon learning of the King's intent to move against them, they struck on the night of July 22–23, 1952. In a nearly bloodless military operation, by morning the Free Officers had seized control of army headquarters and key field units. Within the next few days they purged the upper ranks of the military, dismissed a pro-Palace ministry and in its place installed one staffed by cooperative civilian politicians. On July 26 King Faruq, the monarch they held responsible for many of the country's problems, was hustled into exile.

The Free Officers had no definite agenda for Egypt when they seized power in 1952. Disparate in background, linked individually with civilian parties and movements spanning the political spectrum from the Muslim Brotherhood to Egypt's socialist movements, they were united by little beyond the desire to reform the country's corrupt domestic politics and to end the lingering British occupation. Initially the term "blessed movement," implying both internal purification and external liberation, was the slogan employed to describe their agenda; the more sweeping word "revolution" found its way into their rhetoric only gradually.

Executive decisions after July 1952 were made by a committee of leading Free Officers eventually known as the Revolutionary Command Council (RCC). Over time the RCC assumed a larger and larger role in Egyptian political life. General Muhammad Najib, an older officer not originally part of the military movement but co-opted by the Free Officers on the eve of their coup, was appointed Prime Minister in September 1952 in place of a civilian prime minister. In January 1953 a three-year transitional period, during which the precise nature of a new political order would be defined, was declared; in the interim the RCC was to remain the ultimate decision-making body in Egypt. The last formal link with the old order was broken in June 1953, when the Egyptian monarchy was abolished and Egypt declared a republic with Muhammad Najib as its first President. At the same time other members of the RCC assumed formal cabinet posts. Of these, the most consequential was the appointment of the individual who had been the driving force in the formation of the Free Officers, Colonel Jamal 'Abd al-Nasir (= Nasser), as deputy prime minister and minister of the interior.

Parallel to their assumption of a more direct role in government, the military group now in control of Egypt moved against existing political forces. The swift trial and execution of the leaders of a textile factory strike which had turned violent in August 1952 indicated that the new regime would not tolerate labor unrest. Existing political parties were officially banned in January 1953 and a new pro-regime political organization, the Liberation Rally, established. Much of 1953 was taken up with corruption trials of prominent figures of the old regime, with the banning and closure of partisan publications, and with internal purges of officers too closely identified with civilian movements of either left or right. In January 1954 the organization which was probably the main potential rival to the power of the RCC, the Muslim Brotherhood, was declared by the regime to be a political party and thus subject to the earlier edict outlawing all parties. Many of the components of Egypt's fractious pre-1952 political universe – its established political parties, including the Wafd; its leftist organizations and labor movement; and the Muslim Brotherhood – were largely neutralized between mid 1952 and early 1954.

The most serious challenge to the consolidation of RCC power came in February/March 1954. By that time considerable tension and personal animosity had developed between the official leader of the army's "blessed movement," General/President Najib, and the real dynamo within first the Free Officers movement and later the RCC, Colonel Nasser. Progressively marginalized by Nasser within the RCC, Najib abruptly resigned as President in late February 1954. When his resignation became public knowledge, a storm of protest against the departure of the popular symbol of the new regime erupted. Unprepared for this reaction, Nasser and the RCC beat a hasty retreat; Najib was reinstalled as President of Egypt on March 1, 1954.

This was only the first phase of the Najib–Nasser clash. Through March the RCC quietly rallied support within the military and among civilian groups. Deliberately intending to provoke a new crisis, on March 25 Egypt was stunned by the announcement that the ban on political parties was to be lifted, that the RCC would soon dissolve itself, in effect that the revolution was over. A second round of public turmoil – demonstrations, now sometimes violent, now mounted by both supporters and opponents of the RCC and the revolution – shook Egypt in late March 1954. But this time Nasser and the RCC were ready; the mass mobilization of the regime's new political movement, the Liberation Rally, and the support of much of organized labor eventually won the day for the RCC. Responding to cries of "long live the revolution," on March 29 the RCC announced that it would remain in power. Exhausted by a month of intense struggle, on the same day President Najib collapsed and had to be hospitalized. Nasser and his supporters had won.

The final challenge to RCC domination came in October 1954, when a member of the Muslim Brotherhood attempted to assassinate Nasser. The attempt failed and served as the occasion for a massive crackdown on the last remaining organized body capable of contesting military ascendancy. Thousands of Brotherhood members were arrested and imprisoned; several of its leaders were tried, found complicit in the assassination attempt, and executed. The Brotherhood was too deeply embedded in Egyptian society to be permanently destroyed; but its organizational power was broken for the duration of the Nasser era. Almost as a footnote to the crackdown on the Brotherhood, in November President Najib – "Kerensky with a fez," in the words of one journalist – was dismissed from office and placed under house arrest.

The scaffolding of a new political system was put in place in 1956. A new constitution for Egypt was promulgated by the RCC in January 1956. Declaring Egypt to be "a sovereign independent Arab state," a "democratic Republic," and "part of the Arab Nation," it established a presidential form of government which gave extensive executive powers to an elected President and gave legislative authority to an elected National Assembly. By restricting eligibility for election to the legislature to candidates nominated by the National Union, a mass-based organization which was to replace the Liberation Rally and serve as the only authorized political party in republican Egypt, the Constitution of 1956 in effect created a one-party state. The new Constitution was approved by popular plebicite in June 1956. Upon its ratification the RCC was dissolved.

By 1956, there was little doubt as to whom the new President of Egypt was to be. Parallel to the consolidation of the power of the RCC in 1952–54 went the consolidation of the personal primacy of Nasser. At its inception the RCC had been a genuinely collective leadership. Internal debate was frequent and often heated in the early years of the regime; although Nasser's opinion counted most, it did not always prevail. It appears to have been largely Nasser's tactical skills in leading the struggle against challenges to the position of the RCC in 1952–54 which gradually elevated him above his comrades in arms. Prime Minister from April 1954, Nasser increasingly spoke for Egypt before the world at large. When the Brotherhood at last took on the regime in late 1954, it was Nasser whom it singled out for assassination. By mid 1955 Nasser was making unilateral decisions on behalf of the RCC. His nomination as President of Egypt in 1956 was endorsed by an overwhelming ninety-eight per cent of those voting.

* * *

Although there were adjustments in specifics in subsequent years, the broad outlines of the political structure of Egypt did not change significantly between Nasser's designation as president in 1956 and his death in 1970. The unexpected union of Egypt and Syria in the United Arab Republic (UAR) in 1958 occasioned the drafting of a new provisional constitution for the new state and the expansion of both the National Assembly and the National Union to include Syrian members. The secession of Syria from the UAR in 1961 again necessitated formal adjustments in constitutional arrangements. A Charter for National Action, drafted by Nasser in 1962 and approved by a popular congress, both specified a new socialist agenda for the United Arab Republic as Egypt continued to be known for the rest of the Nasser era, and called for the establishment of a new mass organization for popular mobilization, the Arab Socialist Union (ASU). For the remainder of the 1960s the ASU was the organization within which tussles for political power at the local level were contested. Yet another provisional constitution declaring the UAR to be "a democratic socialist state based on the alliance of the working forces" and further strengthening the powers of the executive was promulgated by presidential decree in 1964; it remained in effect until 1971.

Formal arrangements are one thing, the realities of power another. There was little if any effective check on the power of the executive agencies of state in revolutionary Egypt. Successive assemblies sometimes offered mild criticism of specific policies or ministers; they never took on Nasser or the system. The official designation of Egypt as a democratic state meant little. Legislative elections were conducted within the framework of a one-party system (first the National Union, later the Arab Socialist Union), their results being manipulated and orchestrated by the regime. Political and civil liberties were limited at best. An extensive security and intelligence apparatus created initially with United States assistance and directed by ex-military officers guaranteed regime control of civil society. The muzzling of the press had been part and parcel of the regime's consolidation of power through the mid 1950s. The nationalisation of newspapers in 1960 completed the process of official control of expression. With countervailing checks absent, abuse inevitably accompanied authoritarianism – the capricious incarceration of suspected opponents, routine brutality and occasional sadism in the prisons. To be sure, Nasserist rule was not as heavy-handed as some of its contemporaries of the 1950s and 1960s; but it was unquestionably an autocracy with few restraints on the arbitrary exercise of state power.

Yet the regime was not as monolithic as the above might imply. A key structural feature of revolutionary Egypt after the mid 1950s was the emergence of what are known as "centers of power," autonomous areas of control or influence carved out by leading figures of the regime as personal fiefdoms which they exploited to the private benefit of themselves and their supporters. The largest and most important of these was the Egyptian military under Nasser's close friend and RCC colleague 'Abd al-Hakim 'Amir. Appointed commander of the armed forces in 1953, through control of appointments and the use of military resources to build a clientele, 'Amir over the course of the 1950s succeeded in creating an extensive patronage network within the armed forces, the civilian administration, and the expanding public sector of the economy. "From their positions of power the senior officers were able to trade on their influence, pocket kickbacks on everything from citrus exports to arms purchases, and to acquire property and income through appropriations or management of sequestered properties."[1] In the early 1960s, Nasser attempted to challenge 'Amir's position by depriving him of control of military appointments, but backed off when 'Amir's supporters remained loyal to the latter. Similar but less extensive centers of power emerged within the security and intelligence services, and after 1962, also within the regime's official party, the Arab Socialist Union. Politically, centers of power meant the subdivision of authority and influence among rival coalitions of high officials within an apparently unitary authoritarian regime; economically, it meant the diversion of part of the benefits of economic growth and structural transformation into the pockets of a new elite.

The only significant challenge to Nasserist authoritarianism and the new centers of power which it had spawned came after Egypt's military defeat by Israel in 1967. Not surprisingly, 'Amir and his military clique were discredited by Egypt's humiliation in a war which they had reportedly encouraged by assuring Nasser of

Egyptian readiness. 'Amir himself was immediately sacked after the 1967 war, was later arrested for reportedly planning a coup against his old friend Nasser, and by September 1967 had died in prison apparently at his own hand (although many Egyptians had their doubts; "he was suicided" was the contemporary characterization of his death). Over the next year 'Amir's top associates were dismissed and/or jailed, lesser clients of the former commander in chief purged from the military. Yet the change was one of personnel rather than of structure. After 1967 a similar center of power run by officers loyal to Nasser emerged in place of 'Amir's previous fiefdom.

A broader challenge to Nasserist autocracy developed in 1968. After a decade and a half of civilian docility, sizable student and labor demonstrations critical of a faltering dictatorial regime, and calling for greater democratization within the Arab Socialist Union, erupted in Egypt's cities in February 1968. By March Nasser had responded by promising new ASU elections which would democratize the organization. ASU elections were indeed held in June/July 1968. But Nasser's authoritarian inclinations proved too strong. Manipulated by the regime, the elections resulted in a shuffle of individuals but not in an opening of the country's only political party to alternative voices. It was only after Nasser's death in 1970 that partial movement in the direction of political liberalization occurred in republican Egypt.

ARAB SOCIALISM AND SOCIAL CHANGE

The economic and social approach of the new regime which took power in Egypt in 1952 evolved only gradually. When it did solidify, the Nasserist socio-economic agenda amounted to a program of fundamental change in the character of the Egyptian economy and to a lesser degree its society as both had developed over the course of the nineteenth and early twentieth centuries. It is particularly in the areas of economic and social life that Nasserist policies mark an attempt at "revolution."

The new regime's inital socio-economic approach was far from radical. A liberal and free-market orientation, emphasizing the reduction of expenditure, controlling inflation, and encouraging both private domestic and foreign investment in the economy, prevailed from 1952 to 1956. New initiatives indicating a more pronounced economic role for the state were only tentative at first, including the establishment of a Permanent Council for National Production in 1952 to coordinate development projects and the creation of a National Planning Committee in 1955 to draft a comprehensive plan for economic and social development. State-directed capitalism, not socialism, was the original economic thrust of Egypt's new rulers.

The main exception to this conventional approach to the economy was the regime's policy regarding agriculture. Driven in large part by a desire to break the economic and thus the political power of the landed class whom it regarded as the core of the *ancien régime*, the RCC enacted an agrarian reform law in September 1952. Individual ownership of agricultural land was limited to 200 feddans; an additional 100 feddans could be held by a family in the name of its children. Land above these limits was either to be sold by the landlord or was to be confiscated by the state, previous owners receiving compensation in the form of government bonds. The nationalized land would be redistributed in small lots to tenant families, to agricultural workers, or to the poorest families in the village. Agricultural rents were also limited by the agrarian reform act. Subsequent agrarian reform laws limited individual ownership of agricultural land to 100 feddans (1961) and later to fifty feddans (1969).

The agrarian reform law of 1952, the Nasserist regime's main initiative in the economic sphere in its early years, cut in two directions. On the one hand, it accepted but broadened the system of private ownership of agricultural land which had developed in Egypt since the mid-nineteenth century. On the other, it marked a further extension of state control of Egyptian agriculture. Not all nationalized land was immediately distributed to peasant cultivators; much of it was managed as state farms for a considerable period of time. Redistributed lands also came at a cost, the new owners being required to pay the government an amount equivalent to the compensation paid to the previous owner. Equally significant was a provision that the recipients of redistributed land should join cooperatives which would coordinate agricultural production and marketing. Directed by state functionaries, cooperatives now set the price that cultivators were to receive for their crops. They often did so at artifically low rates. Increased state control of agriculture in effect vitiated much of the meaningfulness of land reform for Egypt's peasantry.

A shift to a new economic order in the urban economy began in the later 1950s. It began in response to an external stimulus. The Suez Crisis of late 1956, in which Great Britain and France joined Israel in war against Egypt, had major economic repercussions. Most British and French properties and holdings in Egypt were nationalized in late 1956 or early 1957, their owners and/or managers simultaneously expelled from the country. Parallel nationalizations of the properties of Egypt's Jewish minority also occurred, with perhaps half of Egyptian Jewry emigrating from Egypt in the wake of Suez. Not only was the sizable foreign presence in the modern sectors of Egypt's economy definitively shattered in 1956–57; in the process, the Egyptian state acquired possession of a sizable chunk of the economy.

The nationalizations of 1956–57 set Egypt on the road to a state-controlled economy. To manage existing as well as newly-acquired enterprises, the government established the Egyptian Economic Organization in 1957. As additional firms were placed under the control of the Economic Organization on a case-by-case basis over the next few years, the state slowly became more prominent in non-agricultural economic production. In February 1960 Bank Misr, the Egyptian-owned financial and industrial conglomerate, was nationalized; nationalization of the Egyptian press followed in June.

What had commenced as a piecemeal and event-driven expansion of state ownership and direction of the economy eventually became more systematic. Egypt became an officially socialist state in the early 1960s. The most sweeping measures were enacted in 1961. A series of new laws in June nationalized all banks and insurance companies, most large-scale import-export, industrial, commercial, and transport firms, and mandated partial state ownership of many medium-sized economic enterprises. Nationalization was accompanied by legislation intended to level socio-economic disparities. On the one hand laws mandating maximum limits on salaries and steep progressive taxation on personal income (ninety per cent on incomes over ten thousand Egyptian pounds) were enacted in an attempt to restrict the future accumulation of private wealth; on the other, measures requiring profit-sharing by firms, setting a minimum wage and a 42-hour work week, and enlarging social security benefits for workers, were promulgated. Socialism in Egypt took on a more punitive tinge in late 1961, when in the wake of Syria's secession from the United Arab Republic Nasser blamed conservative elements for the secession and moved against "reactionaries." The property of several hundred wealthy Egyptians was sequestered in late 1961 to early 1962; simultaneously several thousand former landlords or capitalists were deprived of political rights. Full nationalization of firms which had been only partially nationalized in 1961, as well as additional nationalizations, occurred through 1964.

In the late 1950s and early 1960s, the Egyptian government effectively took control of the leading sectors of the non-agricultural economy. By the mid 1960s the government owned all financial institutions, public utilities, and transport firms except taxis, all large industrial and construction companies, most export-import firms, and the larger firms engaged in retail trade (department stores), many hotels, and the Egyptian publishing industry. This economic colossus was placed under the direction of thirty-nine government-run holding companies or General Organizations, each of which managed a pyramid of individual firms or factories with virtual monopoly status in different productive sectors. By 1965 nearly forty per cent of total economic output, including the still mainly private agricultural sphere, was generated by firms in the public sector.

Parallel to the physical creation of a state-dominated economy came the articulation of an official ideology intended to justify this economy. The Charter of National Action of 1962 provided the Nasserist regime's definitive statement of its socio-economic agenda as it had evolved after a decade in power. After expounding on the failures of indigenous capitalism as a vehicle of economic development, it went on to proclaim that "the socialist solution was a historical inevitability" for Egypt. The public sector would now bear the "main responsibility" for national development, the private sector (once purified of "exploitative" elements) playing only a subordinate role. Planning on a national scale was the only way to assure proper national development; efficient planning in turn depended on the concentration of resources. Therefore, large-scale industry, foreign trade, and the financial sector were henceforth to be under state ownership and direction. In the evolution of what now came to be officially known as Arab Socialism, ideology clearly followed praxis.

There is now a considerable literature elaborating on the structural inefficiencies of Egyptian public sector enterprises. As a result of overstaffing due to the politically driven expansion of the workforce to accommodate a rapidly increasing urban population, per capita labor productivity in industry declined after 1962. Redundancy in the workforce, the faulty installation or substandard quality of machinery, and bottlenecks in the acquisition of imported equipment and/or component parts due to bureaucratic red tape, meant public sector firms often operated at well below capacity. The cumbersomeness of the Egyptian public sector bureaucracy is legendary: a top-heavy administrative structure, the proliferation of regulatory agencies with overlapping and sometimes crosscutting responsibilities, the diversion of human effort into the filling out and stamping of multiple forms and unnecessary paperwork. The example of export requirements illustrates the larger problem: "in the mid-sixties the exportation of any commodity from Egypt was subject to control procedures conducted by thirteen different bodies, through five different stages of customs' checks. At Cairo International Airport, responsibility was divided among ten different government authorities and every parcel was handled through thirty-three processes. The customs system in general was governed by about twenty-six laws and decrees, and the forms that had to be used were still those designed in 1884."[2]

The problems of the public sector soon had an impact. By 1966–67, regime spokesmen occasionally spoke in defense of "non-exploitative" private enterprise. Simultaneously the government once again attempted to attract capitalist foreign investment to Egypt and turned to Western international development agencies for assistance in meeting its foreign debt obligations. Military defeat in 1967 enormously increased the country's economic difficulties and the need for foreign economic assistance. Numerous voices called for measures of domestic economic liberalization and an external reorientation towards the market economy after 1967. While substantial movement in the direction of economic liberalization had to await the death of Nasser, the perception of a need for an "opening" (infitah) to the private sector and to foreign investment, policies which marked Egypt's economic course in the 1970s under Sadat, were being articulated within regime counsels by the later 1960s.

How much did Egypt's economy actually change under Arab Socialism? A leading goal of the creation of the huge public sector which came to dominate the non-agricultural economy by the 1960s was economic growth. Here the record is uneven. Estimates of the annual rate of economic growth indicate a steady rise of close to four per cent a year through the 1950s, prior to the full implementation of Arab Socialism; a surge in the rate of growth to 5.5% annually in the first half of the 1960s, thanks primarily to massive state investments; then a tailing off to slightly over three per cent a year in the later 1960s, as both bottlenecks in the dominant public sector and international complications combined to inhibit growth. The rate of economic growth was negative in 1967–68, the fiscal year after the disastrous war of June 1967.

Industry was the economic poster-child of the Nasser regime. Industrial expansion was most impressive in the period from 1953 to 1963, when the output of Egyptian industry grew by almost ten per cent annually. Due in part to lack of funds for additional investment and in part to the inefficiencies of the public sector, industrial expansion slowed from 1964 onwards. Industry's share of national product increased from fifteen to twenty-three per cent between 1952 and 1970; that of agriculture declined from thirty-five to twenty-five per cent. Manufacturing, mining, and construction enterprises employed approximately 1.3 million workers by the end of the Nasser era, in comparison to over four million still employed in agriculture.

Although textiles, the single largest area of manufacturing prior to 1952, continued to bulk large, by the close of the Nasser years Egypt was producing a wide range of other materials and finished products: steel from a new installation at Helwan and aluminum from a factory at Naj' Hammadi; automobiles, tractors, and television sets using imported components but assembled in Egypt; household appliances, pharmaceuticals, agricultural and electrical equipment. While much of domestic consumption was being met by locally produced goods, problems of quality control, of financial obstacles to the procurement of necessary components resulting in under utilization of capacity, and of cumbersome bureaucratic procedures, severely hampered the external competitiveness of Egyptian industry. Through the 1960s textile products accounted for over half of Egypt's manufactured exports, a clear indication of the difficulties faced by other Egyptian exports in international markets. On the whole, Egyptian industry failed to assume its intended role as saviour of the Egyptian economy in the 1960s.

The regime's focus on industrialization should not be taken to imply a neglect of the agricultural sector. Several major projects were initiated with the aim of extending Egypt's cultivated area. The centerpiece of this effort was the Aswan High Dam, a massive artificial mountain thrown across the Nile just south of the city of Aswan in the 1960s. The High Dam made possible the reclamation for agricultural purposes of an estimated 650,000 acres in the 1960s. Other land reclamation projects, including an ambitious but costly scheme to develop a "New Valley" of agricultural land in the oases which run parallel to the Nile in the Western Desert, accounted for the reclamation of another 150,000 acres.

Impressive as the raw figure of over 800,000 acres opened to agriculture is, it falls below the regime's targets for land reclamation. Ancillary complications – evaporation of the water stored in Lake Nasser, the soil erosion generated by a faster flow of the river, and the loss of the invaluable silt previously deposited by the river's annual flood in the case of the High Dam and high cost and marginal soils in the case of the New Valley – also diminished the benefits of land reclamation efforts. Observing that only sixty per cent of land reclaimed actually came into agricultural production, of which much was below standard, a recent study had identified land reclamation as the "white elephant" of the Nasserist regime.[3]

The character of Egyptian agriculture was changing by the Nasser period. Whereas cotton accounted for eighty-five per cent of agricultural exports in 1950, its share decreased to slightly over forty per cent by 1970. Rice, fruits, and vegetables produced for the European market, along with manufactured products, accounted for a larger proportion of Egyptian exports in 1970 than did raw cotton. To its benefit, Egypt was shedding its monocultural economic base and developing a more diversified economy.

* * *

Growth was only part of the Nasserist economic agenda. Equally important to the regime, at least through the mid 1960s, was restructuring the pyramid of national wealth. Gradually "revolution" came to mean particularly the economic and social – although not the political – empowerment of "the people," in Nasserist rhetoric both the agent and the prime beneficiary of Arab Socialism.

Agrarian reform was one mechanism of socio-economic redistribution. The impact of the agrarian reform laws of 1952, 1961, and 1969, on the Egyptian countryside was considerable but did not totally transform it. Unquestionably, the top layers of the rural pyramid of landed wealth were lopped off. Huge agricultural estates of thousands of feddans ceased to exist as a result of agrarian reform. Yet previously dominant landlord families did not totally lose their economic position or their political clout in Nasserist Egypt. De facto holdings in excess of the statutory limits continued to exist through landlord manipulation (e.g. fictitious bequests to relatives, false buyouts by dependent peasants). The ownership of multiple plots of land by the members of large extended families, and their acting as a corporate unit within village councils and cooperative societies, preserved a considerable measure of the collective power of Egypt's former landlord class in some areas. Their assumption of posts in the bureaucracy, in cooperatives, and in the ASU, reinforced the ability of leading families to continue to influence local affairs.

Perhaps the main beneficiaries of Nasserist agrarian policies were the middle strata of the Egyptian peasantry. Owning between ten and fifty feddans of agricultural land made one relatively well-off in the Egyptian rural context. Landowners owning less than fifty feddans were not subject to land confiscation through agrarian reform and, thanks to their possession of adequate capital to buy land being sold by larger landowners who were, actually increased the percentage of land under their control. Their capital put them in a position to benefit most from agricultural modernization (e.g. buying tractors) and to finance the shift to profitable new export crops such as fruits and flowers. Their local influence and connections similarly enabled them to benefit most from the credit and extension services provided by cooperatives. In the words of one analyst, "the major change in the village-level power structure [since the 1952 revolution] has been the replacement of one class of notables by another."[4]

The retention of a degree of elite power in the countryside and the consolidation of the position of the middle strata of the Egyptian peasantry should not obscure the considerable impact agrarian reform did have on rural society. By 1970, somewhat over 800,000 feddans of agricultural land had been redistributed to about 340,000 rural families in plots of two to five feddans each. About one-eighth of the total cultivated area changed hands as a result of agrarian reform; slightly less than ten per cent of rural families obtained land. Where small landholdings of five acres or less accounted for thirty-five per cent of all ownership in 1952, the percentage of land held in such holdings increased to fifty-two per cent by 1970. The number of landless rural families decreased from 1,270,000 in 1952 to 960,000 in 1965. Landless families had made up fully forty-four per cent of the rural population in 1952, but only twenty-eight per cent in 1965.

The impact of agrarian reform can be viewed in two ways. That the previous landlord class retained part of its wealth and power, that middling peasants increased their acreage and benefited most from cooperative arrangements and from technical improvements, and that less than ten per cent of rural families received land, all indicate that agrarian reform meant less than a revolution in the Egyptian countryside. At the same time, that 340,000 families acquired land, that the percentage of land held by poorer peasants grew by half, and that – despite population growth – there were 300,000 less landless rural families in 1965 than in 1952, are not trivial changes.

In the social sphere, the Arab Socialism which became official dogma in the 1960s was distinctly populist. An increasingly more radical regime whose attitude towards the existing structure of privilege eventually hardened into one of antipathy, its rhetoric repeatedly asserted that its policies were intended to bring the benefits of modernity to the mass of the population of Egypt. Nor was this populist emphasis solely rhetorical; within the constraints imposed by a faltering economy, the Nasserist regime undertook a significant expansion of social services and inaugurated major new social initiatives.

One area of emphasis was education. The total student population of Egypt increased from slightly over two million in
1952–1953 to nearly five million in 1969–70. The boast of the
regime was that it was opening a new school every day somewhere
in Egypt by the 1960s. Educational expansion was most marked at
the university level; there were over three times the number of
Egyptians enrolled in universities in 1969–70 (161,517) than in
1952–53 (51,681). The rapid expansion of the educational system
came at a price: overcrowded facilities, large and sometimes
dysfunctional classes, and shortages of necessary school supplies.
While a larger percentage of Egyptians were benefiting from
formal education under the Nasserist regime than had previously
been the case, the quality of the education they were receiving deteriorated in comparison to the more elitist educational system of the
prerevolutionary era.

Providing improved access to health care was a parallel goal of
Arab Socialism. The Charter of 1962 declared "the right of each
citizen to medical care" and that "health insurance must be
expanded to embrace all citizens." Government employees – the
largest single component of the urban workforce thanks to nationalization – were rapidly enrolled in a state-run and financed comprehensive health care program. Making the benefits of modern medical
care available to the agricultural majority in the countryside was a
more daunting problem. One health initiative directed towards rural
Egypt was preventative: the provision of clean drinking water in
villages. Whereas only a minority of villages had clean drinking
water available in 1952, access to the same was expanded to almost
all rural communities by the late 1960s. A pre-revolutionary project
of establishing rural health centers which could provide basic
medical services to a number of villages in their vicinity was vastly
expanded after 1952; by 1967 the government reported that there
were 1,680 such units scattered across rural Egypt. As with
education, the expansion of health services had problems; long waits
for treatment, inadequate facilities and staff especially in rural areas,
in some cases perfunctory service rendered by physicians more interested in their private practices than in serving the patients that they
were obliged to treat in government-run clinics. Nonetheless, more
Egyptians came to have access to at least a modicum of medical
treatment thanks to the health initiatives of the revolution.

Egypt's population at the time of the census of 1947 was nineteen million; it had increased to thirty million by the census of 1966. Due to overpopulation in the countryside and the rural-to-urban migration which it engendered, the rate of population growth in urban areas was roughly double that in rural communities over the same period. Population growth was clearly outpacing the expansion of employment opportunities in both rural and urban Egypt by the 1960s, in the process fueling an accelerating rate of migration from rural to urban areas and feeding the growth of a burgeoning informal sector of the urban economy composed of underemployed casual labor, peddlers of recycled goods, and hustlers of various stripes.

Population growth was formally acknowledged as a national concern in 1962, when the Charter declared that continued economic progress was contingent on controlling the rate of population growth. A national family-planning program took shape in the mid 1960s. The main thrust of the effort was the distribution at nominal cost of contraceptive pills and devices through government-run health centers as well as via a network of new family-planning clinics to be established across Egypt. Although the rate of population growth declined slightly in the late 1960s, this appears to have been more a function of the difficult economic circumstances of the period than because of the regime's recent efforts to encourage family planning.

Expanding the opportunities available to the largest single group of disadvantaged Egyptians – Egyptian women – was another thrust of the Nasser regime after 1952. One major formal change for women came in the political realm. The right to vote and to run for public office were extended to women in 1956. A limited number of women sat in Egyptian and UAR National Assemblies from 1957 onwards; the first woman cabinet minister was appointed (as Minister of Social Affairs) in 1962. Womens' independent political activity was another matter. Some of the more vigorous womens' groups were closed down when political parties were abolished in 1953, and women had no more scope for political activity than men as the regime became increasingly authoritarian over time. A subsidiary of the all-enveloping ASU, the Women's Organization, served as the officially sanctioned voice of Egyptian women in the 1960s.

The economic position of women changed considerably under Nasser. Populist legislation improved working conditions for all workers and mandated equal pay for equal work. Some legislation took account of women's special needs in the workforce; thus Law 91 of 1959 guaranteed paid maternity leave for mothers. The Charter of National Action of 1962 proclaimed the equality of men and women in the economic sphere: "Woman must be regarded as equal to man and must therefore, shed the remaining shackles that impede her free movement, so that she might take a constructive and profound part in shaping life." This acknowledgement of the importance of women to national development was in part an aspiration, in part a recognition of reality. Thanks primarily to expanding educational opportunities, women were present in virtually all civilian sectors of the labor force – industrial and commercial establishments, teaching, health care, the civil service, engineering, law, journalism, the media – by the 1960s.

In contrast to their formal inclusion in the political system and the expansion of their economic role, the Nasser years saw little change in the legal position of women. Perhaps out of a desire not to encourage further religiously derived opposition to its generally secular policies, the revolutionary regime dodged the issue of legal reform for women. A proposal to bring the revision of personal status law before the National Assembly in 1958 was rejected; later feminist demands that parliament take up the issue were similarly ignored. The enlargement of opportunities for women during the Nasser years occurred primarily in the social and economic rather than in the legal spheres.

In general, the populist goals of Egypt's revolutionary Nasserist regime were certainly only partially realized. Financial constraints, institutional barriers, and social prejudices all worked to limit the degree to which peasants, workers, and women could be empowered and have their lives enriched. Nonetheless, for all their limitations the social initiatives of the Nasserist regime should not be underestimated. Economic disparities did decrease from 1952 to 1970; the social opportunities available to many Egyptians expanded over the same period. The Nasserist era left a legacy of commitment to "the people" and to socioeconomic egalitarianism which many Egyptians recall with fondness.

EGYPT, THE ARABS, AND THE WORLD

To a far greater degree than under the parliamentary monarchy, foreign affairs were a major preoccupation of the revolutionary regime in power in Egypt from 1952 to 1970. As with its internal orientation, the Nasserist government's approach to international issues developed incrementally. Ultimately, however, it marked a dramatic shift in the place Egypt occupied in the Middle East as well as in the world as a whole. The Nasser years were Egypt's heroic era of regional leadership, global prominence, and eventually international overextension.

The main concern of the new regime in its first few years in power were issues specific to the Nile Valley. In 1952 Great Britain still operated a major military base at the Suez Canal. The later memoirs of Egypt's new military masters are unanimous that getting the British out of Egypt was their top priority upon assuming power. A parallel Nile Valley issue was the status of the Sudan, occupied by Egypt in the nineteenth century but effectively under British control since the beginning of the twentieth. Whether the Sudan would return to Egyptian control or would move in another direction was another issue which the RCC had to address.

Both issues were substantially resolved in 1952–54. Viewing the dispute over the Sudan as an obstacle to reaching agreement with the British on the more vital question of British military evacuation, RCC negotiations of late 1952–early 1953 with Sudanese leaders and the British reached agreement on a process whereby the Sudanese people would determine their own future. Although the Egyptian government subsequently and somewhat clumsily attempted to bend that process in the direction of union with Egypt, it failed; the Sudan became an independent state on January 1, 1956. The military regime's acquiescence in Sudanese self-determination effectively marked the end of the longstanding Egyptian claim to sovereignty over the Sudan. Nonetheless, geographical propinquity and Egyptian dependence upon the waters of the Nile gave the Sudan a special place in Egyptian foreign relations in the years that followed.

Anglo-Egyptian negotiations for a revision of the Treaty of 1936, the agreement authorizing a British base along the Suez Canal, extended from early 1953 to mid 1954. Agreement on a new Anglo-Egyptian relationship was finally reached in July 1954 and signed by both governments in October. The Treaty of 1936 was abrogated; the British were allowed twenty months to evacuate their military forces from the Suez Canal area. The last British troops withdrew from Egyptian soil in June 1956. By mid 1956, four years after the military regime came to power, the British occupation of Egypt was over.

With the residual issues of the British occupation and the Sudan substantially settled in 1953–54, what next for Egypt in the world? Initially, the RCC paid little attention to regional affairs. The stimulus to the new regime playing a larger role in Middle Eastern politics came from the West. In 1954–55, Great Britain took the lead in establishing a pro-Western defense organization in the Middle East. Initially known as the Baghdad Pact, the organization linked Great Britain, Turkey, Iran, Iraq, and Pakistan in a defense alliance; the United States was an associate member. The hope of the organization's Western sponsors was to entice additional independent Arab states beyond Iraq into joining the alliance.

To Nasser and his colleagues, the Baghdad Pact smacked of imperialism on the cheap; while formally withdrawing from the Arab world, here was Great Britain attempting to perpetuate its influence through a defense alliance. If extended to the Arab world, the Baghdad Pact would also undercut parallel Egyptian efforts to organize Arab regional defense under the umbrella of the League of Arab States. From 1954 onwards Egypt strenuously opposed Arab participation in any Western alliance system. When the Baghdad Pact grouping took shape in 1955, Egypt denounced Iraq's membership as a betrayal of Arab solidarity and did its diplomatic (and often its undiplomatic) best to insure that other Arab states such as Syria and Jordan would not follow the Iraqi example. For most of 1955 a war of rhetoric, of propaganda, of subversion raged across the Arab East. Egypt's efforts were successful; no Arab state other than Iraq joined the Baghdad Pact. More broadly, by 1955 Egypt was emerging as the champion of Arab solidarity and the leader of opposition to efforts to perpetuate Western influence in the Arab world.

Egyptian-Western confrontation over the issue of regional defense overlapped with another international situation which worsened in 1955. Egypt and Israel had been in a formal state of war since 1948. For much of the period between the cessation of large-scale hostilities in 1949 and 1954, Egyptian-Israeli hostility was low-key; there had even been inconclusive *sub rosa* negotiations between the two countries toward some sort of peace agreement both under the monarchy and during the early years of the new military regime. Largely because of Egypt's new push for Arab solidarity from late 1954 onwards, the potential success of which was viewed in Israel as a tangible threat to Israeli security, the situation between the two countries worsened by 1955. In February 1955 Israeli military forces mounted a major raid in the Egyptian-occupied Gaza Strip; Egypt retaliated by sponsoring more extensive and sustained Palestinian Arab infiltration across the Egyptian-Israeli border. From early 1955 an accelerating spiral of border violence between Egypt and Israel further added to regional instability.

A third development of 1955 related to the Cold War. The younger officers who seized power in 1952 were initially pro-Western and in particular pro-American. Although later claims of US inspiration and direction of the 1952 coup are overstated, they had been in contact with American intelligence agents prior to their coup. The new regime's preferred source of foreign assistance in their early years in power was the United States. Extended and ultimately fruitless negotiations for US aid occurred from 1952 through 1954. By 1955, as both Egypt's wish to establish regional defense leadership and increasing tension with Israel necessitated augmenting Egypt's military strength, an increasingly frantic Egyptian government turned elsewhere for military assistance. A major arms agreement officially concluded with Czechoslovakia, but in reality negotiated with the Soviet Union, was announced in late 1955. The Czech arms deal further soured Egypt's already-frayed relationship with the Western powers. Simultaneously, through demonstrating that there were alternatives to reliance on the West for aid, it enhanced Egypt's and Nasser's position at the forefront of Arab nationalism.

These several developments of 1955 – Egyptian opposition to defense arrangements with the Western powers and its parallel attempts to promote Arab solidarity, increasing Egyptian-Israeli border violence, Egypt's turn to the Soviet Union for military assistance – marked a transformation in Egypt's international position.

Egypt was breaking with the West, was assuming a posture of Arab leadership, and was being sucked into deeper confrontation with Israel. The developments of 1955 form the indispensible background to the even more dramatic sequence of international events which convulsed the Middle East in 1956.

A major domestic project of the new revolutionary regime was the construction of a huge new dam on the Nile at Aswan. Negotiations for American, British, and World Bank financial assistance for the project were conducted in 1955–56. By early 1956, both the American and British governments had come to regard Nasser as the leading opponent of the Western position in the Middle East. In large part to demonstrate both to Nasser and others that one did not challenge Western hegemony with impunity, in mid July 1956 the two governments abruptly terminated aid negotations. Nasser's riposte was a bombshell. On July 26, 1956, in an emotional speech in Alexandria celebrating the anniversary of the exile of King Faruq, Egypt's new President announced that in order to finance the building of the Aswan Dam, Egypt was nationalizing the International Suez Canal Company, arguably the prime symbol of Western economic dominance in the Middle East.

Egypt's nationalization of the Suez Canal – carried out immediately and efficiently, with little disruption of Canal traffic – was the spark for war. Great Britain's Prime Minister Sir Anthony Eden had wished to overthrow the Nasserist regime in Egypt since early 1956; the nationalization of the Canal reinforced his determination to do so. By 1956 the French government had come to view Egypt as a leading source of external assistance to the rebels in French Algeria, and similarly was ready to join in an anti-Nasser operation. For quite different reasons – border violence; the Soviet armaments now flowing to Egypt; and recent Egyptian threats to restrict Israeli maritime access through the Gulf of Aqaba – the Israeli government had been muting large-scale military action against Egypt since 1955. In secret meetings outside Paris in October 1956, representatives of the three governments developed a patchwork plan whereby an Israeli military invasion of Sinai would provide the occasion for Britain and France to dispatch military forces to seize the Suez Canal and in the process to bring about the fall of the Nasser regime.

The Suez Crisis or Sinai Campaign of 1956, as the joint operation is known, was a world crisis of the first order. In late October

Israeli forces crossed the border and within a few days occupied the bulk of the Sinai Peninsula. A day later the British and French began bombing Egypt and announced that they were sending military forces to safeguard the Suez Canal. It took almost a week for an Anglo-French armada to reach the area of the Canal and begin disembarking military forces. This was too late; in the interval between Israeli attack and Anglo-French arrival, the fact of collusion between the three partners had become clear and had generated nearly universal international opposition to what many viewed as blatant aggression against Egypt. World opinion as expressed at the United Nations was overwhelmingly critical; the Soviet Union threatened possible nuclear intervention on behalf of Egypt (this while busy liberating Hungary from the Hungarians); most decisively, the Eisenhower administration in the United States, kept in the dark by its erstwhile allies, viewed the joint attack as counterproductive and used its financial clout to pressure the British in particular to suspend military operations. Facing a domestic firestorm of criticism and financially menaced by a run on the pound, the British buckled. To the consternation of the French, Britain called off military action short of the two allies establishing control of the Suez Canal area.

Although Israel had successfully occupied Sinai, the Anglo-French attempt to assert Western control of the Suez Canal had failed. British and French forces were soon withdrawn. In good part due to American pressure and guarantees, Israel evacuated Sinai by mid-1957. In physical terms, the Suez Crisis and Sinai Campaign was a blip on the screen; the Canal remained nationalized, Nasser remained in power, Egypt regained Sinai. Perceptually, however, the events of late 1956 were the decisive catalyst making Nasser, still in power despite the best efforts of the old imperial powers to unseat him, the leading figure in Arab and Middle Eastern politics for the remainder of his reign.

* * *

Nasser bestrode the Arab world like a colossus in the years after Suez. Leader of first a political and increasingly a socio-economic revolution at home, symbol of opposition to both Western imperialism and Israel abroad, his popularity with the Arab public was enormous. What are known as "Nasserist" parties echoing the domestic approach and international stance of Egypt were to be found in many Arab states. Regardless of their own views, rulers throughout the Arab world had to take account of Egypt's positions in shaping their policies. Nasser did not always get his way; relations with the pro-Western Iraqi regime up to 1958 as well as with the anti-Western but prickly military regime in power in Iraq after 1958, with the conservative monarchies in Jordan and Saudi Arabia, or with pro-Western republican governments in Lebanon, were often tense, sometimes frankly hostile. But for many Arabs in the later 1950s and early 1960s, Egypt and Nasser represented the future, a historical tide of progress sweeping the Arab world.

Egypt's external influence reached well beyond the Arab world from the mid 1950s onwards. The decolonization of Africa coincided with the Nasser years. As an independent and revolutionary African state, Egypt supported independence movements elsewhere in the continent. Cairo Radio offered verbal inspiration; African students were welcomed into Egyptian schools and Egyptian teachers dispatched abroad; various African nationalists came to Egypt to seek support in their struggle for independence. Egypt's prestige and outreach extended beyond Africa. Along with Prime Minister Jawaharlal Nehru of India and Marshal Tito of Yugoslavia, Nasser was one of the central figures in the non-aligned movement of the 1950s and 1960s. Numerous leaders of newly independent Asian and African states visited Egypt to seek Nasser's counsel as well as Egyptian diplomatic and/or material support. The decade after Suez was Egypt's moment in the international sun.

The apogee of the Nasserist tide in the Arab world came with the creation of the United Arab Republic in 1958. Syria was the center of postwar integralist Arab nationalism or "Pan-Arabism" – the perception that existing Arab states were artificial and that the proper course for Arabs was to unify in one greater and more natural Arab polity. Syria was also deeply divided internally, the scene of successive internal coups and external plots. The country may have been on the verge of disintegration by late 1957; Egyptian testimony indicates that Nasser felt that either civil war among military factions or a Communist takeover were distinct possibilities. When a delegation of Syrian officers suddenly arrived in Cairo in January 1958 to plead for the unity of Syria with Egypt, Nasser was placed in a quandary. His own view as well as that of most of his associates was that unity was premature. His new position as champion of Arab nationalism, however, made it difficult for him to turn down an appeal which embodied the aspiration of unity. Reluctantly, and only after imposing conditions which he felt would guarantee his control of the fractious Syrians, did Nasser agree to Egyptian-Syrian unity. He did so with considerable apprehension. To the American Ambassador he characterized the task ahead of him as "a big headache, because we're not set for it. We have to do it but it'll be a big headache."[5]

Nasser's fears were justified. The United Arab Republic, the name given to the major effort at integral unity between two geographically distinct Arab states of the modern era, lasted little more than three years. A unified government headed by Nasser and staffed by Egyptian and Syrian ministers was hastily cobbled together. Genuine Syrian participation in national decision-making was limited, however. By the end of 1959 even the main supporters of union among Syrian politicians, the leaders of the Ba'th Party, had resigned their ministerial appointments in frustration. Equally serious was the failure fully to integrate the military establishments of the new halves of the new state. Although Egyptian officers were assigned to Syrian units and Syrians similarly posted to Egypt, Egyptian and Syrian units remained intact and separate within the armed forces of the UAR.

The posting of Egyptian officials in increasing numbers to Syria and the manipulation by some of the more freewheeling Syrian economy for personal profit; the replication of Egyptian patterns of authoritarian rule in the Northern Region of the UAR, as Syria was now known; by 1961 the application of socialist-inspired measures of nationalization and economic control to Syria as well as to Egypt: various factors contributed to a growing mood of disillusionment with Syria's subordinate position within the UAR. Even nature seems to have conspired against the union, in the form of three successive years of drought in Syria. A quip circulating in 1960 expresses the mood of discontent which had gradually developed in the Northern Region of the UAR: "there's been no rain since the Egyptians came and there'll be none till they go!"[6]

The Egyptians went in late September 1961, when a coup by Syrian army units took control of Damascus and other Syrian cities. Nasser at first considered the use of force to preserve the union, dispatching paratroop forces to Syria in an attempt to do so. Soon the practical difficulties of effective military intervention across the Mediterranean dissuaded him from continuing. Within a few days the government of the UAR was forced to acknowledge the loss of its Northern Region. It was a bitter pill for the man who had symbolized the cause of Arab nationalism in recent years; his most visible Arab nationalist achievement lay in ruins.

*   *   *

Syria's secession from the UAR in 1961 was a watershed in Egypt's position in the Arab world. Although Nasser remained the leading personality in inter-Arab politics until his death in 1970, the decade of the 1960s was one of accumulating regional problems and eventually of a disastrous international setback.

Nasser's immediate response to the secession of Syria from the UAR was a sharp turn to the political left. Accusing "reactionaries" of having been behind the Syrian secession, Nasserist rhetoric now proclaimed that revolution throughout the Arab world was the prerequisite for progress towards Arab unity. UAR policy was perhaps at its most aggressive in the regional arena in the early 1960s, including verbal abuse of conservative and pro-Western Arab regimes and military intervention in support of the republican side when an anti-royalist coup sparked civil war in Yemen in 1962. The intervention in Yemen eventually became an albatross for Egypt. Despite the provision of substantial economic and military aid and the dispatch of tens of thousands of troops in support of the new republican regime, Egypt and the new republican government were unable to resolve the conflict in their favor. At home the intervention drained an already troubled economy; abroad it accelerated an increasingly vitriolic Arab cold war between revolutionary Egypt and monarchical Saudi Arabia. Ultimately the intervention proved a failure. Egyptian forces were withdrawn from Yemen after Egypt's 1967 defeat by Israel without having consolidated the position of Egypt's revolutionary surrogates.

Egyptian radicalism moderated somewhat in the mid 1960s, when Nasser took the lead in arranging a surface reconciliation between conservatives and revolutionaries through the medium of a series of summit conferences of Arab leaders. But this harmony between revolutionaries and conservatives was superficial and fleeting. Steadily pushed to the left by the militancy of fellow revolutionary regimes, especially that in Syria, and possibly perceiving that a concerted campaign to isolate the UAR in the Arab world was being orchestrated by the United States in collaboration with his main conservative rival, King Faysal of Saudi Arabia, by late 1966 Nasser had denounced the summit process and entered into a new military alliance with a radical Syrian regime. The stage was set for the denouement of 1967.

In all probability Nasser neither planned for, nor expected, war with Israel in 1967. His brinksmanship of May which produced an Israeli military riposte in June was undertaken in response to rising Israeli-Syrian border violence. This tactic also appears to have been motivated in good part by extraneous considerations, specifically a desire to regain the initative in the propaganda battle with his conservative Arab rivals. As tension escalated, he seems to have anticipated something like a repeat of the scenario of 1956: either international action would prevent war or international pressure upon Israel would quickly limit and ultimately reverse any Israeli gains. Nasser may also have been gulled by bad advice from his military subordinates, especially Marshal 'Amir, assuring him that Egyptian forces were more prepared, should war erupt, than was the case in reality.

Whatever Nasser's motivations and expectations, the Six-Day War of June 1967 was a disaster both for the UAR and Nasser. UAR armed forces in the Sinai Peninsula and much of its air force were destroyed; Israel occupied all of Sinai; the Suez Canal became the front line and was closed to shipping; to the east the UAR's Jordanian and Syrian allies were defeated and lost significant portions of their territory. Appalled by the magnitude of defeat, Nasser immediately announced his resignation. Massive street demonstrations in support of the man who had become the symbol of Egyptian national dignity led him to reverse his decision and remain in office.

"Reversing the consequences of aggression" and regaining the Sinai Peninsula were Nasser's main preoccupations in his last years in power. Egyptian forces were rapidly withdrawn from Yemen; a rapprochement with conservative Saudi Arabia won financial aid from the oil monarchies; the rivalry between revolutionary and conservative regimes came to an end as all Arab states came together in an effort to deal with the common issue that had been a general Arab defeat in 1967. A good case can be made that Nasser in effect abandoned the Pan-Arabist goal of unity after 1967, implicitly accepting the regional status quo. Although the name "the United Arab Republic" was retained until 1971, in practical terms it was the national interests of Egypt that reemerged as dominant in foreign policy after 1967.

The de facto Israeli-UAR border along the Suez Canal was the scene of frequent fighting through the late 1960s. The UAR mounted a self-proclaimed "War of Attrition" from early 1969 through mid 1970; virtually daily shelling, periodic commando raids, and Israeli bombing of Egyptian installations in the Nile Valley produced an unprecedented level of sustained Arab-Israeli violence. This level of conflict on Israel's western front was paralleled by violence to the east, as Palestinian movements burgeoned in the later 1960s and mounted daily raids into Israel or Israeli-held territory. All this had no territorial effect; Israel remained in control of the territories it had occupied in 1967.

Nasser was not a well man by the later 1960s. The diabetes from which he had suffered since the 1950s eventually produced heart complications. His pace slowed visibly after 1967; a heart attack necessitated medical treatment in the Soviet Union in 1968. The end came in September 1970. The tense situation between the government of Jordan and the Palestinian movements which had emerged as a state within a state in Jordan after 1967 exploded into civil war in September 1970. As premier Arab leader, Nasser presided over several days of intense and exhaustive negotiations in an effort to end the bloodshed. Almost immediately after mediating a Jordanian-Palestinian truce, on September 28 he suffered a major heart attack and died.

Nasser's funeral on October 1, 1970 was an event unparalleled in Egyptian history. Literally millions flooded the streets of Cairo to lament the passing of the man who for so long had been the leader and prime symbol of Egyptian independence as well as of Arab nationalism in the era of decolonization. His recent failures in the international arena and the difficult domestic situation of Egypt in the later 1960s were at least temporarily forgotten, as Egyptians remembered instead his earlier triumphs; the overthrow of an alien monarchy and a greater degree of social justice at home, the final termination of the British occupation, and an unprecedented measure of Egyptian regional and world leadership abroad.

EIGHT

Whose Egypt?

A ny narrative of Egyptian history over the past few decades of necessity has a tentative character. Much of the documentation available for understanding previous eras is missing; the long-term effects of official policies on socio-economic trends in many cases are not yet clear; the perspective afforded by the passage of time is lacking. As a result, this chapter focuses mainly on what can be termed the public history of Egypt during the presidencies of Anwar al-Sadat (1970–81) and Husni Mubarak (1981–). The concluding section attempts to highlight some of the most important features of the Egyptian scene at the close of the twentieth century, and to identify some of the major issues facing the country as it enters the sixth millennium of its long history as a distinct society and polity.

ANWAR AL-SADAT AND THE OPENING, 1970–81

Upon Nasser's death in September 1970, Vice-President Anwar al-Sadat ascended to the presidency of Egypt. A Free Officer and member of the RCC in the early years of the revolution, Sadat had held various high positions under Nasser prior to his appointment as Vice-President in December 1969. His assumption of the presidency was ratified by popular referendum in October 1970.

Sadat's position as president was precarious in the early 1970s. With a prior reputation for obsequiousness ("Nasser's poodle" to some uncharitable critics), and unaffiliated with the clusters of apparatchiks based in the security services and the Arab Socialist

Union which had emerged in the 1960s, Sadat was widely assumed to be a transitional figure. In reality, he proved to be a more skilled political operator than many anticipated. Meetings with officers in which he pledged greater support and autonomy for the military consolidated his base of support in the army; the announcement of plans to return some sequestered property to its previous owners signalled his intention to pursue a less socialist path of development to the Egyptian bourgeoisie. For many Egyptians alienated by the radicalism and police-state techniques of the 1960s, Sadat represented a better alternative than the clique of socialist bureaucrats led by his rival 'Ali Sabri and centered in the ASU. When this cohort challenged his authority over issues of foreign policy in the spring of 1971, Sadat publicly denounced the "centers of power" maneuvering against him, dismissed 'Ali Sabri and his associates from their official positions, and used the claim of an ASU-based plot to replace him as an excuse to have his major rivals arrested and to begin to dismantle their ASU fiefdom. In the later rhetoric of the Sadat years this crisis of April–May 1971 was elevated into a "Corrective Revolution" nearly on a par with the military's assumption of power in July 1952.

The transcendent political issue facing Egypt and Sadat in the early 1970s was the ongoing state of war with Israel. The ambiguous state of "no war – no peace" into which the Egyptian–Israeli confrontation had settled by the early 1970s produced great frustration among Egyptians. Student demonstrations denouncing government immobility against Israel erupted in early 1972; in April 1972 leading political figures of the Nasser years called on the government to reconsider Egypt's dependence on the Soviet Union and its alienation from the West; further student demonstrations occurred in January 1973.

Sadat responded to this ferment with dramatic international moves. Civilian and military resentment over the Soviet presence in Egypt was in part assuaged in July 1972 when, in the first example of the electric-shock diplomacy for which he was to become famous, Sadat abruptly announced the termination of the Soviet military mission and the ousting of Russian military advisors from Egypt. A more startling initiative came a year later. On October 6, 1973 Egypt and Syria mounted coordinated military assaults into the Sinai Peninsula and in the Golan Heights. The military outcome of the three-week war which raged for most of October 1973 was at best ambiguous: initial Egyptian and Syrian advances in Sinai and on the Golan were followed by later Israeli counterattacks which took additional territory from Egypt and Syria before the United States and the Soviet Union, fearing the potential of Middle East war for generating a larger superpower confrontation, imposed a cease-fire in late October. Nonetheless, initial Arab successes in penetrating formidable Israeli defenses, the prolonged fighting which ensued, and the economic and political effects of the war enabled the governments of both Egypt and Syria to present the war of October 1973 as an Arab victory. These effects included a huge increase in the price of oil, augmenting Arab financial power, and subsequent international efforts to arrange peace between Israel and the Arab states on the basis of Israeli withdrawal from territories it had occupied in 1967. In Egypt the date of Egypt's crossing of the Suez Canal into Sinai, October 6, 1973, became a national holiday; Sadat now became "the Hero of the Crossing."

The war of October 1973 brought Sadat out from under Nasser's shadow. His major policies and the mark he put upon Egypt date from 1973 onwards. The overall direction of his initiatives is indicated in a joke circulating in Egypt in the 1970s. Upon Nasser's death Sadat acquired the various perks of office including the presidential limousine. When driving down the highway one day, the new president and his driver came to a fork in the road; the driver inquired whether to turn to the right (i.e. in a conservative direction) or to the left (i.e. towards more radical policies). Sadat's response indicates both his initial verbal fidelity to the revolutionary legacy he had inherited from Nasser, but also his eventual divergence from the course Nasser had set for Egypt: "signal left and turn right."

The most sweeping shift away from Nasserism came in foreign policy. Egypt's international position was transformed over the course of the 1970s. The war of October 1973 marked the beginning of an Egyptian-Israeli peace process. The convoluted cease-fire line resulting from the war – Egyptian forces holding positions on the east bank of the Suez Canal while Israeli forces occupied a bulge on the west bank – was inherently unstable. It offered a unique opportunity for outside mediation between the parties, a role which was quickly assumed by the United States. Between late 1973 and late 1975 American Secretary of State

Henry Kissinger engaged in intensive shuttle diplomacy between Egypt and Israel, brokering two successive agreements for the gradual disengagement of Egyptian and Israeli military forces and in the process inaugurating Egyptian-Israeli negotiations towards peace. By 1975 Egypt had regained western Sinai, allowing it to reopen the Suez Canal to shipping. In turn Israel obtained a pledge that Egypt would not resort to force to resolve their differences.

The peace process stalled from 1975 to 1977. It resumed with a vengeance in late 1977 when Sadat, frustrated by recent lack of movement, made a bold declaration of his willingness to go to Israel for face-to-face negotiations towards peace. After decades of only indirect or clandestine contact between Egypt and Israel, Sadat's dramatic trip to Jerusalem in November 1977 began direct Egyptian-Israeli peace talks. These too were bogged down by mid 1978, but were salvaged by American President Jimmy Carter's inviting Sadat and Israeli Prime Minister Menachen Begin to Camp David for intensive negotiations. Two agreements were concluded at Camp David in September 1978. One, outlining a process for movement towards Palestinian autonomy on the West Bank and in the Gaza Strip, never came to fruition. The other, a bilateral Egyptian-Israeli agreement for Egyptian peace with, and recognition of, Israel in exchange for Israeli withdrawal from the Sinai Peninsula, did. Some final details remained even after Camp David; only in Washington in March 1979 was the formal peace treaty between Egypt and Israel signed. Formal diplomatic relations between Egypt and Israel were opened in February 1980. Israel completed its withdrawal from Sinai in April 1982. After thirty years of war, Egypt had made peace with Israel; after fifteen years of Israeli occupation, it had regained the Sinai Peninsula.

Parallel to the peace process of the 1970s came a redefinition of Egypt's relationship with the superpowers. Even before the 1973 war, the dismissal of Soviet advisors in 1972 indicated Sadat's willingness to move away from dependence on the USSR. Soviet military aid to Egypt continued through the 1973 war but shrunk thereafter. In 1976 Egypt unilaterally abrogated its Treaty of Friendship with the USSR, thereby officially terminating its political orientation towards the Soviet Union.

As Egypt turned away from the east, it looked to the west. Diplomatic relations with the United States, severed in June 1967, were restored in November 1973. The central role played by the United States in the Egyptian-Israeli peace process after 1973 was accompanied by steadily improving US-Egyptian bilateral relations, the most substantial aspect of which for Egypt was American economic and military aid. Egypt received over three billion dollars in US aid between 1974 and 1979. Annexes to the Camp David accords of 1978 provided for 1.5 billion dollars annually in US aid for Egypt, a sum which grew to over two billion dollars in the 1980s.

Possessing a strong sense of identification with Egypt as a distinct and separate historical entity, Anwar al-Sadat did not share Nasser's commitment to Arab nationalism. Sadat also operated in a different political context, one in which the pan-Arabist enthusiasms of the 1950s and 1960s were giving way to recognition of the reality of the existing regional state structure and of the necessity to work with, rather than against, other Arab regimes. A shifting orientation towards the Arab world was evident as early as 1971, when a new Egyptian Constitution formally changed the country's name from "the United Arab Republic" to "the Arab Republic of Egypt." Egypt was back on the international map.

Through the mid 1970s "cooperation" with other Arab regimes – with Syria in the October war; with the Sudan, where Egyptian assistance in 1971 and 1976 propped up a friendly military regime and was repaid by the conclusion of a joint defense agreement; with the newly-affluent oil states of the Gulf in economic matters – replaced the drive for Arab unity of the Nasser years. Although he initially attempted to achieve a comprehensive Arab-Israeli settlement which would address Palestinian as well as Egyptian grievances, at Camp David Sadat in effect broke Arab ranks and concluded a separate peace agreement with Israel. Egypt paid a heavy regional price for going it alone: the suspension of much Arab aid, the severance of diplomatic relations with most Arab states, and expulsion from the Arab League as well as the larger Organization of the Islamic Conference. Sadat personally paid an even heavier price. Peace with Israel was a central grievance prompting a small band of Islamists to assassinate Egypt's president on October 6, 1981.

* * *

Sadat's initiatives in regard to Egypt's internal politics were not as as definitive as the international volte-face which he carried out in the

1970s. The "Corrective Revolution" of 1971 began a process of moving away from the authoritarianism and abuses of power which had become more pronounced over the Nasser era. Many of those jailed for political reasons in the 1960s were released from prison in the early 1970s. Surveillance and harassment by the security services decreased. A process of desequestration extended over the decade, as new laws passed by the National Assembly gradually returned some sequestered property to its previous owners or provided for the payment of compensation. The primary fiefdom of the later Nasser years, the Arab Socialist Union, was subjected to public criticism, gradually stripped of real power, and in 1980 officially shut down when an amendment to the Constitution declared its abolition. The destruction of the institutional structure of Nasserism was accompanied by an intellectual assault on the Nasserist legacy. A wave of "de-Nasserization" struck Egypt in the mid 1970s, as the publication of exposés of the abuses of the Nasser years written by both former officials and victims of the security apparatus became a growth industry in the media.

Presiding over the transition to a more pluralist political order proved to be a more difficult operation than dismantling Nasserism. Egypt did see greater freedom of expression in the 1970s. Press censorship formally ended in 1974. While their continued operation was precarious, opposition journals of both left and right made their appearance from time to time. The scope of allowable criticism of government policies widened in the early and mid 1970s, before contracting from 1977 onward as growing opposition to Sadat's international initiatives generated a government counterattack against critics of the regime.

The years from 1974 to 1977 were the heyday of political liberalization under Sadat. In 1974 the government permitted the creation of "platforms" advocating different political approaches under the formal umbrella of the still-existent ASU. By 1975 four such groupings – "right," "center," "Nasserist," and "left" – had emerged. In October 1976 the "center" platform, supporting Sadat's policies and in turn benefiting from state support, won the overwhelming majority of seats in relatively open National Assembly elections. The highpoint of political liberalization came early in 1977, when the government announced its intention to authorize the creation of formal political parties in Egypt.

Several political parties emerged in the next few years. The most important was the pro-regime National Democratic Party (NDP) established in 1978, a broad but shallow coalition led by state officials, professionals, technocrats, and rural notables, most connected in one way or another with the state or profiting from association with it. National in scope and benefiting from state backing, both overt (access to the media and the ability to deliver government patronage at the local level) and covert (intimidation of opposition candidates and outright fraud), the NDP won decisive majorities in every parliamentary election from 1979 to 1995.

Several opposition parties also emerged in the later 1970s. The most important have been the National Progressive Unionist Party (NPUP), consisting of a coalition [Arabic *Tajammu'*] of former Nasserists and leftists championing the economic and social approach of the Nasser era; the Socialist Labor Party (SLP), a center-right body advocating populist and somewhat Islamist policies; and the New Wafd Party, a professionally and commercially-based movement echoing the liberal outlook of the pre-1952 era and calling for more extensive political as well as economic liberalization. Lacking the resources and access to patronage of the NDP and subject to periodic government harassment, opposition parties have been little more than gadflies in the more superficially democratic political universe existing in Egypt since the late 1970s. None have won more than a fraction of the seats in parliamentary elections; many fail to reach threshhold required for inclusion in the Assembly; and some have preferred to boycott manifestly rigged elections.

The trend towards political pluralism of 1974–77 was soon reversed. In mid-January 1977 the government's announcement of its intention to reduce government subsidies for basic consumer goods set off massive rioting in Egyptian cities. Almost immediately thereafter, the pluralist window partially opened earlier began to close. The Parties Law of May 1977 specifying guidelines for the formation of political parties set stringent requirements for the legal recognition of parties. In 1978 government pressure and harassment compelled the New Wafd, arguably the most popular opposition movement, to suspend operations. The parliamentary elections of June 1979, in which the NDP won 330 of 392 seats, are generally regarded to have been more fraudulent than those of 1976.

Criticism of Sadat became more widespread after the conclusion of Egyptian-Israeli peace in early 1979. Sadat in turn responded with increased repression. A Higher Press Council was created in 1980 to enforce a government-approved code of ethics for the press. A "Law of Shame" of the same year, which imposed an open-ended ban on any speech or activity which would "set a bad example" for youth and which specified criminal penalties for the same, in effect amounted to a government hunting license for use against its critics. By now an international politician, the darling of the Western media because of his pro-Western foreign policy, Sadat himself became more short-tempered after 1979 as domestic and Arab criticism of his policies mounted. His response to a question at a press conference of 1981 – "In the old days, I could have had you shot for that" – demonstrated a grimmer persona than the avuncular image he had cultivated in happier years.[1] By September 1981, when the government carried out a massive wave of arrests in which over fifteen hundred critics and opponents of the regime from across the political spectrum were incarcerated, Sadat had forfeited much of the legitimacy his earlier efforts at political liberalization had won for him. This is the local context in which to appreciate the apathy and indifference with which the bulk of Egyptians responded to his assassination in October 1981. Nasser's funeral had been a genuine demonstration of mass grief by millions of Egyptians. In contrast, Sadat's was a sombre affair attended by numerous foreign dignitaries, but was unaccompanied by any appreciable outpouring of popular emotion.

* * *

Already by the late 1960s the socialist experiment of state-controlled and directed economic growth was experiencing serious difficulties. Economic stagnation due to the flaws of Egypt's cumbersome and inefficient public sector was unquestionably exacerbated by Egypt's international situation; loss of Sinai and its oil resources after 1967, the closure of the Suez Canal, continuing and draining conflict with Israel. The global environment of the 1970s was also significantly different from that of the 1950s or 1960s. The Soviet economy was itself experiencing problems and thus less attractive as a model; closer to home the conservative oil states were accumulating gigantic inflows of capital which presumably could be tapped for regional investment if conditions were favorable. Sadat himself – from a reasonably well-off peasant family and with a definite appreciation for the good things of life – lacked Nasser's burning sense of indignation against privilege. Domestic imperatives, the global context, and his own predelictions, thus led Sadat in the direction of an "opening" of the formally-socialist economy of Egypt: an opening to the previously marginalized private sector, an opening to Western investment and expertise, an opening to Arab oil money.

Egypt's new economic approach was articulated especially in a body of legislation passed by the National Assembly from 1974 onwards. The basic framework of what now became known as "the Opening" was set down in Law 43 of June 1974 which eliminated many existing restrictions on foreign investment, which authorized joint ventures between local and foreign businesses, and which gave tax breaks and guarantees against future nationalization to foreign investors. Legislation passed over the rest of the decade fleshed out the new economic approach: foreign exchange controls were loosened; Egyptians were allowed to enter partnerships with foreign companies; the private sector was given more scope to conduct business without government interference; and the sale of shares in public sector companies was authorized. Collectively, the laws of the 1970s on the one hand attempted to make Egypt a more hospitable environment for international capital; on the other, they gave the local private sector more freedom domestically and more encouragement to work in collaboration with foreign enterprises.

The impact of Sadat's new economic approach on Egypt in the 1970s was appreciable. What the Opening did not do should perhaps be noted first. Most importantly, it did not immediately eliminate the massive public sector which had emerged as the dominant component of Egypt's non-agricultural economy under Nasser. Most of the enterprises which had nationalized before 1970 remained under government ownership. Nor were the endemic institutional problems of the public sector eliminated; with some exceptions, overstaffing, under-utilization of facilities, and cumbersome bureaucratic bottlenecks, continued to hamper productivity. What did change was the character of public sector operations. The General Organizations which had directed public sector enterprises were abolished in 1975, giving individual public sector firms more autonomy. In effect, public sector companies now operated like private ones, their goal being to maximize profits rather than to realize broader social or national goals; the Egyptian state now became one entrepreneur – the biggest – among many. It was to take until the 1990s before the Egyptian government mounted a concerted effort to dismantle the public sector it had created in the 1960s.

Egypt's private sector did expand somewhat as a result of the Opening. Relaxed regulations drew some foreign capital into collaboration with dynamic private enterprises either begun or reinvigorated as a result of now having more freedom of operation. Joint ventures between foreign investors and public sector firms also acted to shift assets from the public to the private sector due to the Egyptian partner using its existing plant and real estate as its contribution to the combined operation. The private sector on the whole experienced little structural change. The growth which did occur did so largely in traditional industries (textiles, food production), and even more markedly in what economists identify as non-productive areas of economic activity (banking, commerce, real estate, services, tourism). What an Egyptian analyst has termed "'commercialism' – whereby money may change hands but little production is carried out" – became "the dominant 'economic' activity" spawned by the Opening in the private sector.[2]

The primary goal of the new approach was of course economic growth and greater prosperity. Egypt did experience an impressive rate of economic growth – five to eight per cent annually, depending on the year – from the mid 1970s through the early 1980s. However, little of this newfound prosperity was the result of the expansion of the country's productive capacity. Through the 1970s, less foreign investment than its architects had hoped for materialized under the new regime of the Opening. Egyptian economists estimated that only roughly one-tenth of new investment over the second half of the 1970s could be directly traced to the Opening; one source asserts that "by 1980 *infitah* projects had produced only twenty thousand new jobs."[3]

The primary cause of Egypt's post-1973 prosperity was a surge in the receipt of revenues from external sources. In the 1970s Egypt benefited from the return of its oil fields in Sinai, from the exploitation of new fields, and most of all from the explosion of world petroleum prices which occurred over the decade. The Suez Canal was reopened to shipping in 1975, income from tolls growing steadily thereafter. An estimated million and a half Egyptians were working in other Arab countries by 1980, sending or bringing much of their salaries to their families in Egypt. The global expansion of tourism, a late twentieth century growth industry, also worked to Egypt's benefit especially as the country's relations with the West and Israel improved. In 1980–81, Egypt obtained over seven billion dollars in foreign currency from oil revenues, Suez Canal tolls, tourism, and remittances; over two billion dollars in foreign aid further sweetened the pot. Egypt became a dependent economy – both in the narrow sense of dependence upon foreign largesse and in the wider sense of dependence on world prosperity – under Sadat.

The Opening had significant effects on Egyptian society. The import of consumer goods, especially foreign luxuries for a new bourgeoisie profiting from the opportunities which came with economic opening, boomed during the Opening. Where imported consumer goods were about ten per cent of imports in the late 1960s, they accounted for fully one-third in the mid 1970s. New classes of people emerged alongside, and in some cases out of, the previously ascendant state bourgeoisie: "openers" engaged in the import trade, in financial speculation, or serving as middlemen for foreign investors; "suitcase merchants" peddling designer fashions or electronic gadgets on the streetcorners; a new layer of indigenous millionaires being chauffeured in Mercedes and residing in opulent villas near the Pyramids. For Egypt's now-sizable urban middle class emerging from over a decade of socialist austerity, foreign was 'in'; for the country's upper stratum, expensive weddings at the Hilton or Sheraton, at which hundreds of guests were regaled with imported delicacies, demonstrated the host's manifest success under the Opening. An Egyptian cartoonist's vision in which two Egyptians admiring the Great Pyramid were prompted to exclaim "Fantastic, it must be imported!", encapsulates much of the ambiance of the 1970s.[4]

While much of the upper and part of the middle class did well out of the Opening, the same is not true for the bulk of Egyptians at the lower levels of the urban social pyramid. The main culprit was inflation, which reached an annual rate of twenty-five to thirty per cent in the later years of the 1970s and in the process produced great pressure especially on salaried workers whose wages failed to keep up. Part of the slack was assumed by government price subsidies for basic consumer goods, such as wheat, sugar, tea, and cooking oil. Whereas such subsidies accounted for less than eight per cent of government expenditure in 1970, they ate up almost sixty per cent of the state budget by 1980. As noted earlier, a projected reduction in subsidies in 1977 produced Egypt's most serious round of civil unrest of the decade (the proposal was quickly shelved). With instant fortunes being made at the top and inflation eroding incomes at the bottom, urban social cleavages widened under the Opening.

The same was less true in rural Egypt. The fifty-feddan limitation on landownership was now declared not to apply to reclaimed land, and some state-held land was now auctioned off on the open market. Both measures led to a degree of reconcentration of ownership of agricultural land in the 1970s. But a larger process occurring simultaneously brought significant financial benefits for much of the rural population. The outflow of Egyptian laborers to work in other Arab countries produced a significant shortage of agricultural labor which in turn led to a rise in agricultural wages. The concomitant flow of remittance money to the families of laborers working abroad also benefited rural society. Almost by accident – the spillover of oil affluence from abroad – rural Egypt may have done better than urban Egypt in the Sadat years.

Many observers also found a sleazy quality to the Opening. Much of the prosperity enjoyed by at least some Egyptians in the 1970s was generated by questionably legal or flatly illicit means. Commissions and kickbacks were a normal part of doing business. Corruption permeated all levels of the economy: payoffs to and embezzlement by higher officials, evasion of safety requirements in housing construction (resulting in the periodic collapse of tenements and the death of their inhabitants), the payment of bakshish to government functionaries for the performance of their stipulated duties. In the judgement of one Egyptian analyst, "corruption had to a large extent been 'institutionalized' in the seventies."[5] The same author's comparison of the Sadat years to the reign of the Khedive Isma'il a century earlier, similarly an era of foreign penetration and domestic extravagance, is an apt one.

* * *

The negative social ramifications of the Opening form much of the context for the surge in Islamist activism in Egypt in the 1970s. The contemporary Islamic "revival" in Egypt and elsewhere in the Muslim world is a complex phenomenon. Efforts at Westernization and secularization over the nineteenth and twentieth centuries notwithstanding, loyalty to Islam and adherence to Islamic values remained the bedrock identity of the bulk of Egyptian Muslims. The manifest shortcomings of the secular state from the 1960s onward – economic stagnation and humiliating defeat by Israel (in six days) under Nasser, widening socio-economic disparities, the Coca-Cola-ization of Egypt, and the apparent abandonment of the Arab-Muslim cause of Palestine under Sadat – indicated to many Egyptians that a secular approach modelled on Western guidelines was a failure. Among the Muslim majority, "Islam is the solution" became the slogan of increasing numbers of Egyptians.

Thanks to the greater pluralism of the 1970s, the advocates of religious solutions had also more room for maneuver than they had possessed under Nasser. The Sadat regime initially encouraged the reemergence of Islamic sentiment and activism as a counterweight to leftist trends. Many Islamic activists were released from prison as part of the Corrective Revolution. The relaxation of police controls and surveillance meant more freedom for independent political advocacy and organizing, Islamists included. Sadat himself endeavored to envelop himself in a more religious aura than his socialist predecessor; ostentatious mosque attendance and prayer, the patronizing of popular preachers who would defend his policies, a public persona as "the believer president." The partial liberalization of political life in the mid 1970s continued the process of opening a window for the expression of an alternative Islamic vision of society.

Much Islamist activism was not explicitly or primarily political in character. Egypt witnessed a surge in the building of "popular" mosques erected through private initiative and not under the supervision of the official religious establishment. A number of Islamic banks – investment companies which attempted to follow Islamic strictures against usury – were formed and attracted sizable amounts of capital in the boom economy of the later 1970s. The most pervasive dimension of the Islamization of society was the emergence of a huge network of social service organizations – private schools and adult literacy training programs, religious study groups, medical clinics and hospitals, child day-care centers, women's counselling offices, and more. In terms of having an impact on the daily lives of millions of Egyptians, this "social Islam" which began to develop under Sadat, and which has expanded under his successor Husni Mubarak, is probably the most important aspect of the Islamic revival.

Many popular mosques and Islamic organizations in turn became recruiting grounds for the welter of politically oriented groups with an explicitly Islamic agenda which emerged or reemerged in the more tolerant atmosphere of the 1970s. Muslim Brotherhood journals resumed publication from the mid 1970s onwards, calling for a more Islamic structuring of Egyptian society but also supporting many of Sadat's generally conservative initiatives. On university campuses Islamic "societies" [Arabic *jama'at*] burgeoned. Providing valuable social services for students (study sessions; the free distribution of lecture notes; transport to campus by which women students could avoid Egypt's congested public transport), student *Jama'at* were dominating elections for some college governing bodies by the late 1970s.

The outer edge of the religious revival was militance. For thoroughly committed Islamists, the overwhelming power of the state and – despite the superficial religiosity of Sadat and his policies – its generally Westernizing and pro-Western character was interpreted to mean that only force could recreate an Islamic order. Egypt witnessed intermittent bouts of Islamist violence directed against state institutions or personnel from the mid-1970s onwards, the most notable of which were a quixotic attack on a military school as a prelude to an attempted coup in 1974 and the kidnapping and murder of a government minister in 1977 in an effort to attain the release of imprisoned militants.

An ominous feature of Egyptian public life in the 1970s was greater Muslim-Coptic tension. Egypt's Coptic community – between six and fifteen per cent of its population, depending on source – were also undergoing a partial if less thorough communal awakening. In part due to the emergence of new and more politicized organizations, in part in reaction to the Muslim call for an Islamic order which would have the effect of marginalizing non-Muslims in Egyptian public life, Egypt's Copts led by a new and more assertive Pope Shenouda III became more vocal under Sadat. Muslim claims of aggressive Coptic proselytization and Coptic complaints of underrepresentation and discrimination in state agencies agitated sectarian opinion on both sides. The flash-point for physical violence between the two communities was often the building of new churches by Copts, which Muslim activists then attempted to pull down while Copts resisted. In Upper Egypt in particular, where the Coptic population is thickest on the ground and where communal tension overlapped with long-standing village rivalries and feuds, Muslim-Coptic animosity and violence was now articulated in the language of religion.

Religious militancy and communal violence eventually led the state to adjust its attitude towards religious activism. Egypt's unilateral peace treaty with Israel in 1979 was rejected as a sell-out by the bulk of Islamist opinion; correspondingly, it generated greater criticism of the regime from Islamist spokesmen in particular. By the beginning of the 1980s periodic Muslim-Coptic violence led an increasingly short-tempered president to denounce extremists on both sides of the religious divide. Sadat's massive crackdown on critics in September 1981 included the arrest of both Muslim and Coptic activists (including Pope Shenouda III on the Coptic side) as well as the dissolution of ten Muslim and three Coptic religious organizations.

It was this clampdown on religious activism which brought Sadat's own assassination. A small cohort of individuals associated with one militant Islamist grouping, the *Tanzim* ("organization") or *Jihad*, hastily cobbled together a combined operation for the assassination of the president and an Islamist uprising in Upper Egypt. Where the latter failed, the former succeeded. On October 6, 1981, while reviewing the armed forces on the eighth anniversary of the crossing of the Suez Canal, Anwar al-Sadat died in a hail of bullets fired by Islamist members of the army which he had led to victory eight years earlier.

EGYPT UNDER HUSNI MUBARAK, 1981–PRESENT DAY

A half-generation younger than Nasser and Sadat, Muhammad Husni Mubarak (1928–) was uninvolved either in the core cadre of the Free Officers or the politics of the Nasser years. An air force officer who rose to the post of commander of the Egyptian air force by the time of the October war, Mubarak was designated as Sadat's Vice-President in April 1975. He became president immediately upon Sadat's assassination in October 1981. As had been the case with Sadat's succession to Nasser, Mubarak's assumption of the presidency was promptly ratified by popular referendum. Additional referenda in 1987, 1993, and 1999 have extended his tenure as President.

A career military officer rather than a political activist, Mubarak's style of rule is distinctly non-ideological. For most of his tenure in office Mubarak has eschewed bold new initiatives and concentrated on the more prosaic task of maintaining internal stability (and his own position). The Egyptian perception of the thrust of his administration in his early years in office was expressed in a recycled version of the joke about Nasser, Sadat, and the fork in the road cited previously. In the updated version current in Egypt in the mid 1980s, Mubarak was faced with the same choice of turning right (conservatism) or left (radicalism) upon arriving at the fork in the road. His response, delivered after considerable cogitation, indicated a distinct preference for continuity over change: "signal left, signal right, and park." At least until the 1990s, when major new economic departures were initiated, continuity has been the hallmark of the Mubarak era.

The greatest area of continuity has been in Egyptian foreign relations. Egypt's place in the world in the 1980s and 1990s has largely remained as Sadat reconfigured it. A close linkage with the United States and beyond that with the West have been maintained throughout the Mubarak years. American financial assistance has been a major prop of both the Egyptian military and the Egyptian economy. Lesser amounts of economic assistance have also come from other Western countries and from international financial organizations. Joint military exercises between the armed forces of Egypt and the United States became an annual exercise in the 1980s. The litmus test of Egypt's relationship with the West came in 1990–91, at the time of the Gulf crisis and war. Firmly committed to a Western orientation and reportedly angered by Saddam Husayn's mendacity as to his intentions vis-à-vis Kuwait, Mubarak quickly took Egypt into the anti-Iraqi coalition being constructed by the United States. An estimated thirty-five thousand Egyptian troops participated in the military operation which liberated Kuwait in early 1991.

Although unaltered in its broad outlines, Egypt's relationship with Israel in the 1980s and 1990s has demonstrated more volatility. The formal state of peace between the two countries has never been in question. Diplomatic contretemps notwithstanding, the Egyptian-Israeli border remained open for trade (limited) and tourism (considerable from the Israeli side, less from the Egyptian). A lingering border dispute over Taba, a minuscule chunk of land on the Gulf of 'Aqaba, disturbed bilateral relations for much of the 1980s until resolved by arbitration in Egypt's favor. The diplomatic relationship between the two countries fluctuated from warm to cool largely on the basis of the level of tension existing between Israel and other Arabs at different points in time – decidedly cool through most of the 1980s as a consequence of Israel's 1982 invasion of Lebanon and its ongoing repression of the Palestinians, and progressively warmer in the 1990s as Israel and the Palestinians plodded towards accommodation.

The major change in Egyptian foreign relations under Mubarak has occurred in relation to the Arab world. Egypt was ostracized by most Arab states after its unilateral peace with Israel. It took most of the 1980s for it to be reintegrated into the Arab fold. Mubarak's less arrogant posture towards Arab critics of peace with Israel facilitated the process. Egypt was readmitted to the Organization of the Islamic Conference in 1984. The main breakdown in Egypt's regional isolation came in 1987–89, when in the context of the final stages of the Iran-Iraq war and the opening of the Palestinian Intifada most Arab states acknowledged the inevitability of Egyptian participation in inter-Arab politics and reestablished diplomatic relations. Egypt was readmitted to membership in the Arab League in 1989. In the Gulf crisis and war of 1990–91 Egypt and Mubarak were active first in Arab diplomatic efforts aimed at avoiding confrontation between Iraq and Kuwait, later in mobilizing Arab governmental support for the anti-Iraqi coalition. Egypt has continued to play an integral role as counsellor and mediator in the central inter-Arab issue of the 1990s, the unfolding peace process between Israel and the rest of the Arab world. An important exception to the pattern of improving Egyptian relations with other

Arab states concerns the Sudan. The ascendancy of a military regime with an Islamic orientation in the Sudan after 1989, and reported Sudenese support for Egypt's domestic Islamist opposition, generated repeated political tensions between Egypt and its southern neighbor in the 1990s.

* * *

After a surge in prosperity produced largely by exogenous factors in the late 1970s and early 1980s, the mid and late 1980s were years of economic contraction. Thoroughly integrated into and dependent upon the world economy, Egypt suffered from several economic trends beyond its control. The world oil glut and the precipitous decline in oil prices over the 1980s meant less revenue from Egyptian oil exports as well as relative stagnation in receipts from Suez Canal tolls. Declining oil revenues also meant less work for Egyptians in the oil states and a dropoff in the money they sent home. Tourism, hostage to public perceptions of the rise of "terrorism" in the Middle East as a whole, proved an erratic source of income which varied considerably from year to year. The shortfall in revenue had to be met by external borrowing. Egypt's external debt rose steadily over the 1980s, reaching a sum estimated at about fifty billion dollars in 1990.

With economic contraction came growing privation. Inflation – in the range of twenty to thirty per cent annually over the 1980s – remained a serious problem for the financial wellbeing of the salaried majority of urban workers. While the average wage is estimated to have increased by sixty per cent between 1978 and 1988, prices increased by three hundred and fifty per cent. Government subsidies continued to be an indispensable buffer for the urban population in particular, but were a costly burden for the state. A further economic shock came at the beginning of the 1990s. The Gulf crisis led to an exodus of perhaps half a million Egyptian workers from their jobs in the Gulf states and Iraq, producing an immediate drop in revenue from remittances and adding to domestic unemployment.

It was these internal and external stresses which compelled the Egyptian government to bite the bullet of economic reform. It did so only incrementally. An effort to reduce subsidies began in 1986; by 1991 it was announced that the bill for direct subsidies had been reduced from thirteen to six per cent of GDP over the preceding five years. A limited effort at privatization – reducing the size of the inefficient public sector through the leasing or sale of government-owned enterprises to private operators in the hope of stimulating greater efficiency – also commenced in the late 1980s. The spur to the effort to cut subsidies and privatize the public sector was largely external, specifically pressure from the International Monetary Fund and the World Bank for major structural adjustments which would create a leaner public sector, a smaller budget deficit, and a more open Egyptian economy. Prolonged negotiations between Egypt and the IMF towards restructuring debt repayment stretched on through the late 1980s, the IMF demanding greater commitment and more rapid movement toward reform and Egypt resisting because of fear of the adverse social consequences of accepting the IMF package. Economic liberalization remained halting through the 1980s; a "search for soft spots" rather than a wholehearted commitment to significant structural reform.[6]

Movement towards economic liberalization accelerated in the 1990s. Egypt's participation in the anti-Iraqi coalition during the Gulf crisis and war was promptly rewarded by Western debtors, forgiving fourteen billion dollars of Egypt's foreign debt. In May 1991 a major agreement on debt restructuring which wrote off half of Egypt's debt to the "Paris Club" of creditor nations, and which restructured repayment of the remainder on terms more favorable to Egypt, was concluded with the IMF. Egypt's foreign debt was reduced to manageable dimensions in the early 1990s.

The price for debt restructuring has been a greater Egyptian commitment to the liberalization of its state-controlled economy. There are several components to the economic reforms which have been introduced or accelerated in the 1990s. One is eliminating most currency controls and making Egypt's currency almost fully convertible in foreign exchange markets. Another is the deregulation of economic procedures internally to allow more scope for both private sector initiative and foreign investment. The government has continued its efforts to reduce its budget deficit through various means, the most important of which has been the further reduction of both direct and indirect subsidies.

The centerpiece of structural adjustment is privatization of public sector enterprises. Along with cuts in subsidies, privatization is one of the more politically sensitive aspects of economic liberalization. For state bureaucrats it means insecurity, possible redundancy, and a more uncertain future; for workers in public sector firms it portends a loss of jobs in leaner and more efficient enterprises as well as a reduction in the social benefits which they had been guaranteed under Arab Socialism. Privatization has been resisted by both groups, more subtly by bureaucratic back-room politics within officialdom, more actively by direct labor agitation and protest against cutbacks and the loss of prior entitlements. As a result privatization proceeded slowly through the early 1990s, gaining momentum only in the second half of the decade. Much of the privatization has involved the sale to private investors of part rather than all of the assets of state-owned firms. Over half of a total of 314 public sector firms selected for privatization were reported to have been wholly or partially privatized by 1999, and the Egyptian government has announced that the private sector will account for eighty per cent of the Egyptian economy by 2000.

It is too early to draw firm conclusions about the results of Egypt's economic liberalization of the 1990s. A preliminary assessment indicates that structural reform has been a two-edged sword. On one side, Egypt's macro economic performance over the past decade has been a robust one. The country's external debt is a much smaller percentage of GDP than the burden it had become in the 1980s. Revenue from external sources also improved over much of the 1990s. Receipts from tourism have normally ranged from three to four billion dollars annually in the late 1990s, depending on political conditions; Suez Canal tolls brought in almost two billion dollars and petroleum exports were worth almost $1.5 billion in 1995; foreign aid remained steady in the three billion-dollar range for most of the 1990s. As a result of a smaller burden of debt repayment, rising external revenues, and the cutback in subsidies, Egypt's budget deficit was reduced from around twenty per cent of GDP at the beginning of the decade to the vicinity of one per cent at its close. Inflation, which according to official estimates stood at over twenty per cent in 1991, had dropped to nine per cent in 1993 and may have been under five per cent annually by 1998. The annual rate of economic growth has been five per cent or better for much of the decade (slightly lower in 1998, due to low oil prices and a huge dropoff in tourist revenues due to Islamist violence). Reported per capita GDP (always a slippery indicator in a developing country where wages may be low but the price of basic necessities and services is also low) doubled over the 1990s, from $600 in 1990 to $1290 in 1998. A 1999 survey of Egypt in *The Economist* opened by proclaiming Egypt to be "the very model of a modern emerging market, the International Monetary Fund's prime pupil."[7]

But there is also a darker side to economic liberalization. Unemployment has remained high through the decade; officially in the ten-to-fifteen per cent range, in actuality almost certainly higher. Because of inflation and the resultant wage-price gap, the real wages – i.e. the buying power of salaries – of workers has declined since the 1970s. On a national level salaries and wages, which were about fifty per cent of GDP in 1970, had fallen to less than a third by the early 1990s. The situation is most serious for public sector workers. In the effort to make public sector companies a more attractive investment for private investors, the drive to privatize has meant less hiring in public sector enterprises as well as a slowdown in public sector wage increases. By 1992 the real wages of government employees had declined to about one-half of what they had been at the start of the Opening in the mid 1970s, and it is questionable if the deterioration in wages reversed itself when economic liberalization accelerated thereafter. The theory behind economic liberalization is that a rising tide lifts all boats. Through most of the 1990s there was little indication that this process began to occur in regard to the vessels in which most Egyptians are compelled to row.

Perhaps most serious for many people is the reduction of government subsidies since the late 1980s. By the end of the 1990s the bulk of subsidies on basic necessities had been scaled back or eliminated. Subsidies on basic consumer goods were scheduled to consume between five and six per cent of government expenditure in 1998–99, a far cry from what they had accounted for through the 1980s. What was a blessing for the state was hardly such for its citizens. The same *Economist* survey, cited above, calculated that "half the food eaten by the poor doubled in price in two years" largely due to the termination of subsidies, and went on to note that "services that had been free since the 1952 revolution are becoming less so."[8] The Nasserist welfare state has partially evaporated in the 1990s.

* * *

The texture of Egyptian internal politics has witnessed less change than the recent shift in the country's economic posture. Allowing for generational attrition, many of the same high officials as had served Sadat have filled the key posts of state under Mubarak. By the 1990s some observers were commenting on what amounted to regime gerontocracy, an entrenchment in office by a cadre of aging officials whose service in high posts reaches back into the early Mubarak years. Egypt's Prime Minister from late 1987 to the end of 1995, Dr. 'Atif Sidqi, had an uninterrupted tenure as premier longer than any other prime minister since independence; the Prime Minister in office at the close of the 1990s, Dr. 'Atif Muhammad 'Ubayd, had been a fixture of Egyptian cabinets since 1984.

Political parties demonstrate the same continuity. The National Democratic Party remains Egypt's preferred and dominant party, the victor by a wide margin in every National Assembly election of the 1980s and 1990s. The cast of main opposition parties remains much the same as had emerged under Sadat in the later 1970s; the National Progressive Unionist Party (*Tajammu'*) on the left, the Socialist Labor Party to the center-right, and the New Wafd and the Muslim Brotherhood espousing liberal and Islamist agendas respectively.

The sectarian genie let out of the bottle in the Sadat years was by far the major problem perturbing Egyptian domestic politics under Husni Mubarak. The overall orientation of the regime – adhering to and eventually broadening an economic opening internally, maintaining a pro-Western outlook and peace with Israel externally – has largely remained within the same parameters which under Sadat had contributed to the articulation and spread of Islamist opposition. The regime's economic policies especially in the 1990s have widened rather than narrowed the socio-economic disparities which fuel lower class alienation from the established order and provide the foot-soldiers for Islamist militancy. In short, rather than mitigating in intensity, many of the socio-economic causes behind the growth of the Islamist trend have acquired greater salience under Husni Mubarak. As a result, Islamism itself has flourished. The central dynamic of Egyptian internal politics in the 1980s and 1990s was the contest between the secular state and organized Islamism.

Mubarak initially presided over a more relaxed political atmosphere than that which had existed during Sadat's final years in power. While the Islamist militants associated with the assassination of Sadat and a subsequent attempt at popular uprising in Upper Egypt were hunted down and brought to trial, the numerous non-violent critics of Sadat who had been jailed in September 1981 were soon set free. A well publicized crackdown on corruption, which included the arrest, trial, and incarceration of Sadat's brother Ismat, was another way in which Egypt's new president attempted to distance himself from the record of his predecessor. The 1984 parliamentary elections are considered to have been one of the freer electoral contests of recent decades. Together opposition parties gained over one-quarter of the reported vote; a New Wafd-Muslim Brotherhood coalition won 59 seats in the Assembly and emerged as a vigorous opposition voice to the compliant NDP.

The political pendulum swung in the other direction from the mid 1980s. Now represented in parliament, Islamist spokesmen and groups mounted a public campaign for the immediate implementation of Islamic law in 1985. Although the Assembly rejected the demand, it did nod to Islamist sensibilities by watering down previously passed legislation of the Sadat era which had restricted a husband's right to polygamy. Muslim-Coptic confrontation once again appeared in public life, more benignly in the form of a "stickers war" in which adherents of the two faiths displayed their communal loyalties through putting bumper stickers with verses from Qur'an or Bible on their autos, but more ominously in a renewal of Muslim-Coptic violence in Upper Egypt. A brief but frightening bout of rioting in February 1986 by the poorly paid and miserably treated members of the regime's Central Security Services required army intervention to reassert order. Reports of attacks on video stores distributing immoral material, of clashes between police and Islamists outside mosques and on university campuses, and of Islamist attacks on government installations and attempts to assassinate high officials, were a recurrent item in the Egyptian press in the later 1980s.

This turmoil in turn produced a movement towards political closure. Government efforts to control the activities of popular mosques, and periodic police sweeps of Islamic militants, increased. Despite their results in which opposition parties gained a reported thirty per cent of the vote and ninety-one seats in the Assembly, the parliamentary elections of April 1987 saw more government manipulation and intimidation than those of 1984.

The constriction of political opportunity continued into the 1990s. Three features of the domestic and international scene during the decade all pushed the Egyptian government towards a more authoritarian stance: a major regional crisis in which the anti-Iraqi and pro-Western stance of the Egyptian government was considered controversial with various segments of Egyptian opinion; new economic initiatives which involved greater popular privation and consequently fed alienation from the regime; most importantly an ongoing civil war between the government and the extreme fringes of the Islamist movement. Emergency laws giving the security services extensive powers of detention and providing for the trial of civilians in military courts, that were first enacted in the wake of Sadat's assassination in 1981, were repeatedly extended through the 1990s. The parliamentary elections of late 1990, conducted in the tense atmosphere of the Gulf crisis, were boycotted by the main opposition parties save the NPUP in protest against electoral restrictions. As a result, all but twenty-nine of 444 contested seats were won by NDP candidates or "independents" affiliated with the party. New legislation of the early 1990s brought election to office in professional syndicates under greater government regulation in order to prevent occupational bodies from becoming centers of opposition. A well publicized national "dialogue" mounted by the government in 1994 turned into a purely cosmetic exercise when the government excluded the Muslim Brotherhood from participation and the New Wafd in turn boycotted its deliberations.

The parliamentary elections of late 1995 are generally evaluated as the most fraudulent and violent since the political opening of the 1970s. They were preceded by an extensive security crackdown on the Muslim Brotherhood and a lesser one against other opposition parties. The elections themselves were marked by official intimidation, blatant fraud, and an unprecedented level of local conflict (an estimated fifty-one dead and 878 injured, according to the Independent Commission for Electoral Review). The results followed suit: the victory of 316 NDP candidates, 115 "independents," and only thirteen representatives of opposition parties. Shortly after the election, ninety-nine of the 115 "independents" promptly joined the NDP, giving it over ninety per cent of seats in the National Assembly. Subsequent to the election Egypt's highest court, investigating complaints about the conduct of the contest, recommended voiding the election of over 200 of the winning candidates on grounds of irregularities. The Assembly took no action on the court's recommendation.

Simultaneous with this shrinkage of the scope of legitimate political activity, Egypt experienced a low-level Islamist insurgency against the regime in the 1990s. Why then? The recession of the 1980s and the state's partial abandonment of its social contract with its population in the 1990s (e.g. the provision of basic necessities in exchange for political passivity) provide the material context for state-Islamist confrontation. The social makeup of Islamist militance also seems to have evolved over time. Now drawing more heavily from the urban lower class living in the shanty-towns or belts of poverty surrounding greater Cairo, from the pauperized provincial cities of Upper Egypt, and from rural communities where adherents bear ancient grudges especially against their Coptic neighbors, Islamist extremism gradually became more proletarian in composition, more Balkanized in structure, and more indiscriminate in strategy. A nebula of clandestine and ephemeral Islamist groupings with floating memberships and transitory alliances formed and reformed, compounding the difficulties of state penetration and control. The main militant groupings were the *Jihad*, a Cairo-based outgrowth of the movement which assassinated Sadat in 1981, and the "Islamic Societies" or *Jama'at Islamiyya*, a coalition of largely-autonomous militant cells drawn particularly from the Upper Egyptian provinces. The overall strategy of the militants of the 1990s also seems to have shifted from a primary focus on assaulting the commanding heights of the state (e.g. the assassination of Sadat) to one of seeking the gradual destabilization of society and the eventual collapse of the system through the sustained use of violence against a wider range of targets.

In the early 1990s Egypt experienced an exponential increase in attacks on government officials (eventually including President Mubarak) and installations, against secular intellectuals, and against foreign tourists. At the local level, militants were sometimes able to establish bases in some of the sprawling shantytowns surrounding greater Cairo as well as in various urban quarters and villages especially in Upper Egypt, communities which they temporarily turned into no-go zones under militant control. In localities in Upper Egypt, renewed Muslim-Coptic violence was a concomitant of the Islamist militance of the 1990s. The height of Islamist violence appears to have been between 1993 and 1995. In 1993 alone, an independent source estimated over 250 attacks on government officials and facilities, video shops and cinemas, Coptic churches and communities, and foreign visitors to Egypt.

The government responded to Islamist insurgency with repression. Massive security sweeps brutalized the populations of entire quarters or villages. Thousands of Egyptians were detained often without charge or trial; when in custody some were subjected to systematic torture. Military courts heard the cases of those accused of complicity in violence and issued death sentences which had no appeal. A 1993 report by Amnesty International spoke of the "frightening brutality" of the security forces, concluding that they had been given "a license to kill with impunity" and terming the military courts "a travesty of justice." As the authorities responded to Islamic violence with indiscriminate repression, the pool of alienated potential recruits of the Islamic alternative grew. A vicious cycle of violence-repression, repression-violence, persisted in Egypt for much of the 1990s.

Islamist insurgency had both human and economic costs. The toll of dead grew through the early 1990s, rising from over 100 killed either by militants or security forces in 1991 and 1992 to well over 200 in 1993 and 1994. By 1997, well over a thousand people – Egyptians and foreigners – had died in the struggle between Islamists and state. The financial consequences were also appreciable. Tourism to Egypt dropped off significantly in the mid 1990s, depriving the state of foreign currency and cutting into the incomes of Egyptians dependent on the tourist industry.

The tide turned from 1995 onwards. However brutal, government security operations gradually bit into the base of Islamist militance. In time attrition took its toll on militant leadership; some were killed in gun battles with the authorities, others apprehended and executed, others forced into exile. Although there was appreciable violence from 1995 through 1997, the frequency of Islamist attacks slowly diminished in comparison to the years from 1992 to 1994. By 1997 the leadership of the main Islamist movements involved in the insurgency were splitting over strategy, some calling for a truce with the authorities while others maintained the need for continued struggle. The single most tragic episode of the violence of the 1990s, the massacre of fifty-eight foreign tourists and four Egyptian police near Luxor in November 1997, appears to have been a desperate operation by a movement now on the run. By 1998–99 Islamist-inspired violence had diminished greatly and the government was declaring victory in its war against "terrorism." Given that it is questionable if the social disparities and economic privation which fed Islamist alienation and insurgency decreased over the course of the 1990s, it is too early to judge if the claim is correct.

* * *

While Egyptian Islamists appear to have lost the physical battle against the secular state, on a deeper level Islam may be winning. In contrast to its repression of anti-state Islamist activism and violence, other actions by the Mubarak regime have gone a long way towards reinforcing and deepening the broader trend known as "social Islam" in Egypt. A gradual and peaceful Islamization of Egyptian society has occurred under Mubarak, partially with the acquiescence and encouragement of the state.

There is unquestionably a coercive dimension to the contemporary Islamization of Egyptian society. It is most obvious in the use of violence by militant Islamists in an attempt to silence secularist voices (the murder of the outspoken secularist champion Faraj Fauda in 1992; the assault upon and wounding of Egypt's Nobel Prize-winning author Najib Mahfuz in 1994). But coercion need not always involve violence. Egypt's official religious establishment, centered around al-Azhar, has long been dominated by the state and pressured into giving support to its policies. Recently it has become more assertive in censoring the expression of Egyptian opinion relating to religion. While continuing to endorse the state's struggle against militant Islam, the shaykhs of al-Azhar have also assumed a more active public role by calling for the banning of books and films which they view as "un-Islamic." Partially dependent upon the moral sanction of the religious establishment for its own legitimacy, the regime has concurred in this process. In 1994 Egypt's State Council, the body which evaluates the constitutionality of laws, recognized al-Azhar's authority to monitor cultural production in Egypt. Another tactic of Islamists in the 1990s was the use of Egyptian courts to intimidate secularist authors and artists. Basing their actions on the Islamic principle of *hisba* – the injunction for believers to command the good and forbid the evil – Islamist spokesmen have hauled "apostate" writers, film producers and distributors, and performers, before the courts and demanded the banning of their works. Faced with constant badgering, some secularist spokesmen have left the arena of public contestation; others have tempered their publicly expressed positions.

But at base Islamization is the consequence of religion becoming more popular within civil society. Numerous features of the contemporary Egyptian scene testify to the appeal of Islamic symbols and referents to the Muslim majority of Egyptians. Enrollment in the religious faculties of al-Azhar increased at a higher rate than enrollment in arts and humanities faculties of secular universities in the 1980s. The proliferation and expanding social outreach of Islamically oriented social service agencies first visible in the 1970s has continued; already in the 1980s one study found some three thousand such organizations in operation in Egypt. There is no indication that this popular demand for religious resources has diminished in the 1990s.

Given the manifest appeal of Islamic subjects and symbols to the public, the regime has been compelled to compete on turf which is perhaps not of its own choosing or to its best advantage. In the process of doing so, it reinforces the Islamic current flowing within civil society. The enlargement of the curricula of the state-run school system to include such themes as "Islamic Society" or "Faith, Morals, and Social Solidarity" reinforces the religious orientation of Egyptian students; the annual "Religious Awareness Caravan" jointly sponsored by several state agencies continues to do the same for youth during the summer recess; the publication of religious journals such as "The Islamic Banner" or "The Little Muslim" by the ruling NDP serve to promote an Islamic outlook on the part of both children and adults. The rhetoric of government officials has increasingly assumed a religious coloration, simultaneously attempting to persuade Egyptians of the "Islamic" bona fides and character of the regime, and at the same time soberly warning against the dangers of religious "extremism." At the same time as combatting militant Islam, the state is also complicit in the gradual Islamization of society.

To draw on the perceptive analysis of Gregory Starrett, three factors together – the popular reorientation towards religion, the Islamist turning of some of the institutions of the secular state against secularism, and the regime's attempt to demonstrate its own Islamic credentials to a more religiously inclined public – have worked to transform what was previously an Egyptian trend into an Egyptian context. By the 1990s Islamism was "pervasive, persistent, and normal, an immense counterculture" within Egyptian society: Islam had become "the language in which cultural and political battles are fought by the vast majority of interested parties."[9] The generally secular course of development which marked Egyptian public life since the nineteenth century has not been totally reversed; but it has certainly been overlaid by a counter-current emphasizing the continuing relevance of Egypt's millennial Islamic heritage.

CONTEMPORARY EGYPT

Egypt faces numerous problems at the beginning of the third millennium. With a population in the range of sixty-five million in 2000, human pressure on finite resources is enormous. Land reclamation efforts from the 1950s through the 1980s brought the area of cultivable land to over eight million feddans by 1990, and ambitious further reclamation projects – the al-Salam canal intended to carry Nile water to Sinai and to reclaim almost half a million acres of desert, the Toksha canal which will bring water from Lake Nasser to the oases of the Western Desert and hopefully reclaim an even larger area for habitation and agriculture – have been inaugurated in the 1990s. From these and other projects, the government hopes to add another two million feddans to Egypt's usable land area by 2010.

Yet Egypt is no longer mainly an agricultural country. In the late 1990s agriculture accounted for one-sixth of GDP, industry for one-third, services for fully half of national output in financial terms. Until recently the country has depended primarily on the productivity of its hitherto relatively uncompetitive industrial and overregulated commercial sectors, and on revenue from exogenous sources (petroleum exports, Suez Canal tolls, remittances from Egyptians working abroad, tourism, foreign aid) to stay afloat. Its economy, gradually being deregulated and privatized in the 1990s, has demonstrated appreciable improvement in its macro economic performance over the past decade. Whether that improvement will sustain itself in a global environment in which Egypt competes with many other countries for markets and investment is an open question.

Recent economic liberalization has also carried a heavy social price. Direct state subsidies for basic consumer goods have been cut. The social safety net put in place under Nasser (job security and fringe benefits for workers in public sector firms, rent controls and protection against arbitrary eviction for tenants in the agricultural sector) is being eroded in an effort to improve productivity. Government expenditure on social services such as education and health facilities now consume a smaller share of the state budget than in the past. The patron state is gradually relinquishing responsibility for both the management of the economy and the social welfare of its citizens.

There is no doubt that, in terms of basic statistical indicators, Egypt has experienced considerable "progress" in recent decades. Reported per capita income doubled over the 1990s (income distribution, where trends are less favorable, will be discussed later). The expansion of the educational system has improved literacy; whereas over three-quarters of Egyptians beyond childhood had been estimated to be illiterate in 1947 (seventy-seven per cent), the figure had dropped to under half by 1997 (forty-eight per cent). Increased life expectancy resulting from the control of epidemic diseases, the provision of clean drinking water, and the extension of health care to poorer Egyptians through the construction of state-supported clinics is perhaps the most telling single statistic. Whereas life expectancy had stood at forty-one for men and forty-four for women in the 1950s, it had risen to sixty-five for men and sixty-eight for women in the late 1990s.

Quantitative indicators alone are an inadequate guide to qualitative realities. In the countryside, where something over half of the population still resides, it appears that more continuity than change prevails in spite of a half-century of revolution, opening, and structural adjustment. Change, and indeed major change, there has been, to be sure: new schools make primary and secondary education available to many village children; health care is better and life expectancy improved; electronic access to a wider world is gained through radio and television. The temporary migration of millions of Egyptians to work abroad and the remittances they have sent home have resulted in the construction of new red-brick rather than mud-brick houses and a greater dissemination of manufactured consumer goods in rural areas.

Yet fundamental structural conditions in the countryside seem to have changed less than material ones. The revolution of 1952 gave land to a minority of peasants but did not mean the end of social stratification in the countryside. Farmers in what used to be the middle range of ownership between ten to fifty feddans, possessing enough land to support their families and to rent or hire labor to work part of their holdings, have replaced the former large landlord class as the rural elite. Government programs have not eliminated patronage and clientage, nor the subordination of the landless or the land-poor to the landed. At best land reform replaced "patron monogamy" (a peasant's dependence on a single large landlord) with "patron polygamy."[10] Kinship bonds and obligations remain strong, the extended family or clan acting as a social body (intermarriage), an economic unit (patrons finding tenants and hiring laborers from within their clan), and a political entity (voters favoring relatives in local or national elections; village feuds and vendettas).

Urban Egypt has different social cleavages and stresses. Almost half the country's population (forty-five per cent) was estimated to be living in urban areas by 1998. The overcrowding and urban difficulties existing in Egypt's main metropolis, Cairo, are legendary. At a hundred thousand residents per square kilometer in some older quarters, population density in parts of Cairo is amongst the highest in the world. Traffic is both jammed and chaotic. The concept of the lane has yet to make its way to Egypt; the horn is its functional substitute. In the 1980s and 1990s the government made a concerted attempt to improve the urban infrastructure through the construction of new roads and a metro system, as well as through updating telephone and sanitation services. Whether these efforts are keeping pace with growth is problematic.

While formal education is now available to most urban as well as rural children, urban population growth and the inability of the educational budget to keep pace with enrollment has resulted in a decline in the teacher-pupil ratio and severely overcrowded classrooms (over a hundred students per class in some urban primary schools). As a result, a parallel privatized educational system in which teachers supplement their low income by offering tutorial sessions for pay has emerged. The tutorial system has deleterious national consequences; corruption in examinations, recently a reported increase in the school drop-out rate due to the inability of parents to pay for the necessary private lessons.

Housing is perhaps the most pressing problem for Egyptian urban dwellers. Rent controls have until recently discouraged new urban residential construction. The inability to find an affordable flat is a major life dilemma for many younger Egyptians in particular, often resulting in multi-year delays in marriage plans. When residential construction does occur it is sometimes illegal and substandard. Collapsed apartment buildings erected (or added to) by shoddy construction techniques are a periodic scandal. Huge new squatter communities, populated partially but not exclusively by rural migrants, have emerged on the outskirts of greater Cairo as a result of the housing shortage, one survey estimating over six million people living in such "spontaneous communities" by the late 1990s.[11] To alleviate overcrowding in Cairo, since the 1970s the government has put considerable capital into the construction of planned and theoretically more attractive new cities on the edges of the desert. Many of these, however, remain devoid of the necessary infrastructure and remain largely unpopulated.

The economic conditions in which many urban Egyptians live are deteriorating. The salaries of many if not most workers in the public sector have long been inadequate to meet living expenses. As a result many urban dwellers are compelled to find second or even third jobs often in the huge, unregulated, and poorly paid informal sector of peddlers, handymen, and service personnel which has blossomed in recent decades. Studies of urban income distribution indicate that the percentage of urban income received by the poorest segments of the urban population have declined from the 1970s into the early 1990s, while the share obtained by the top layers has – with occasional plateaus – increased over the long term. Surveys of the level of urban poverty offer slightly different estimates depending on their definition of "poverty," but concur that the number of Cairenes living below the poverty line has increased from the 1970s into the 1990s. One such survey found fully one-third of Cairenes living below a poverty line of $1114 per year for a family of 4.6 members in 1991.

The current situation of Egyptian women is a huge topic which can only be briefly addressed here. The main impact of the state upon women has been through the provision of formal education and better health care. Reported school enrollment statistics show a steady rise in female primary and secondary school enrollments. By the end of the 1980s four-fifths of girls of the relevant age groups were enrolled in primary school and three-fifths in secondary school; over one-third of Egyptian university students in 1990 were women. The female illiteracy rate decreased from seventy-one per cent in 1976 to sixty per cent in 1998, but still is well above that of men (forty-three per cent in 1976, thirty-five per cent in 1998). State and private family planning programs have gradually encouraged a sizable minority – possibly now close to a majority – of Egyptian women to adopt the use of birth control methods, producing a decline in the rate of population growth from near three per cent annually a few decades ago to an estimated 2.1% in the late 1990s.

Studies of Egyptian rural society indicate a slower pace of change for women in the countryside than in urban areas. Save for education and health care, rural women have remained largely outside the scope of state-initiated efforts to improve rural life over the past half-century. The land redistribution efforts of the 1950s and 1960s generally gave ownership of land to men. Local studies show women's inheritance rights under Islamic law sometimes being usurped by male relatives. The family remains the dominant corporate unit, structuring much of life for both its male and female members. Its patriarchal character continues to invest formal authority (although not necessarily all influence) for family affairs in the hands of men. Labor migration by Egyptian men to work in other countries has had appreciable side-effects for rural women, both increasing the participation of women (and children) in the labor force because of the shortage of male labor and giving wives a greater role in family decision-making due to the temporary absence of their husbands.

In urban Egypt women now span the spectrum of civilian occupations – everything from domestic service through secretarial work and factory jobs to employment in professional specialities (doctors, lawyers, teachers) for educated women. Although equal wages for equal work are guaranteed by law, in practice women in many non-professional occupations often hold less skilled or demanding jobs, and thus receive less pay than men. In the urban economy women are concentrated particularly in service jobs in the private sector; in teaching, clerical, and health care positions in the public sector; and in commerce in the booming informal sector. One-sixth of Egypt's industrial work force was female in the late 1980s. This percentage declined with the structural adjustment of the 1990s. Women have been more vulnerable than men to lay-offs when firms reduce redundant staff and, as "expensive labor" with guaranteed maternity leave, tend not to be hired for new openings. Preliminary estimates of the effects of structural adjustment also indicate that real wages have fallen most severely in the lower-level, or unskilled, positions that are held disproportionately by women.

It is difficult to say if womens' place in Egyptian public life has altered appreciably in recent decades. A smaller percentage of women than men have traditionally voted in Egyptian local and national elections since women obtained the franchise in the 1950s. Women continue to be represented in token numbers in parliament (the 1990–95 National Assembly had ten women members) and in political parties. Genuinely independent womens' organizations appear to have suffered the same periodic harassment and marginalization as has been experienced by many non-establishment bodies in the fitful and contracting pluralism of the 1980s and 1990s.

Women have both participated in, and been influenced by, the Islamic trend of recent decades. The assumption or reassumption of "modest" or "Islamic" dress – depending on the individual, the covering of the hair, the limbs, sometimes the face – by Muslim women is arguably the most visible indicator of the growing rise of religion in Egypt. Islamist social service agencies of course reach out to women and often perform valuable social services for them. Autonomous women's organizations – Qur'an study groups for women, day-care centers, counselling groups – have been a sub-set of "social Islam" which have expanded womens' horizons and life-opportunities. On the other side, the Islamist agenda includes items which portend the restriction of womens' social space and ability to make independent life choices (emphasis on woman's primary duties as being in the home; the designation of some types of work, and sometimes all work outside the home, as unsuitable for women; strident opposition to abortion).

Amending Egypt's personal status law to give women greater say in marriage and divorce was the occasion for an extended public controversy in the 1970s and 1980s. Impatient with parliament's inability to move forward on what was a hotly debated issue, in 1979 Sadat by presidential decree amended Egypt's sixty-year-old personal status law to require greater court supervision of divorce proceedings, to make a husband's taking a second wife sufficient grounds for the first wife to obtain a divorce, and to give the first wife the right to possession of the family residence in cases of divorce occasioned by polygamy. Popularly known as "Jihan's law" because of the advocacy of the initiative by the President's wife, the measure generated repeated protest over the next several years by conservative spokesmen and Islamist organizations. When in 1985 the court declared the decree invalid because of its implementation by presidential fiat, a substitute measure enacted by parliament significantly reduced a wife's rights in divorce by mandating that injury be proved (rather than assumed) in cases where a husband took a second wife, and by eliminating the first wife's automatic right to the family residence. The gradual Islamization of society since then has in effect placed a lid on substantial change in the legal status of Egyptian women.

What of the political arena? Contemporary Egyptian politics seem to have reached a state of what might be termed low-level equilibrium. An aging political leadership, entrenched in office and increasingly unresponsive to external input, soldiers on in power. From the outside, frustrated critics in opposition parties and independent intellectuals of various stripes call for "radical constitutional and political reform" (the words of a manifesto issued by several opposition parties and intellectuals on the eve of the referendum giving President Mubarak his fourth term in office in late 1999); but they are unable to budge the establishment. At the mass level a declining rate of participation in national and local elections seems to testify to a popular loss of faith and interest in a manifestly manipulated political process. In the words of one recent study of Egyptian local politics, for most people "the state has reduced politics to the issue of distribution;" how the average Egyptian can obtain, by hook or by crook, access to the material resources controlled by the state apparatus.[12]

Yet the structure as a whole appears quite stable. Several factors combine to make it so. The uneven prosperity of the 1990s has given some – although by no means all – Egyptians a positive stake in the system and a reason for supporting its perpetuation. Perhaps more significant is the massive weight and thus staying-power of the state and the public sector; still largely intact, still controlled by the establishment, and still the source of the livelihood of much of the population. A comparatively privileged military and (at its upper levels) an adequately compensated bureaucracy have done relatively well out of the system and conse-quently remain loyal to it.

A lack of viable alternatives also plays a role. Secular opposition parties are fragmented, have only limited appeal on a mass basis, and lack the power of patronage available to supporters of the system. The Islamist alternative is similarly fractured, has been contained by force, and more recently appears to have been discredited with much of the public due to the tactics of its militant edge. Equally importantly, with the popular growth and official tolerance of social Islam, Egyptian public life in general is gradually assuming a more Islamic coloration. These factors rather than any inherent Egyptian proclivity to "fatalism" or "resignation" provide sufficient explanation for the durability of a political order which, although much criticized by its most politically articulate citizens and viewed as a reservoir to be exploited for personal benefit by the rest of the population, continues to creak along.

Notes

CHAPTER ONE

1. Barry J. Kemp, "Old Kingdom, Middle Kingdom and Second Intermediate Period," in B. G. Trigger, *et. al.*, *Ancient Egypt: A Social History* (Cambridge: Cambridge University Press, 1983), p. 87.
2. The above is based on the argument in Donald B. Redford, *Egypt, Canaan, and Israel in Ancient Times* (Princeton: Princeton University Press, 1992), pp. 257–280, 387–392, 406–422.

CHAPTER TWO

1. Alan K. Bowman, *Egypt After the Pharaohs* (Berkeley: University of California Press, 1986), p. 93.
2. Quoted in ibid., 61.
3. Naphtali Lewis, *Greeks in Ptolemaic Egypt* (Oxford: Oxford University Press, 1986), p. 154.
4. Quoted in Naphtali Lewis, *Life in Egypt Under Roman Rule* (Oxford: Oxford University Press, 1983), p. 23.
5. Roger S. Bagnell, *Egypt in Late Antiquity* (Princeton: Princeton University Press, 1993), p. 324.

CHAPTER THREE

1. Hugh Kennedy, *The Prophet and the Age of the Caliphates* (London: Longman, 1986), pp. 342–344.
2. P. M. Holt, *The Age of the Crusades* (London: Longman, 1986), p. 196.
3. Quoted in David Ayalon, *Gunpowder and Firearms in the Mamluk Kingdom* (London: Mitchell Valentine, 1956), p. 94.
4. See the discussion in Robert Irwin, *The Middle East in the Middle Ages: The Early Mamluk Sultanate, 1250–1382* (Carbondale: Southern Illinois University Press, 1986), pp. 152–156.

5. Ira Lapidus, *Muslim Cities in the Later Middle Ages* (Cambridge, MA: Harvard University Press, 1967), p. 51.
6. Ibid., p. 177.

CHAPTER FOUR

1. Jane Hathaway, *The Politics of Households in Ottoman Egypt* (Cambridge: Cambridge University Press, 1997), p. 6.
2. Ibid., pp. 116, 166–167.
3. Quoted in Michael Winter, "The Reemergence of the Mamluks After the Ottoman Conquest," in Thomas Philipp and Ulrich Haarmann, eds., *The Mamluks in Egyptian Politics and Society* (London: Routledge, 1998), p. 98.
4. Quoted in Michael Winter, *Egyptian Society under Ottoman Rule, 1517–1798* (London: Routledge, 1992), pp. 243–244.
5. Nelly Hanna, *Making Big Money in 1600: The Life and Times of Isma'il Abu Taqiyya, Egyptian Merchant* (Syracuse: Syracuse University Press, 1998), pp. 12, 82–86.
6. Kenneth M. Cuno, *The Pasha's Peasants: Land, Society, and Economy in Lower Egypt, 1740–1858* (Cambridge: Cambridge University Press, 1992), pp. 48–84.
7. Afaf Lutfi al-Sayyid Marsot, *Women and Men in Late Eighteenth-Century Egypt* (Austin: Texas University Press, 1995), p. 37.
8. Hathaway, op. cit., p. 124.

CHAPTER FIVE

1. Khaled Fahmy, *All the Pasha's Men: Mehmed Ali, His Army and the Making of Modern Egypt* (Cambridge: Cambridge University Press, 1997), p. 116.
2. Cuno, op. cit., p. 164.
3. Afaf Lutfi al-Sayyid Marsot, *Egypt in the Reign of Muhammad Ali* (Cambridge: Cambridge University Press, 1984), p. 122.
4. Fahmy, op. cit., p. 280.
5. Roger Owen, *The Middle East in the World Economy, 1800–1914* (London: Methuen, 1981), p. 138.
6. Quoted in P. J. Vatikiotis, *The Modern History of Egypt* (New York: Praeger, 1969), p. 74.
7. Juan R. I. Cole, *Colonialism and Revolution in the Middle East: Social and Cultural Origins of Egypt's 'Urabi Movement* (Princeton: Princeton University Press, 1993), pp. 195–203.
8. Owen, op. cit., p. 126.
9. Quoted in Robert L. Tignor, *Modernization and British Colonial Rule in Egypt, 1882–1914* (Princeton: Princeton University Press, 1966), p. 65.
10. Ibid., p. 190.
11. See Owen, op. cit., pp. 225, 236–239.

12. Quoted in Afaf Lutfi al-Sayyid Marsot, *Egypt and Cromer: A Study in Anglo-Egyptian Relations* (New York: Praeger, 1969), p. 173.
13. Quoted in Israel Gershoni and James Jankowski, *Egypt, Islam, and the Arabs: The Search for Egyptian Nationhood, 1900–1930* (Oxford: Oxford University Press, 1986), p. 12.
14. Quoted in Vatikiotis, op. cit., p. 216.
15. Sir Thomas Russell Pasha, *Egyptian Service, 1902–1946* (London: John Murray, 1949), p. 33.
16. Albert Hourani, *A History of the Arab Peoples* (Cambridge, MA: Harvard University Press, 1991), p. 297.
17. Ehud Toledano, *State and Society in Mid-Nineteenth-Century Egypt* (Cambridge: Cambridge University Press, 1990), pp. 11, 83–87.
18. Judith E. Tucker, *Women in Nineteenth-Century Egypt* (Cambridge: Cambridge University Press, 1985), p. 43.
19. Ibid., p. 101.
20. Ibid., p. 198.
21. Marsot, *Women and Men in Late Eighteenth-Century Egypt*, p. 147.

CHAPTER SIX

1. Jacques Berque, *Egypt: Imperialism and Revolution* (London: Faber and Faber, 1972), p. 488.
2. Charles Issawi, *Egypt at Mid-Century: An Economic Survey* (Oxford: Oxford University Press, 1954), p. 242.
3. Quoted in Magda Baraka, *The Egyptian Upper Class between Revolutions, 1919–1952* (Reading: Ithaca Press, 1998), pp. 152–153.
4. Quoted in Marius Deeb, *Party Politics in Egypt: The Wafd and Its Rivals, 1919–39* (Reading: Ithaca Press, 1979), p. 12.
5. Quoted in Baraka, op. cit., p.154.

CHAPTER SEVEN

1. John Waterbury, *The Egypt of Nasser and Sadat: The Political Economy of Two Regimes* (Princeton: Princeton University Press, 1983), p. 337.
2. Nazih Ayubi, *Bureaucracy and Politics in Contemporary Egypt* (Reading: Ithaca Press, 1980), pp. 281–282.
3. Bent Hansen, *Egypt and Turkey: The Political Economy of Poverty, Equity, and Growth* (Oxford: Oxford University Press, 1991), pp. 120–123, 154–155.
4. Mahmoud Abdel-Fadil, *Development, Income Distribution and Social Change in Rural Egypt, 1952–1970* (Cambridge: Cambridge University Press, 1975), p. 117.
5. Eisenhower Library, Raymond Hare Oral History.
6. Letter from A. J. Edden, British Embassy, Beirut, September 13, 1960; Great Britain, Public Record Office, FO371/150901, VG1015.18.

CHAPTER EIGHT

1. Quoted in Waterbury, *The Egypt of Nasser and Sadat*, p. 384.
2. Nazih Ayubi, *The State and Public Policies in Egypt Since Sadat* (Reading: Ithaca Press, 1991), p. 28.
3. Raymond J. Hinnebusch Jr., *Egyptian Politics under Sadat* (Cambridge: Cambridge University Press, 1985), pp. 272–273.
4. Cited in ibid., p. 286.
5. Ayubi, *The State and Public Policies in Egypt Since Sadat*, p. 286.
6. Iliya Harik, *Economic Policy Reform in Egypt* (Gainesville, FL: University of Florida Press, 1997), pp. 47–48.
7. "Egypt: New and Old," *The Economist*, March 20, 1999, p. 3.
8. Ibid., p. 11.
9. Gregory Starrett, *Putting Islam to Work: Education, Politics, and Religious Transformation in Egypt* (Berkeley: University of California Press, 1998), pp. 90, 192, 219.
10. Richard H. Adams, *Development and Social Change in Rural Egypt* (Syracuse: Syracuse University Press, 1986), p. 145.
11. Asaf Bayat, "Cairo's Poor: Dilemmas of Survival and Solidarity," *Middle East Report*, Winter 1996, p. 5.
12. Diane Singerman, *Avenues of Participation: Family, Politics, and Networks in Urban Quarters of Cairo* (Princeton: Princeton University Press, 1995), p. 245.

Further Reading

PHARAONIC EGYPT

Edwards, I.E.S. *The Pyramids of Egypt*. London, Penguin, 1947.
Hoffman, Michael A. *Egypt Before the Pharaohs: The Prehistoric Foundations of Egyptian Civilization*. New York, Alfred E. Knopf, 1979.
Kemp, Barry J. *Ancient Egypt: Anatomy of a Civilization*. London, Routledge, 1983.
Redford, Donald B. *Egypt, Canaan, and Israel in Ancient Times*. Princeton, Princeton University Press, 1992.
Rice, Michael, *Egypt's Making: The Origins of Ancient Egypt, 5000-2000 BC*. London, Routledge, 1990.
Trigger, Bruce G., *et al. Ancient Egypt: A Social History*. Cambridge, Cambridge University Press, 1983.
Tyldesley, Joyce. *Daughters of Isis: Women of Ancient Egypt*. London, Penguin, 1994.
Wilson, John A. *The Culture of Ancient Egypt*. Chicago, Chicago University Press, 1951.

GRECO-ROMAN EGYPT

Bagnell, Roger S. *Egypt in Late Antiquity*. Princeton, Princeton University Press, 1993.
Bowman, Alan K. *Egypt after the Pharaohs: 332 BC-AD 642: from Alexander to the Arab Conquest*. Berkeley, University of California Press, 1986.
Green, Peter *Alexander to Actium*. Berkeley, University of California Press, 1990.
Lewis, Naphtali *Greeks in Ptolemaic Egypt*. Oxford, Oxford University Press, 1986.
Lewis, Naphtali *Life in Egypt under Roman Rule*. Oxford, Oxford University Press, 1983.

Peters, F.E. *The Harvest of Hellenism: A History of the Near East from Alexander the Great to the Triumph of Christianity.* New York, Simon and Schuster, 1970.

ISLAMIC EGYPT

Abu-Lughod, Janet *Cairo: 1001 Years of the City Victorious.* Princeton, Princeton University Press, 1971.

Berkey, Jonathan *The Transmission of Knowledge in Medieval Cairo: A Social History of Islamic Education.* Princeton, Princeton University Press, 1992.

Holt, P.M. *The Age of the Crusades: The Near East from the Eleventh Century to 1517.* New York, Longman, 1986.

Irwin, Robert *The Middle East in the Middle Ages: The Early Mamluk Sultanate, 1250-1382.* Carbondale, IL, Southern Illinois University Press, 1986.

Kennedy, Hugh *The Prophet and the Age of the Caliphates: The Islamic Near East from the Sixth to the Eleventh Centuries.* London, Longman, 1986.

Lapidus, Ira *Muslim Cities of the Later Middle Ages.* Cambridge, MA, Harvard University Press, 1967.

Lev, Yaacov *State and Society in Fatamid Egypt.* Leiden, Brill, 1991.

Petry, Carl F. (ed.) *The Cambridge History of Egypt, vol. I: Islamic Egypt, 640–1517.* Cambridge, Cambridge University Press, 1998.

Petry, Carl F. *The Civilian Elite of Cairo in the Later Middle Ages.* Princeton, Princeton University Press, 1982.

Philipp, Thomas and Haarmann, Ulrich (eds.) *The Mamluks in Egyptian Politics and Society.* Cambridge, Cambridge University Press, 1998.

Sanders, Paula *Ritual, Politics, and the City in Fatamid Cairo.* Albany, State University of New York Press, 1994.

Shoshon, Boaz *Popular Culture in Medieval Cairo.* Cambridge, Cambridge University Press, 1993.

OTTOMAN EGYPT

Crecelius, Daniel *The Roots of Modern Egypt: A Study of the Regimes of 'Ali Bey al-Kabir and Muhammad Bey Abu al-Dhahab, 1760–1775.* Minneapolis, Bibliotheca Islamica, 1981.

Cuno, Kenneth M. *The Pasha's Peasants: Land, Society, and Economy in Lower Egypt, 1740–1858.* Cambridge, Cambridge University Press, 1992.

Daly, M.W. (ed.) *The Modern History of Egypt, vol. II: Modern Egypt from 1517 to the End of the Twentieth Century.* Cambridge, Cambridge University Press, 1998.

Hanna, Nelly *Making Big Money in 1600: The Life and Times of Isma'il Abu Taqiyya, Egyptian Merchant.* Syracuse, Syracuse University Press, 1997.

Hathaway, Jane *The Politics of Households in Ottoman Egypt: The Rise of the Qazdaglis*. Cambridge, Cambridge University Press, 1996.
al-Sayyid Marsot, Afaf Lutfi *Women and Men in Late Eighteenth-Century Egypt*. Austin, TX, Texas University Press, 1995.
Shaw, Stanford J. *The Financial and Administrative Organization of Ottoman Egypt, 1517–1798*. Princeton, Princeton University Press, 1958.
Winter, Michael *Egyptian Society under Ottoman Rule, 1517–1798*. New York, Routledge, 1992.

MODERNIZING EGYPT/COLONIZING EGYPT

Abu-Lughod, Janet *see "Islamic Egypt."*
Ahmed, Jamal Mohammed *The Intellectual Origins of Egyptian Nationalism*. Oxford, Oxford University Press, 1960.
Baer, Gabriel *Studies in the Social History of Modern Egypt*. Chicago, Chicago University Press, 1969.
Baron, Beth *The Women's Awakening in Egypt*. New Haven, Yale University Press, 1994.
Berque, Jacques *Egypt: Nationalism and Revolution*. London, Faber and Faber, 1972.
Cole, Juan R.I. *Colonialism and Revolution in the Middle East: Social and Cultural Origins of Egypt's 'Urabi Movement*. Princeton, Princeton University Press, 1993.
Cuno, Kenneth M. *see "Ottoman Egypt."*
Daly, M.W. (ed.) *see "Ottoman Egypt."*
Fahmy, Khaled *All the Pasha's Men: Mehmed Ali, His Army and the Making of Modern Egypt*. Cambridge, Cambridge University Press, 1997.
Hunter, F. Robert *Egypt under the Khedives, 1805–1879*. Pittsburgh, PA, University of Pittsburgh Press, 1984.
Mitchell, Timothy *Colonizing Egypt*. Cambridge, Cambridge University Press, 1988.
Owen, E.R.J. *Cotton and the Egyptian Economy, 1820–1914*. Oxford, Oxford University Press, 1969.
Owen, Roger *The Middle East in the World Economy, 1800–1914*. London, Methuen, 1981.
al-Sayyid Marsot, Afaf Lutfi *Egypt and Cromer*. New York, Praeger, 1969.
al-Sayyid Marsot, Afaf Lutfi *Egypt in the Reign of Muhammad Ali*. Cambridge, Cambridge University Press, 1984.
Schölch, Alexander *Egypt for the Egyptians: The Socio-Political Crisis in Egypt, 1878–1882*. Reading, Ithaca Press, 1981.
Tignor, Robert L. *Modernization and British Colonial Rule in Egypt, 1882–1914*. Princeton, Princeton University Press, 1966.
Toledano, Ehud R. *State and Society in Mid-Nineteenth-Century Egypt*. Cambridge, Cambridge University Press, 1990.
Tucker, Judith E. *Women in Nineteenth-Century Egypt*. Cambridge, Cambridge University Press, 1985.
Vatikiotis, P.J. *The Modern History of Egypt*. New York, Praeger, 1969.

LIBERAL EGYPT

Baraka, Magda *The Egyptian Upper Class between Revolutions, 1919–1952*. Reading, Ithaca Press, 1998.

Beinin, Joel and Lockman, Zachary *Workers on the Nile: Nationalism, Communism, Islam, and the Egyptian Working Class*. Princeton, Princeton University Press, 1987.

Berque, Jacques *see "Modernizing Egypt."*

Botman, Selma *Egypt from Independence to Revolution, 1919–1952*. Syracuse, Syracuse University Press, 1991.

Daly, M.W. (ed.) *see "Ottoman Egypt."*

Deeb, Marius *Party Politics in Egypt: The Wafd and Its Rivals, 1919–1939*. Reading, Ithaca Press, 1979.

Gershoni, Israel and Jankowski, James *Egypt, Islam, and the Arabs: The Search for Egyptian Nationhood, 1900–1930*. Oxford, Oxford University Press, 1986.

Gershoni, Israel and Jankowski, James *Redefining the Egyptian Nation, 1930–1945*. Cambridge, Cambridge University Press, 1995.

Goldberg, Ellis *Tinker, Tailor, and Textile Worker: Class and Politics in Egypt, 1930–1954*. Berkeley, University of California Press, 1986.

Issawi, Charles *Egypt at Mid-Century: An Economic Analysis*. Oxford, Oxford University Press, 1954.

Jankowski, James *Egypt's Young Rebels: Young Egypt, 1933–1952*. Stanford, Hoover Institution Press, 1975.

Kramer, Gudrun *The Jews in Modern Egypt, 1914–1952*. Seattle, University of Washington Press, 1989.

Mitchell, Richard P. *The Society of the Muslim Brothers*. Oxford, Oxford University Press, 1969.

al-Sayyid Marsot, Afaf Lutfi *Egypt's Liberal Experiment, 1922–1936*. Berkeley, University of California Press, 1977.

Smith, Charles D. *Islam and the Search for Social Order in Modern Egypt: a Biography of Muhammad Husayn Haykal*. Albany, State University of New York Press, 1983.

Tignor, Robert L. *State, Private Enterprise, and Economic Change in Egypt, 1918–1952*. Princeton, Princeton University Press, 1984.

Vatikiotis, P.J. *see "Modernizing Egypt."*

REVOLUTIONARY EGYPT

Ansari, Hamied *Egypt: The Stalled Society*. Albany, State University of New York Press, 1986.

Ayubi, Nazih *Bureaucracy and Politics in Contemporary Egypt*. Reading, Ithaca Press, 1980.

Baker, Raymond *Egypt's Uncertain Revolution under Nasser and Sadat*. Cambridge, MA, Harvard University Press, 1978.

Beattie, Kirk J. *Egypt during the Nasser Years: Ideology, Politics, and Civil Society*. Boulder, CO, Westview, 1994.

Dawisha, A.I. *Egypt in the Arab World: The Elements of Foreign Policy.* New York, John Wiley, 1976.

Gordon, Joel *Nasser's Blessed Movement: Egypt's Free Officers and the July Revolution.* Oxford, Oxford University Press, 1992.

Heikal, Mohamed Hassanein *The Cairo Documents.* Garden City, NY, Doubleday, 1973.

Issawi, Charles *Egypt in Revolution: An Economic Analysis.* Oxford, Oxford University Press, 1963.

Kerr, Malcolm *The Arab Cold War: Jamal 'Abd al-Nasir and His Rivals, 1958–1970.* Third ed. Oxford, Oxford University Press, 1971.

Mabro, Robert *The Egyptian Economy, 1952–1972.* Oxford, Oxford University Press, 1974.

Nutting, Anthony *Nasser.* New York, Dutton, 1972.

Stephens, Robert *Nasser: A Political Biography.* London, Allen Lane, 1972.

Vatikiotis, P.J. *The Egyptian Army in Politics.* Bloomington, IN, Indiana University Press, 1961.

Vatikiotis, P.J. *Nasser and His Generation.* New York, St Martin's, 1978.

Wahba, Mourad Magdi *The Role of the State in the Egyptian Economy, 1945–1981.* Reading, Ithaca Press, 1994.

Waterbury, John *The Egypt of Nasser and Sadat: The Political Economy of Two Regimes.* Princeton, Princeton University Press, 1983.

Woodward, Peter *Nasser.* London, Longman, 1992.

WHOSE EGYPT?

Abed-Kotob, Sana and Sullivan, Dennis J. *Islam in Contemporary Egypt: Civil Society vs. the State.* Boulder, CO, Lynne Rienner, 1999.

Adams Jr, Richard H. *Development and Social Change in Rural Egypt.* Syracuse, Syracuse University Press, 1986.

Ayubi, Nazih *The State and Public Policies in Egypt Since Sadat.* Reading, Ithaca Press, 1991.

Baker, Raymond *Sadat and After.* Cambridge, MA, Harvard University Press, 1990.

Harik, Iliya *Economic Policy Reform in Egypt.* Gainesville, FL, University of Florida Press, 1997.

Heikel, Mohamed Hassanein *Autumn of Fury: The Assassination of Sadat.* New York, Random House, 1983.

Hinnebusch, Raymond A. *Egyptian Politics under Sadat.* Cambridge, Cambridge University Press, 1985.

Hirst, David and Beeson, Irene *Sadat.* London, Faber and Faber, 1981.

Karam, Azza M. *Islamists and the State: Contemporary Feminisms in Egypt.* New York, St Martin's, 1998.

Kepel, Gilles *Muslim Extremism in Egypt: The Prophet and Pharaoh.* Berkeley, University of California Press, 1986.

MacLeod, Arlene Elowe *Accommodating Protest: Working Women, the New Veiling, and Change in Cairo,* New York, Columbia University Press, 1993.

Posusney, Marcia Pripstein *Labor and the State in Egypt, 1952–1994.* New York, Columbia University Press, 1997.

Rugh, Andrea *Family in Contemporary Egypt.* Syracuse, Syracuse University Press, 1984.

Singerman, Diane *Avenues of Participation: Family, Politics, and Networks in Urban Quarters of Cairo.* Princeton, Princeton University Press, 1995.

Springborg, Robert *Mubarak's Egypt: Fragmentation of the Political Order.* Boulder, CO, Westview, 1989.

Starrett, Gregory *Putting Islam to Work: Education, Politics, and Religious Transformation in Egypt.* Berkeley, University of California Press, 1998.

Sullivan, Earl L. *Women in Egyptian Public Life.* Syracuse, Syracuse University Press, 1986.

Talhami, Ghada Hashem *The Mobilization of Muslim Women in Egypt.* Gainesville, FL, University of Florida Press, 1996.

Waterbury, John *see "Revolutionary Egypt."*

Index